The
Reference
Shelf

The Internet

Edited by Gray Young

The Reference Shelf
Volume 70 • Number 5

The H.W. Wilson Company
New York • Dublin
1998

The Reference Shelf

The books in this series contain reprints of articles, excerpts from books, addresses on current issues, and studies of social trends in the United States and other countries. There are six separately bound numbers in each volume, all of which are usually published in the same calendar year. Numbers one through five are each devoted to a single subject, providing background information and discussion from various points of view and concluding with a subject index and comprehensive bibliography that lists books, pamphlets, and abstracts of additional articles on the subject. The final number of each volume is a collection of recent speeches, and it contains a cumulative speaker index. Books in the series may be purchased individually or on subscription.

Visit H.W. Wilson's Web site: www.hwwilson.com

Library of Congress Cataloging-in-Publication data

The Internet/edited by Gray Young
             p. cm—(Reference shelf; v. 70, no. 5)
      Includes bibliographical references and index
      ISBN 0-8242-0945-1
      1. Internet (Computer network) 2. Internet (Computer network)—Social aspects.
      I.Young, Gray.   II. Series.
TK5105.875.I57I536   1998   98-48498
004.67'8—dc21   CIP

Printed in the United States of America

Contents

Preface

"WWW dot..."

At the beginning of this decade, that phrase had absolutely no meaning, but now, as the decade (and century) are drawing to a close, it is one of the most ubiquitous terms in the world. It would be unusual to make it through a day without hearing or seeing it somewhere, whether in an advertisement directing people to some company's Web site for information about its products, or in a television newscast referring to its Web site for more coverage on a topic, or a newspaper pointing towards its Web page for up-to-the-minute reporting.

As we approach the new millennium, the Internet is proclaimed by many to signal a renaissance in which free flowing information will bring more equality and freedom to the world. This new medium will stimulate economies to new levels, improve health care through better access to information, enlighten people through never-before-available contact with people from different cultures, and maybe even alleviate loneliness through the myriad new means of socializing online. Others, meanwhile, see the Internet portending the downfall of civilized society. The Internet will corrupt children through a bombardment of pornography, obliterate any semblance of privacy as businesses and governments track our online movement, tarnish journalism by letting anyone post a so-called news site that may be filled with misinformation, destroy the economy by taking away copyright protections, and physically endanger us by allowing criminals and terrorists to easily and confidentially communicate regardless of their physical proximity.

So what exactly is this pervasive new technology that has become an integral part of our lives and that people see as the pivotal force in the direction our society is headed? Can the Internet really improve our quality of life? Is there a legitimate reason to fear that it may ruin our quality of life? Can governments do anything to help steer this in the right direction? Should they? Why are businesses both embracing and fearing the Internet? Who is actually using the Internet, and what are they using it for? Because of the relative youth of this new medium, these questions have no definitive answers. The Internet is much like a precocious child, with governments, academics, and businesses being the parents, proud yet filled with uncertainty: It is obvious to the entire family that this child is very special, but the child's insatiable inquisitiveness sometimes leads it to places that terrify the parents; the parents are unsure whether they should punish the child for these acts or let him explore freely, fearing that punishing the child for curiosity may stifle the unlimited potential but also fearing that not punishing it may lead it to more and more dangerous behavior; will the child grow to be a Nobel Prize winner or an uncontrollably brilliant psychopath?

The articles in this issue of *The Reference Shelf* examine these issues, illustrating the unique challenges that this technology is presenting us.

We begin this book with a section entitled "What Is the Internet?" which includes articles that give a short history of this technology, explain some of the structure of the Internet, and touch on some of the broad social and political issues concerning the Internet. That is followed by "The Internet and Business," which explores some of the ways in which the Internet is affecting the business world and the closely related issues of how governments are treating this new method of commerce, which in many ways violates most of the premises our laws concerning commerce were built on. The third section, "The Internet and Society," contains articles concerning the ways in which society is being affected by the Internet, touching on such issues as privacy, censorship, equality, and human rights. Finally, we close with a section asking "What's Next?" which includes articles speculating on where the Internet is heading and discussing the challenges—technical, political, philosophical, and otherwise—it must face to even have a future.

As can be surmised by the conflicting views of the Internet as either savior or menace, practically all issues related to the Internet bring strongly felt and conflicting opinions from different groups; hence, several of the articles in this book present strong opinions. With this book, however, we are not attempting to further any of those opinions. The articles were chosen because they either presented a diverse variety of issues or because they examined various aspects of a particular issue. If you would like to read articles presenting different perspectives, please refer to the "Additional Periodical Articles with Abstracts" section of this book. Many of the citations, which have been grouped according to the chapters for which they are most relevant, have been chosen largely because they offer views that differ from those in the articles in this book or because they present some issues that were not touched on in this book.

I would like to thank Michael Schulze for giving me the opportunity to edit this book. I would also like to thank Beth Levy, production editor, and Sandra Watson, editorial assistant, for their assistance in compiling this book.

Gray Young
November 1998

I. What Is the Internet?

Editor's Introduction

There are probably few people who by this time haven't heard the terms Internet, World Wide Web, and e-mail, and most people are at least vaguely aware of what they are. But how did the Internet so suddenly appear? How does it work? Who runs it? Even for people who use the Web or e-mail practically every day, these most basic details remain a complete mystery. Luckily, technical knowledge is becoming less and less vital for using the power of the Internet, and knowing how it got started is in no way important in using it. Nevertheless, as the Internet becomes more and more entwined with our daily lives as a primary communication and information gathering tool, a knowledge of its structure may be beneficial in understanding who is making decisions that control our future. In this chapter, we will shed some light on the history and basic structure of the Internet, and introduce some of the political and personal issues that the growth of the Internet is forcing us to confront.

Although to most people, it may appear that the Internet emerged out of nowhere in the mid-1990s, it has been around since the 1960s. Only with the advent of the World Wide Web (the portion of the Internet with graphics and hyperlinks) in the past few years, and with the recent proliferation of home computers, has the Internet become an integral part of most people's day-to-day life. "A Brief History of the Internet" provides an overview of this history and some of the basic structure of the Internet. Following that is "How Servers Find Needle in Haystack of the Internet," an article that describes some of the technical structure of the Internet, and some of the political issues surrounding the control of that structure.

After the historic and technical overviews are three articles introducing many of the issues that will be revisited in later chapters. Each looks at these issues from a different perspective: The first is looking more at how the issues will affect our lives; the second tells how government is struggling with these issues; and the third is a view from people working intimately with the Internet.

The first, "Taming the Beast," paints a very broad picture of the myriad issues that the Internet is forcing us to confront, on a personal or political level. "Congress Finds No Easy Answers to Internet Controversies," from *Congressional Quarterly* looks at many of the same issues, but from the perspective of how the federal government is attempting to handle them. Among other issues, it raises the question of whether members of Congress are qualified to handle matters that, in many cases, they don't have the technical knowledge to fully understand. The final article in this chapter is a plea for rationality concerning these issues from a broad coalition of Internet experts who call themselves Technorealists. Worried that the common perceptions of the Internet as either the path to utopia or the road to hell will obscure the less exciting, but more realistic, middle ground, the Technorealists wish to emphasize that neither extreme is accurate and that the Internet is a tool to be used for many different purposes. Without the acknowledgment that it is not some magical cure all for society's ills, nor is it some evil force that must be stopped, the Technorealists believe it will be difficult for government to make wise judgements concerning the medium.

A Brief History of the Internet[1]

The Internet was started in 1969 under a contract let by the Advanced Research Projects Agency (ARPA) which connected four major computers at universities in the southwestern US (UCLA, Stanford Research Institute, UCSB, and the University of Utah). The contract was carried out by BBN of Cambridge, MA and went online in December 1969. By June 1970, MIT, Harvard, BBN, and Systems Development Corp (SDC) in Santa Monica, Cal. were added. By January 1971, Stanford, MIT's Lincoln Labs, Carnegie-Mellon, and Case-Western Reserve U. were added. In months to come, NASA/Ames, Mitre, Burroughs, RAND, and the U. of Illinois plugged in. After that, there were far too many to keep listing here.

The Internet was designed to provide a communications network that would work even if some of the sites were destroyed by nuclear attack. If the most direct route was not available, routers would direct traffic around the network via alternate routes.

The early Internet was used by computer experts, engineers, and scientists. There was nothing friendly about it. There were no home or office personal computers in those days, and anyone who used it, whether a computer professional or an engineer or scientist, had to learn to use a very complex system.

Ethernet, a protocol for many local networks, appeared in 1974, an outgrowth of Harvard student Bob Metcalfe's dissertation on "Packet Networks." The dissertation was initially rejected by the University for not being analytical enough. It later won acceptance when he added some more equations to it.

The Internet matured in the 70's as a result of the TCP/IP architecture first proposed by Bob Kahn at BBN and further developed by Kahn and Vint Cerf at Stanford and others throughout the 70's. It was adopted by the Defense Department in 1980 and universally adopted by 1983.

The Unix to Unix Copy Protocol (UUCP) was invented in 1978 at Bell Labs. Usenet was started in 1979 based on UUCP. Newsgroups, which are discussion groups focusing on a topic, followed, providing a means of exchanging information throughout the world. While Usenet is not considered as part of the Internet, since it does not share the use of TCP/IP, it linked unix systems around the world, and

---

1.   Article by Walt Howe, from www.delphi.com Web site Jl 3, '98.
Copyright © 1998 Walt Howe. Reprinted with permission.

many Internet sites took advantage of the availability of newsgroups. It was a significant part of the community building that took place on the networks.

Similarly, BITNET (Because It's Time Network) connected IBM mainframes around the educational community and the world to provide mail services beginning in 1981. Listserv software was developed for this network and later others. Gateways were developed to connect BITNET with the Internet and allowed exchange of e-mail, particularly for e-mail discussion lists. These listservs and other forms of e-mail discussion lists formed another major element in the community building that was taking place.

As the commands for e-mail, FTP, and telnet were standardized, it became a lot easier for non-technical people to learn to use the nets. It was not easy by today's standards by any means, but it did open up use of the Internet to many more people in universities, in particular. Other departments besides the computer, physics, and engineering departments found ways to make good use of the nets—to communicate with colleagues around the world and to share files and resources. Libraries, which had been automating their catalogs, went a step further and made their automated catalogs available to the world.

As more and more universities and organizations connected, the Internet became harder and harder to track.

While the number of sites on the Internet was small, it was fairly easy to keep track of the resources of interest that were available. But as more and more universities and organizations connected, the Internet became harder and harder to track. There was more and more need for tools to index the resources that were available.

The first effort to index the Internet was created in 1989, as Peter Deutsch and his crew at McGill University in Montreal created an archiver for ftp [file transfer protocol] sites, which they named Archie. This software would periodically reach out to all known openly available ftp sites, list their files, and build a searchable index of the software. The commands to search Archie were unix commands, and it took some knowledge of unix to use it to its full capability.

McGill University, which hosted the first Archie, found out one day that half the Internet traffic going into Canada from the United States was accessing Archie. Administrators were concerned that the University was subsidizing such a volume of traffic, and closed down Archie to outside access. Fortunately, by that time, there were many more Archies available.

At about the same time, Brewster Kahle, then at Thinking Machines, Corp., developed his Wide Area Information Server (WAIS), which would index the full text of files in a database and allow searches of the files. There were several versions with varying degrees of complexity and capability developed, but the simplest of these were made available to everyone on the nets. At its peak, Thinking Machines maintained pointers to over 600 databases around the world which had been indexed by WAIS. They included such things as the full set of Usenet Frequently Asked Questions files, the full documentation of working papers by those developing the Internet's standards, and much more. Like Archie, its interface was far from intuitive, and it took some effort to learn to use it well.

In 1991, the first friendly interface to the Internet was developed at the University of Minnesota. The University wanted to develop a simple menu system to access files and information on campus through their local network. A debate followed between mainframe adherents and those who believed in smaller systems with client-server architecture. The mainframe adherents "won" the debate initially, but since the client-server advocates said they could put up a prototype very quickly, they were given the go-ahead to do a demonstration system. The demonstration system was called a gopher after the U. of Minnesota mascot—the golden gopher. The gopher proved to be very prolific, and within a few years there were over 10,000 gophers around the world. It takes no knowledge of unix or computer architecture to use. In a gopher system, you type or click on a number to select the menu selection you want. You can use the U. of Minnesota gopher today to pick gophers from all over the world.

In 1991, the first friendly interface to the Internet was developed

Gopher's usability was enhanced much more when the University of Nevada at Reno developed the VERONICA searchable index of gopher menus. It was purported to be an acronym for Very Easy Rodent-Oriented Netwide Index to Computerized Archives. A spider crawled gopher menus around the world, collecting links and retrieving them for the index. It was so popular that it was very hard to connect to, even though a number of other VERONICA sites were developed to ease the load. Similar indexing software was developed for single sites, called JUGHEAD (Jonzy's Universal Gopher Hierarchy Excavation And Display).

Peter Deutsch, who developed Archie, always insisted that Archie was short for Archiver, and had nothing to do with the comic strip. He was disgusted when VERONICA and JUGHEAD appeared.

In 1989 another significant event took place in making the nets easier to use. Tim Berners-Lee and others at the European Laboratory for Particle Physics, more popularly known as CERN, proposed a new protocol for information distribution. This protocol, which became the World Wide Web in 1991, was based on hypertext—a system of embedding links in text to link to other text, which you have been using every time you selected a text link while reading these pages. Although started before gopher, it was slower to develop.

The development in 1993 of the graphical browser Mosaic by Marc Andreessen and his team at the National Center For Supercomputing Applications (NCSA) gave the protocol its big boost. Today, Andreessen is the brains behind Netscape Corp., which produces what has been so far the most successful graphical type of browser and server, a condition which Microsoft is trying very hard to overcome.

Commercial uses were prohibited unless they directly served the goals of research and education

Since the Internet was initially funded by the government, it was originally limited to research, education, and government uses. Commercial uses were prohibited unless they directly served the goals of research and education. This policy continued until the early 90's, when independent commercial networks began to grow. It then became possible to route traffic across the country from one commercial site to another without passing through the government funded Internet backbone.

Delphi was the first national commercial online service to offer Internet access to its subscribers. It opened up an e-mail connection in July 1992 and full Internet service in November 1992. All pretenses of limitations on commercial use disappeared in May 1995 when the National Science Foundation ended its sponsorship of the Internet backbone, and all traffic relied on commercial networks. AOL, Prodigy, and CompuServe came online. Since commercial usage was so widespread by this time and educational institutions had been paying their own way for some time, the loss of NSF funding had no appreciable effect on costs.

Today, NSF funding has moved beyond supporting the backbone and higher educational institutions to building the K-12 and local public library accesses on the one hand, and the research on the massive high volume connections on the other.

Microsoft's full scale entry into the browser, server, and Internet Service Provider market completed the major shift over to a commercially based Internet. The release of Windows 98 in June 1998 with the Microsoft browser well integrated into the desktop shows Bill Gates' determination to capitalize on the enormous growth of the Internet. Microsoft's success over the past few years has brought court challenges to their dominance. We'll leave it up to you whether you think these battles should be played out in the courts or the marketplace.

A current trend with major implications for the future is the growth of high speed connections. 56K modems and the providers who support them are spreading widely, but this is just a small step compared to what will follow. 56K is not fast enough to carry multimedia, such as sound and video except in low quality. But new technologies many times faster, such as cablemodems, digital subscriber lines (DSL), and satellite broadcast are available in limited locations now, and will become widely available in the next few years. These technologies present problems, not just in the user's connection, but in maintaining high speed data flow reliably from source to the user. Those problems are being worked on, too.

During this period of enormous growth, businesses entering the Internet arena are scrambling to find economic models that work. Free services supported by advertising have shifted some of the direct costs away from the consumer. Services such as Delphi are now offering free web pages, chat rooms, and message boards. Online sales are growing rapidly for such products as books and music CDs and computers, but the profit margins are slim when price comparisons are so easy, and public trust in online security is still shaky.

We live in interesting times!

How Servers Find Needle In Haystack of the Net[2]

The Defense Department created the Internet and so the nature of its offspring should come as no surprise—it's a vast hierarchy with redundancy added in case of war.

That is most evident in the conventions for creating Web addresses like www.nytimes.com, which are, of course, aliases for the strings of numbers that computers use for addresses. The addresses are called domain names; they are converted into numbers known as I.P. (for Internet protocol) addresses. I.P. addresses come as sets of four numbers, like 199.181.172.241.

The domain name system, or D.N.S., is the Internet telephone book that allows computers to convert names into numbers. Of all the computers that make up the Internet, the machines that are ultimately responsible for keeping track of all the names are called the root servers.

The pieces of site names fall into a hierarchy. To parse a name in descending hierarchical order, you start at the right. Americans are most familiar with addresses that end with .com, the designation for commercial ventures. That is called a top-level domain. Other top-level domains are .org for groups like nonprofit organizations, .gov for government agencies, .edu for educational institutions, .mil for military sites and .net for companies that are more closely related to providing Internet services.

Outside the United States, the top-level domains are usually related to a country. For instance, many addresses in the United Kingdom end with .uk. Some addresses in the United States also end in .us, but they are less common.

Top-level domains are just the beginning, even though they come at the end of addresses. Computers decode addresses by examining them from right to left. The machine running the top-level domain answers questions about the smaller domains in the address, and these smaller domains may be broken up even more.

The Web addresses most known to Americans have three levels, but ones with four or even five levels are quite common. For instance, nytimes-gw.customer.ALTER.NET is the name of a machine that helps provide network access to The *New York Times*. The machine belongs to a company

---

2. Article by Peter Wayner, from the *New York Times* G11 My 21, '98. Copyright © 1998 The New York Times Company. Reprinted by Permission.

named Alternet, which uses four levels to name its computers

Most companies stick their Web servers in the third-level domain and name it with www. This is not a requirement. Some of my Web pages are parked on a machine called www.access.digex.net. The Web server does not have to be named www; treesaver.nytimes.com would have worked just as well.

The hierarchy gives computers a clue about how to convert domain names into numbers. Each D.N.S. server is responsible for answering questions about all the machines a step down in the hierarchy. Consider how a computer might look up the www.nytimes.com address. First, it goes to a root server that maintains the list for the top-level domain at the end of the name, in this case, a .com server. It asks for the address for nytimes, then goes to that address and asks for the www address.

One glitch in the database can make someone disappear or send that person's traffic to someone else

What happens when the root server suffers a glitch? Is all the Internet frozen if someone trips over the plug to this machine? No. There are actually nine root servers for the .com domain and more for others. If a computer cannot find the right answer from one, it asks the others.

It should be immediately clear how valuable it can be to control this first step in looking up an address. One glitch in the database can make someone disappear or send that person's traffic to someone else. The power of this location has caused great political turmoil lately because a single company, Network Solutions, controls the information going into the root servers for some of the most popular top-level domains, like .com and .org, and charges fees— $50 a year to list a name—that have been criticized as unfairly high.

Network Solutions runs the primary top-level server for the .com domain. Each day around 3:30 A.M. Eastern Daylight Time, that primary server takes its master list of names and I.P. addresses and converts it into a database that is then copied to the eight other servers.

Many people are offering proposals for how to reorganize the root servers. Some are pushing for the creation of new top-level domains like .firm, which will provide competition for companies like Network Solutions and reduce the concentration in one major database like .com. Others have already started running their own servers with extensions like .xxx. Not all computers recognize these addresses because most are programmed to start with only the standard top-level domains.

Roots and Branches of a Web Address

To the uninitiated, Web addresses seem like a jumble of letters, numbers and punctuation. But it does not take long to discern order in the chaos. Most addresses begin with http://, which reflects how computers on the Web trade information: a method called hypertext transfer protocol. That may be followed by www and may end in one of five suffixes: com, org, net, mil, edu or gov. In between are names identifying the desired site. Most Web addresses follow this hierarchy so the root servers keeping track of each Web site's location can find it quickly when a user goes looking. Here's how those servers work [to find the Web site www.nytimes.com].

(1) Request—When you type the address of a Web site into your browser, your computer asks other computers, known as servers, for directions.

(2) com—The first stop is actually the last part of the Web site's name. Nine computers, which are called root servers and are located around the country, keep track of the location of every Web address that ends in com.

(3) The root server directs you to another computer, nytimes, which acts like a telephone operator forwarding requests to yet another server owned by The *New York Times*.

(4) www is the last stop the request makes. The www server will bring up the requested Web page. If, instead, the request had something to do with e-mail, it would have traveled to either the mail or pop servers.

Finding Each Site

Old Way—The request for a Web page used to go first to the root server called "A" and work its way around to the one called "I" until it found the right address.

New Way—Now, most Web browsers remember which of the root servers gave them the response most quickly the last time the question was asked, and they ask that root server first.

Updating Addresses—The "A" root server keeps a master list of every Web address, and each night the master list is copied onto the other root servers.

Some proposals would even make it easier for people to control which root servers they use. That would provide the most competition, but some people are uneasy about that idea because it could fragment the Internet. A used-car lot might not want to advertise on a site named like-new.used.car unless every computer was programmed to recognize the .car root server.

The role and future of root servers already has the attention of government officials in Washington and abroad. Governments view this job as one role they can serve in cyberspace. Other people, however, say that market-based solutions, where people are free to list with and use the root servers they like, can be just as effective, if not better.

Taming the Beast[3]

The lure of the Internet disguises a welter of issues—privacy, commerce, free speech

Grandpa's got a screen name, your daughter's sending e-mail to Leonardo DiCaprio, and Matt Drudge, a Hollywood gossip with a gonzo Web site, suddenly has become your favorite source of breaking news.

Holy cyberspace! The Internet is hot

Think of it: Five years ago, it was perfectly acceptable to admit you didn't know what the Internet was. Today, 62 million Americans 16 and older are on line, according to a national survey released last week, and 7 million more expect to click onto computer networks in the next six months. "How-to" guides introducing the Internet are out; books that probe Internet addiction are in.

Words like "revolutionary" and "transforming" and "fundamental" roll off the tongues of cyberscholars to describe the surging medium. Futurist and author Esther Dyson writes in "Release 2.0" that the Internet will do nothing short of reshaping the world: "The Net's impact—the widespread availability of two-way electronic communications—will change all of our lives," Dyson writes. "It will suck power away from central governments, mass media, and big business.... It gives power to the powerless. That is, it undermines central authorities whether they are good or bad."

But for all the predictions of computer nirvana and for all the millions signing onto Web sites, weighty questions still surround the Internet: how to control access, how to sell products through it, how to keep it secure, and how to fit it into American law, which has never seen anything like it. Lawsuits (including one involving the so-hot Drudge) will take years to decide anything.

For good or bad, hype about the medium continues to travel with the speed of the Internet. Michael Kinsley, a longtime Washington journalist who is now editor of *Slate*, Microsoft Corp.'s online magazine, declared last week that the story of President Clinton's alleged sexual relationship

---

3. Article by Mary Leonard, from *The Boston Globe* C1 + Fe 8, '98. Copyright © 1998 *The Boston Globe*. Reprinted with permission.

with former White House intern Monica Lewinsky, rumored first on the Drudge Report Web site and later reported in the mainstream media, "is to the Internet what the Kennedy assassination was to TV news: its coming of age as a media force."

Any technology that changes the ways we communicate—witness the printing press, the telephone, and the television—has a profound impact on the culture. The Internet is no exception, and with its speed, its content (500,000 Web sites of information, growing every hour), its global reach, its integration in the workplace, its libertarian nature, and, perhaps most important, its talk-back capacity, the Net has the potential to be at once empowering and engaging, decentralizing and isolating, and even right and wrong, as in the Web site reporting on the Lewinsky case.

The Internet culture has its risks (not just the sensationalized ones, such as pornography home pages and prowling pedophiles), including the veracity question: Does a medium that lets everybody anonymously act like an authority ultimately have no authority at all? The biggest rap on the Internet's virtual reality is that it isn't real. People can't trust it.

Does a medium that lets everybody anonymously act like an authority ultimately have no authority at all?

This has become painfully obvious to those expecting a commercial payoff from the Internet. Most Web sites that market products or services aren't profitable yet, says Donna Hoffman, a management professor and codirector of Project 2000 at Vanderbilt University, because consumers don't trust the security of transactions in cyberspace and have no confidence that online businesses will protect their privacy.

"Until these issues get ironed out, Internet commerce is not ready for prime time, and the cultural revolution isn't going to be realized," Hoffman says. "It's stuck on the consumer side because businesses, at their own peril, are ignoring these very serious human issues of privacy and trust."

Are traditional news organizations also ignoring those issues as they clamber to create and market Web sites? Intense competition to score cyberscoops has brought retractions (The *Dallas Morning News* on Jan. 26) and corrections (The *Wall Street Journal* on Wednesday) to online stories by reputable news organizations, but only after the flawed stories got wide airing on television, radio, and in newspapers.

Tom Rosenstiel, a media analyst who directs the Project for Excellence in Journalism in Washington, says moving onto the never-static Internet is natural for the news busi-

---

Casting the Internet

- 62 million Americans, or 30 percent of the population over age 16, say they use the Internet. That's up 32 percent from a year ago.
- 7 million adults say they plan to go online in the next six months.
- Nearly 70 percent of all Internet users go online from their homes. They engage in many activities, including sending and receiving e-mail; getting information about hobbies or products; and reading the news.
- The newest members of the online community are "middle Americans": They are older, less well-educated, and less affluent than the first wave.
- A profile of the Internet user in 1996 was: male (64 percent), bachelor's degree or higher (46 percent); and income of more than $50,000 (60 percent). In 1997, the profile was: male: (54 percent); bachelor's degree or higher (36 percent), and income over $50,000 (53 percent).
- In 1997, the average Internet user spent 9.8 hours a week on line. That grew from 6.9 hours in 1996.
- While only 17 percent of Internet users buy products on line, about 60 percent shop on line, comparing products' features, prices, and places to purchase them.

Source: IntelliQuest Information Group

---

ness, but is also a cultural change causing heartburn in newsrooms.

"The issue mostly is speed; it's axiomatic that the less time you have to prepare a news account, the more mistakes you'll make," Rosenstiel said. "But you also see when journalists shift mediums—from newspapers to television, for example—their level of sourcing vanishes, and they become a lot more willing to speculate."

Some worry that the Drudge standard—that what you post on the Internet doesn't always have to be accurate, as long as it's exclusive and entertaining—will nudge cyberjournalists in the same direction and further erode the low level of public confidence in the press. Americans say repeatedly in polls that they deplore the media's graphic, nonstop coverage of the Lewinsky-Clinton story; at the same time, they showed enormous interest in its titillating details, visiting or "hitting" more media Web sites in the week after the story broke than at any time in the Net's history.

In striking down the 1996 Communications Decency Act, which made it a federal crime to send or display indecent material to children on line, the Supreme Court last summer affirmed that Internet speech is protected by the First Amendment. But can that speech go too far, particularly if it's untrue or can't be proved?

White House adviser Sidney Blumenthal is suing both Drudge and America Online, the Internet service provider that sends out the Drudge Report, for alleging on line last August that Blumenthal had "a spousal abuse past." Drudge quickly retracted the false charge and claimed it came from GOP sources. But once it was on the Net, it was in the public domain, and Blumenthal has pressed ahead with a $30 million suit.

It's one sign of the Internet's cultural coming of age that it's entering the legal crosshairs, increasingly the target of litigation and legislation, as lawyers, businessmen, and ethicists try to build it into the media framework. Cyberlaw is suddenly a hot field; universities offer courses in it, and lawyers sign up for seminars on Internet contract, privacy, and intellectual-property law. The hallowed Harvard Law School announced just Friday that it would offer a course to the public on "Privacy in Cyberspace"—and would offer it on line.

It's one sign of the Internet's cultural coming of age that it's entering the legal crosshairs

Daniel Weitzner, deputy director of the Center for Democracy and Technology in Washington, suggests that the rush to find legal solutions is really a substitute for addressing cultural issues posed by the Net. "The cultural challenge for our society is trying to figure out what to make of the Internet, what to do with the Internet and, most important, how people can come to trust what others say and write and offer as opinion on the Internet," Weitzner said.

Timothy McVeigh, a chief petty officer in the Navy, apparently believed that he could trust America Online to protect his privacy when he described himself as "gay" but didn't reveal his real name in an Internet user profile. Last month, the company acknowledged it had disclosed the identity of McVeigh (no relation to the Oklahoma City bomber) to Navy investigators, who dismissed him for violating the service's "don't ask, don't tell" policy on homosexuality. McVeigh has sued successfully to be reinstated and resume his Navy career.

Online aficionados predict that curiosity—the main reason people start surfing the Net—will give way over time to a greater sophistication that allows users to establish "electronically mediated relationships—and find comfort, identity, and trust in shared-interest online communities.

. Until that utopia arrives, of course, most people will embrace the Internet for what is by far its most popular function: sending and receiving e-mail. E-mail now is nearly essential for communicating in the workplace, but it's swiftly becoming the technology of choice for more casual communication, from keeping up with friends overseas to tracking children at college.

Peter Zandan, chairman of IntelliQuest in Austin, Texas, a company that collects marketing data for the technology industry, says he is surprised by the phenomenal growth of those who say they use the Internet and by the amount of time many are spending on line: 9.8 hours a week now, up from 6.9 hours a year ago.

"I know there aren't two additional hours in the day since the last time we surveyed, so the Internet is clearly taking away from something," Zandan said. "Is it shopping? Is it being with your family? Is electronic communication taking away from face-to-face interaction?" Yes, Clifford Stoll says. The author of *Silicon Snake Oil*, Stoll says the Internet is the television of the '90s, saying, "It's entertainment, a terrific way to waste time and satisfy a craving for knowledge without learning anything.

"What good does it do our society to take us away from a close, physical community and put us in touch with distant strangers," Stoll asks. "The things people yearn for most—a community, a relationship with commitment and trust—are exactly what you don't have on line. I'm very skeptical of it, in every way."

Congress Finds No Easy Answers to Internet Controversies[4]

On matters of censorship, privacy, taxation and commerce, Hill struggles to regulate new industry without stifling it.

Internet surfers who inadvertently log on to "www.whitehouse.com" are in for a big surprise.

Instead of finding information about the president and the executive branch, visitors will find an X-rated Web site complete with flashing pictures of scantily clad women and ways to link up to live video strip shows.

This is exactly the type of site that worries members of Congress who are concerned about the relatively easy access children have to pornography online. Internet users will find themselves connected to the X-rated White House just by typing "com" instead of "gov" at the end of the Internet address.

As lawmakers return for the second session of the 105th Congress, they will likely take up a wide range of Internet-related issues.

From taxes to gambling to unsolicited e-mail, dozens of bills have been introduced to restrict or in some way govern the growth of the Internet, a global communications network that links people via computers and telephone lines worldwide.

Republican Rep. Rick White of Washington, co-founder of the Congressional Internet Caucus, said Congress' watchword is, "When in doubt, regulate it. [But] that's not always the right approach."

But Congress is finding there are no easy answers in dealing with this new medium.

Although developed with the help of the federal government, the Internet is not owned by anyone, and it is not confined by geographical borders. Many lawmakers may be familiar with the Internet but know little of its workings.

"There are very many members of Congress who know the Internet as a word but don't have any idea how it works and the potential it has for changing economic and human behavior," said Democratic Rep. Zoe Lofgren of California.

Degrees of Freedom

But the high-tech industry and its supporters say the Internet must remain free of regulation in order to grow and prosper.

"I think that the heart of the challenge is to expand the access of the new technology without expanding government intervention," said Sen. Ron Wyden, D-Ore., who has sponsored a bill (S 442) that would impose a moratorium on taxation aimed directly at the Internet.

For the most part, the Clinton administration has said it is willing to let industry lead the way. In a report released in July 1997, the White House endorsed the idea of keeping the Internet as free of regulation as possible. "We don't want to govern the Internet," said Larry Irving, administrator of the Commerce Department's National Telecommunications and Information Administration.

In his State of the Union address on Jan. 27, Clinton said, "We must give parents the tools they need to help protect their children from inappropriate material on the Net, but we also must make sure that we protect the exploding global commercial potential of the Internet"

Some members are determined that Congress not give special treatment to the Internet merely because it is a new form of communication

But some members are determined that Congress not give special treatment to the Internet merely because it is a new form of communication.

"The Internet can ride over a phone line, cable wire or broadcast over a television signal.... It is not qualitatively better than other communications media," said Democratic Rep. Edward J. Markey of Massachusetts, who has raised questions about the fairness of imposing a moratorium on Internet taxes.

Other lawmakers argue that Congress must establish ground rules in some areas such as limiting children's access to pornographic sites and not expanding gambling via the Internet to states where it is currently illegal.

"You have to have some kind of rules; you just can't have totally unfettered commerce," said Rep. Michael G. Oxley, R-Ohio, who has supported restrictions on encryption—data scrambling technology used to prevent unauthorized access to electronic data on the Internet. (*1997 Weekly Report*, p. 3003)

Republican Rep. Robert W. Goodlatte of Virginia said Congress needs to examine each issue on a case by case basis.

He has proposed legislation (HR 2380) that would ban gambling on the Internet and require Internet service providers to discontinue service to gambling sites identified by the Federal Communications Commission.

At the same time, Goodlatte also is the chief sponsor of a bill (HR 695) to relax current restrictions on the export of encryption products. He and others say securing information through encryption is a critical element in the growth of Internet commerce because many people are not willing to send sensitive information, such as their credit card numbers or Social Security numbers, over the Internet unless they can be sure it is kept private.

Government Origins

A study . . . estimated that the value of goods and services traded over the Internet would grow from $8 billion in 1997 to $327 billion by 2002

The Internet was developed in the late 1960s by the Pentagon's Advanced Research Projects Agency (ARPA) as an experimental computer network aimed at withstanding a military attack and communicating with universities and researchers.

As use of this network (known as ARPAnet) grew, it was divided into a military and civilian network. The civilian network was managed by the National Science Foundation. After generally being reserved for use by universities and government agencies, it was eventually opened to commercial use in the 1980s.

Today, the Internet is quickly becoming a ubiquitous part of society. One of the most popular aspects of the Internet is the World Wide Web (WWW), where companies, government agencies and even individuals can post "web pages" with news, entertainment and other information.

But the Internet is more than just a means of disseminating information. In fact, it is increasingly a way for businesses to conduct transactions.

A study in July 1997 by Forrester Research, a technology research company based in Cambridge, Mass., estimated that the value of goods and services traded over the Internet would grow from $8 billion in 1997 to $327 billion by 2002. That does not include consumers who are increasingly shopping on the Internet.

According to a joint survey by CommerceNet, an industry association that promotes electronic commerce, and Nielsen Media Research, the media research firm that produces the Nielsen ratings of television viewership, released in March 1997, about 5.6 million people reported using the Internet to purchase products.

Dealing With Pornography

Among the first issues lawmakers will take up this year is pornography on the Internet. The Senate Commerce Science and Committee has scheduled a hearing Feb. 10 on online pornography and on [Dan] Coats' [R-Ind.] bill (S 1482), which would prohibit Internet distribution of material harmful to minors, including material that depicts, describes or represents sexual acts.

"I'm the last person who wants to impose regulation on what I think is a marvelous technology," Coats said. But "I do think that society has a responsibility" to protect minors.

Congress banned dissemination to minors of "indecent" or "patently offensive" material on the Internet in the 1996 telecommunications law (PL 104-104). The Supreme Court struck down that provision in June 1997, saying its broad wording also imposed impermissible limits on adults. (*1997 Weekly Report*, p. 1519)

Many of the high-tech free speech groups that fought that anti-pornography provision all the way to the Supreme Court have come out against S 1482 as well. "Given the fact that parents already have tools available to control what their children see [on the Internet], the [Coats'] legislation would be unconstitutional," said James X. Dempsey, senior staff counsel for the Center for Democracy and Technology, a group that promotes online civil liberties.

Web of Issues

Prodded by the administration, which originally defended the communications act in court, the center co-sponsored a three-day summit in December 1997 to promote the use of software to block out Web sites that parents may not want their children to access. (*1997 Weekly Report*, p. 3028)

Senate Commerce, Science, and Transportation Committee Chairman John McCain, R-Ariz., has not said whether he will support Coats' bill, but he plans to introduce legislation that would tie funding for schools and libraries to hook up to the Internet to the use of some type of blocking technology that would limit minors' access to online smut.

"I believe the minimum of regulation is in order, but there are some things you simply can't ignore," McCain said, citing child molesters who get information about children from the Internet.

Legislation introduced by Sen. Lauch Faircloth, R-N.C., (S 1356) and Rep. Marge Roukema, R-N.J., (HR 2791) would prohibit Internet service providers from giving an account to those registered as convicted sexual predators under Megan's Law (PL 104-236), which allowed the FBI to provide the names of sexual offenders released from jail to local authorities.

But pornography is not the only cyber-sin that is creating problems for Congress. Lawmakers may also take action this year on legislation to crack down on Internet gambling. The House Judiciary Committee's Crime Subcommittee is scheduled to hold hearings Feb. 4 on Goodlatte's legislation. In the Senate, Republican Jon Kyl of Arizona will be pushing for floor action on a similar bill (S 474). Kyl's bill was approved by the Judiciary Committee in October. (*1997 Weekly Report, p. 3010*)

While many high-tech companies have been reluctant to take a stand on the issue, the Interactive Services Association, which represents Internet service providers and other high-tech companies, opposes the bill, arguing that the legislation will open the door to further regulation of the Internet.

Data Scrambling

While pornography and gambling remain two areas of concern for lawmakers, encryption is one of the most contentious issues to surface in this Congress. Many high-technology companies are backing Goodlatte's bill, which would allow U.S. companies to export encryption products that are equal in strength to those generally available overseas. They say current restrictions are hampering their ability to compete with foreign companies who can export much stronger forms of encryption.

The administration has opposed relaxing export controls because of concerns by law enforcement officials that widespread use of robust encryption will hamper law enforcement and intelligence-gathering. But FBI Director Louis J. Freeh set off alarms last summer in the high-tech community by also advocating that Congress require manufacturers to include a feature in encryption products sold domestically that would allow law enforcement, under warranted circumstances, to gain access to the keys needed to decode encrypted communications—an idea opposed by industry.

While pornography and gambling remain two areas of concern for law-makers, encryption is one of the most contentious issues to surface in this Congress

Five committees in 1997 approved various forms of HR 695 that would impose the domestic controls Freeh has advocated. House Rules Committee Chairman Gerald B. H. Solomon, R-N.Y., whose panel must decide which version to send to the House floor, has said he will not allow HR 695 to go to the floor unless it includes the provisions backed by law enforcement officials.

But the high-tech industry representatives say they would prefer no bill to one that imposes new controls on encryption.

So far, some lawmakers and even some industry officials question whether Congress can settle the matter.

Debra Waggoner, a vice president for international affairs at the American Electronics Association, said encryption "is where the rubber meets the road" for the Clinton administration and its declaration of avoiding any legislation that could hamper the growth of Internet commerce.

Informing Congress

Many lawmakers and industry executives say it is no surprise that Congress is having a difficult time dealing with the Internet.

"The issues tend to be fairly complex and technical from a legal and from a technological perspective," said John Scheibel, vice president and general counsel for the Computer and Communications Industry Association.

Democratic Sen. Patrick J. Leahy of Vermont, who has been active on many Internet issues, recalled how he recently was describing to some colleagues how he uses e-mail to communicate with his children and realized afterward that many of his colleagues were not familiar with what he was talking about.

"I think at some point on some of these things, we have to stop pretending we know everything," Leahy said.

Dave McClure, executive director of the Association of Online Professionals, said whenever a medium has emerged that has "so much potential for both good and evil, it's going to come to the attention of government and the attention of Congress." But McClure and others have expressed concern about some of the approaches lawmakers have taken. In particular, they are concerned about efforts to force Internet service providers to stop an undesirable practice, as the sexual predator and Internet gambling bills would do.

"I don't think Internet service providers should be deputized as cops on the Net," said Dempsey of the Center for Democracy and Technology.

Meanwhile, high-technology companies have been moving aggressively to inform lawmakers about how the technology works in an effort to stop troublesome legislation and promote bills favorable to their industry.

Among the measures they are pushing is Wyden's legislation (S 442) and a similar bill introduced in the House (HR 1054) that would establish a moratorium on taxes specifically aimed at the Internet, while excluding such traditional levies as property and payroll taxes. Its supporters say it is necessary to call a time out so that the Internet is not handicapped by overzealous state and local officials who see an opportunity to reap tax revenues. Opponents see a moratorium as an unnecessary pre-emption of state and local taxing authority.

Sen. Byron L. Dorgan, D-N.D., believes that some in the high-tech community are trying to take advantage of the complexity and the novelty of the issues surrounding the Internet by pushing legislation that will be profitable to their industry. He points to the Internet tax bill as an example, saying it is an attempt "to do an end run around state and local tax jurisdictions."

The Internet "is raising all sorts of policy issues," Dorgan said. "There will be people who want to take advantage of that."

Technorealism Overview[5]

In this heady age of rapid technological change, we all struggle to maintain our bearings. The developments that unfold each day in communications and computing can be thrilling and disorienting. One understandable reaction is to wonder: Are these changes good or bad? Should we welcome or fear them?

The answer is both. Technology is making life more convenient and enjoyable, and many of us healthier, wealthier, and wiser. But it is also affecting work, family, and the economy in unpredictable ways, introducing new forms of tension and distraction, and posing new threats to the cohesion of our physical communities.

Despite the complicated and often contradictory implications of technology, the conventional wisdom is woefully simplistic. Pundits, politicians, and self-appointed visionaries do us a disservice when they try to reduce these complexities to breathless tales of either high-tech doom or cyber-elation. Such polarized thinking leads to dashed hopes and unnecessary anxiety, and prevents us from understanding our own culture.

Over the past few years, even as the debate over technology has been dominated by the louder voices at the extremes, a new, more balanced consensus has quietly taken shape. This document seeks to articulate some of the shared beliefs behind that consensus, which we have come to call technorealism.

Technorealism demands that we think critically about the role that tools and interfaces play in human evolution and everyday life. Integral to this perspective is our understanding that the current tide of technological transformation, while important and powerful, is actually a continuation of waves of change that have taken place throughout history. Looking, for example, at the history of the automobile, television, or the telephone—not just the devices but the institutions they became—we see profound benefits as well as substantial costs. Similarly, we anticipate mixed blessings from today's emerging technologies, and expect to forever

---

5. This document was introduced on March 12, 1998, by a group of 12 technology writers—David Bennahum, Brooke Shelby Biggs, Paulina Borsook, Marisa Bowe, Simson Garfinkel, Steven Johnson, Douglas Rushkoff, Andrew Shapiro, David Shenk, Steve Silberman, Mark Stahlman, and Stefanie Syman (based on a concept and draft document by Shapiro, Shenk and Johnson). It was accompanied by an open invitation for any interested individuals to endorse the technorealist approach. For more information on technorealism, visit the Web site at www.technorealism.org.

be on guard for unexpected consequences—which must be addressed by thoughtful design and appropriate use

As technorealists, we seek to expand the fertile middle ground between techno-utopianism and neo-Luddism. We are technology "critics" in the same way, and for the same reasons, that others are food critics, art critics, or literary critics. We can be passionately optimistic about some technologies, skeptical and disdainful of others. Still, our goal is neither to champion nor dismiss technology, but rather to understand it and apply it in a manner more consistent with basic human values.

Below are some evolving basic principles that help explain technorealism.

Principles of Technorealism

1. Technologies are not neutral.

A great misconception of our time is the idea that technologies are completely free of bias—that because they are inanimate artifacts, they don't promote certain kinds of behaviors over others. In truth, technologies come loaded with both intended and unintended social, political, and economic leanings. Every tool provides its users with a particular manner of seeing the world and specific ways of interacting with others. It is important for each of us to consider the biases of various technologies and to seek out those that reflect our values and aspirations.

2. The Internet is revolutionary, but not Utopian.

The Net is an extraordinary communications tool that provides a range of new opportunities for people, communities, businesses, and government. Yet as cyberspace becomes more populated, it increasingly resembles society at large, in all its complexity. For every empowering or enlightening aspect of the wired life, there will also be dimensions that are malicious, perverse, or rather ordinary.

3. Government has an important role to play on the electronic frontier.

Contrary to some claims, cyberspace is not formally a place or jurisdiction separate from Earth. While governments should respect the rules and customs that have arisen in cyberspace, and should not stifle this new world with inefficient regulation or censorship, it is foolish to say that the public has no sovereignty over what an errant citizen or fraudulent corporation does online. As the representative of the people and the guardian of democratic values,

For every empowering or enlightening aspect of the wired life, there will also be dimensions that are malicious, perverse, or rather ordinary

the state has the right and responsibility to help integrate cyberspace and conventional society.

Technology standards and privacy issues, for example, are too important to be entrusted to the marketplace alone. Competing software firms have little interest in preserving the open standards that are essential to a fully functioning interactive network. Markets encourage innovation, but they do not necessarily insure the public interest.

4. Information is not knowledge.

The art of teaching cannot be replicated by computers

All around us, information is moving faster and becoming cheaper to acquire, and the benefits are manifest. That said, the proliferation of data is also a serious challenge, requiring new measures of human discipline and skepticism. We must not confuse the thrill of acquiring or distributing information quickly with the more daunting task of converting it into knowledge and wisdom. Regardless of how advanced our computers become, we should never use them as a substitute for our own basic cognitive skills of awareness, perception, reasoning, and judgment.

5. Wiring the schools will not save them.

The problems with America's public schools—disparate funding, social promotion, bloated class size, crumbling infrastructure, lack of standards—have almost nothing to do with technology. Consequently, no amount of technology will lead to the educational revolution prophesied by President Clinton and others. The art of teaching cannot be replicated by computers, the Net, or by "distance learning." These tools can, of course, augment an already high-quality educational experience. But to rely on them as any sort of panacea would be a costly mistake.

6. Information wants to be protected.

It's true that cyberspace and other recent developments are challenging our copyright laws and frameworks for protecting intellectual property. The answer, though, is not to scrap existing statutes and principles. Instead, we must update old laws and interpretations so that information receives roughly the same protection it did in the context of old media. The goal is the same: to give authors sufficient control over their work so that they have an incentive to create, while maintaining the right of the public to make fair use of that information. In neither context does information want "to be free." Rather, it needs to be protected.

7. The public owns the airwaves; the public should benefit from their use.

The recent digital spectrum giveaway to broadcasters underscores the corrupt and inefficient misuse of public resources in the arena of technology. The citizenry should benefit and profit from the use of public frequencies, and should retain a portion of the spectrum for educational, cultural, and public access uses. We should demand more for private use of public property.

8. Understanding technology should be an essential component of global citizenship.

In a world driven by the flow of information, the interfaces—and the underlying code—that make information visible are becoming enormously powerful social forces. Understanding their strengths and limitations, and even participating in the creation of better tools, should be an important part of being an involved citizen. These tools affect our lives as much as laws do, and we should subject them to a similar democratic scrutiny.

II. The Internet and Business

Editor's Introduction

The Internet was designed for national security and for many years was used almost exclusively by academics and scientists. Less than five years ago, there was even a debate concerning whether or not advertisements should be allowed on the Web. But as the world became connected, businesses saw the Web to be a ripe medium for connecting with customers in new ways and to sell and distibute their products in new, more efficient ways. The Internet has added a new dimension to business: companies have put marketing and promotional information on the Web; online stores sell books, CDs, flowers, or anything else; online magazines display flashing and constantly changing ads; businesses handle business-to-business transactions online. Practically every type of business is trying to figure out how to make money using the Internet, and the government is attempting to ensure that no obstacles are placed in the way of this new economic driver. At the same time, the government is trying to ensure that when these companies are invited into our homes on our computers they aren't leaving with more information about us than we would like to share. Making government's role more difficult is the fact that the same traits that make the Internet very attractive to legitimate businesses also make the Internet a haunting ground for con artists.

Business touches on many issues in which the government has traditionally had a say: privacy, censorship, fraud, copyrights, taxation, and many more. The old rules set for these areas are often obsolete in regard to the Internet. This presents a huge challenge for governments (not just the United States government, but all governments), because like never before, business can be transacted easily between people in different parts of the world, all with varying and sometimes conflicting economic, social, political, and religious ideals. The first article in this chapter is a policy statement from the White House announcing the goals the United States is to pursue concerning regulation of the Internet.

"The Promise of One to One (A Love Story)" is not the story of an online romance. Instead, it describes many of the ways in which companies are trying to make money through the Internet, and the levels of success they have achieved toward reaching their goals. The "promise" referred to in the title is the dream of marketers that the Internet will be able to determine what products a consumer is interested in from his or her online behavior, and then present the consumer with offers for products that there is a very good chance she or he will be interested in.

Following that is an article discussing how some companies that have well established clout in non-electronic commerce have had trouble achieving similar success in electronic commerce. That article is followed by "The American Way of Spam." No, it's not about the canned food; instead, it's an article about a basically new (and, to many, bothersome) business that has grown out of the Internet: direct marketing through unsolicited bulk e-mail.

The Web has had profound effects on journalism, possibly moreso than on any other type of business. Most news agencies, whether newspapers, news magazines, or television networks, have actively embraced the Web as a new way to distribute the news. The immediacy of news distribution on the Web is forcing them to confront new challenges that threaten some of their long-held ethical practices. "Why Web Warriors Might Worry" discusses three of the main issues that journalists are now facing: interactivity, credibility and authority, and the editorial versus advertising conflict.

We end the chapter with a short lesson in common sense for the electronic age. With a computer and a credit card, you can purchase practically anything over the Internet from many legitimate businesses, big and small, but there are also people who have set up professional looking Web sites that give every impression of being the work of a legitimate business. These flashy online storefronts, however, can be a mere facade for unscrupulous con artists. The non-profit Internet Fraud Watch has produced a list of "Basic Internet Tips" to help consumers avoid becoming victims of one of the non-legitimate businesses lurking on the Web.

A Framework for Global Electronic Commerce[1]

BACKGROUND

The Global Information Infrastructure (GII), still in the early stages of its development, is already transforming our world. Over the next decade, advances on the GII will affect almost every aspect of daily life—education, health care, work and leisure activities. Disparate populations, once separated by distance and time, will experience these changes as part of a global community.

No single force embodies our electronic transformation more than the evolving medium known as the Internet. Once a tool reserved for scientific and academic exchange, the Internet has emerged as an appliance of every day life, accessible from almost every point on the planet. Students across the world are discovering vast treasure troves of data via the World Wide Web. Doctors are utilizing tele-medicine to administer off-site diagnoses to patients in need. Citizens of many nations are finding additional outlets for personal and political expression. The Internet is being used to reinvent government and reshape our lives and our communities in the process. As the Internet empowers citizens and democratizes societies, it is also changing classic business and economic paradigms. New models of commercial interaction are developing as businesses and consumers participate in the electronic marketplace and reap the resultant benefits. Entrepreneurs are able to start new businesses more easily, with smaller up-front investment requirements, by accessing the Internet's worldwide network of customers.

Internet technology is having a profound effect on the global trade in services. World trade involving computer software, entertainment products (motion pictures, videos, games, sound recordings), information services (databases, online newspapers), technical information, product licenses, financial services, and professional services (businesses and technical consulting, accounting, architectural design, legal advice, travel services, etc.) has grown rapidly in the past decade, now accounting for well over $40 billion of U.S. exports alone.

---

1. This article is a White House policy paper dated July 1, 1997. It can be viewed online at www.ecommerce.gov/framewrk.htm

An increasing share of these transactions occurs online. The GII has the potential to revolutionize commerce in these and other areas by dramatically lowering transaction costs and facilitating new types of commercial transactions.

The Internet will also revolutionize retail and direct marketing. Consumers will be able to shop in their homes for a wide variety of products from manufacturers and retailers all over the world. They will be able to view these products on their computers or televisions, access information about the products, visualize the way the products may fit together (constructing a room of furniture on their screen, for example), and order and pay for their choice, all from their living rooms.

Commerce on the Internet could total tens of billions of dollars by the turn of the century

Commerce on the Internet could total tens of billions of dollars by the turn of the century. For this potential to be realized fully, governments must adopt a non-regulatory, market-oriented approach to electronic commerce, one that facilitates the emergence of a transparent and predictable legal environment to support global business and commerce. Official decision makers must respect the unique nature of the medium and recognize that widespread competition and increased consumer choice should be the defining features of the new digital marketplace.

Many businesses and consumers are still wary of conducting extensive business over the Internet because of the lack of a predictable legal environment governing transactions. This is particularly true for international commercial activity where concerns about enforcement of contracts, liability, intellectual property protection, privacy, security and other matters have caused businesses and consumers to be cautious.

As use of the Internet expands, many companies and Internet users are concerned that some governments will impose extensive regulations on the Internet and electronic commerce. Potential areas of problematic regulation include taxes and duties, restrictions on the type of information transmitted, control over standards development, licensing requirements and rate regulation of service providers. Indeed, signs of these types of commerce-inhibiting actions already are appearing in many nations. Preempting these harmful actions before they take root is a strong motivation for the strategy outlined in this paper.

Governments can have a profound effect on the growth of commerce on the Internet. By their actions, they can facilitate electronic trade or inhibit it. Knowing when to act and—at least as important—when not to act, will be crucial to the development of electronic commerce. This report articulates the Administration's vision for the emergence of the GII as a vibrant global marketplace by suggesting a set of principles, presenting a series of policies, and establishing a road map for international discussions and agreements to facilitate the growth of commerce on the Internet.

PRINCIPLES

1. The private sector should lead.

Though government played a role in financing the initial development of the Internet, its expansion has been driven primarily by the private sector. For electronic commerce to flourish, the private sector must continue to lead. Innovation, expanded services, broader participation, and lower prices will arise in a market-driven arena, not in an environment that operates as a regulated industry.

Accordingly, governments should encourage industry self-regulation wherever appropriate and support the efforts of private sector organizations to develop mechanisms to facilitate the successful operation of the Internet. Even where collective agreements or standards are necessary, private entities should, where possible, take the lead in organizing them. Where government action or intergovernmental agreements are necessary, on taxation for example, private sector participation should be a formal part of the policy making process.

2. Governments should avoid undue restrictions on electronic commerce.

Parties should be able to enter into legitimate agreements to buy and sell products and services across the Internet with minimal government involvement or intervention. Unnecessary regulation of commercial activities will distort development of the electronic marketplace by decreasing the supply and raising the cost of products and services for consumers the world over.

Business models must evolve rapidly to keep pace with the break-neck speed of change in the technology; government attempts to regulate are likely to be outmoded by the time they are finally enacted, especially to the extent such regulations are technology-specific.

Accordingly, governments should refrain from imposing new and unnecessary regulations, bureaucratic procedures, or taxes and tariffs on commercial activities that take place via the Internet.

3. Where governmental involvement is needed, its aim

Innovation, expanded services, broader participation, and lower prices will arise in a market-driven arena, not in an environment that operates as a regulated industry

should be to support and enforce a predictable, minimalist, consistent and simple legal environment for commerce.

In some areas, government agreements may prove necessary to facilitate electronic commerce and protect consumers. In these cases, governments should establish a predictable and simple legal environment based on a decentralized, contractual model of law rather than one based on top-down regulation. This may involve states as well as national governments. Where government intervention is necessary to facilitate electronic commerce, its goal should be to ensure competition, protect intellectual property and privacy, prevent fraud, foster transparency, support commercial transactions, and facilitate dispute resolution.

Electronic commerce faces significant challenges where it intersects with existing regulatory schemes

4. Governments should recognize the unique qualities of the Internet.

The genius and explosive success of the Internet can be attributed in part to its decentralized nature and to its tradition of bottom-up governance. These same characteristics pose significant logistical and technological challenges to existing regulatory models, and governments should tailor their policies accordingly.

Electronic commerce faces significant challenges where it intersects with existing regulatory schemes. We should not assume, for example, that the regulatory frameworks established over the past sixty years for telecommunications, radio and television fit the Internet. Regulation should be imposed only as a necessary means to achieve an important goal on which there is a broad consensus. Existing laws and regulations that may hinder electronic commerce should be reviewed and revised or eliminated to reflect the needs of the new electronic age.

5. Electronic commerce over the Internet should be facilitated on a global basis.

The Internet is emerging as a global marketplace. The legal framework supporting commercial transactions on the Internet should be governed by consistent principles across state, national, and international borders that lead to predictable results regardless of the jurisdiction in which a particular buyer or seller resides.

ISSUES

This paper covers nine areas where international agreements are needed to preserve the Internet
as a non-regulatory medium, one in which competition and consumer choice will shape the marketplace. Although there are significant areas of overlap, these items can be divided into three main subgroups: financial issues, legal issues, and market access issues.

Financial Issues
- customs and taxation
- electronic payments

Legal Issues
- "Uniform Commercial Code" for electronic commerce
- intellectual property protection
- privacy
- security

Market Access Issues
- telecommunications infrastructure and information technology
- content
- technical standards

I   Financial Issues

1   CUSTOMS AND TAXATION

For over 50 years, nations have negotiated tariff reductions because they have recognized that the economies and citizens of all nations benefit from freer trade. Given this recognition, and because the Internet is truly a global medium, it makes little sense to introduce tariffs on goods and services delivered over the Internet.

Further, the Internet lacks the clear and fixed geographic lines of transit that historically have characterized the physical trade of goods. Thus, while it remains possible to administer tariffs for products ordered over the Internet but ultimately delivered via surface or air transport, the structure of the Internet makes it difficult to do so when the product or service is delivered electronically. Nevertheless, many nations are looking for new sources of revenue, and may seek to levy tariffs on global electronic commerce.

Therefore, the United States will advocate in the World Trade Organization (WTO) and other appropriate international fora that the Internet be declared a tariff-free environment whenever it is used to deliver products or services. This principle should be established quickly before nations

The Internet lacks the clear and fixed geographic lines of transit that historically have characterized the physical trade of goods

impose tariffs and before vested interests form to protect those tariffs.

In addition, the United States believes that no new taxes should be imposed on Internet commerce. The taxation of commerce conducted over the Internet should be consistent with the established principles of international taxation, should avoid inconsistent national tax jurisdictions and double taxation, and should be simple to administer and easy to understand.

Any taxation of Internet sales should follow these principles:

- *It should neither distort nor hinder commerce.* No tax system should discriminate among types of commerce, nor should it create incentives that will change the nature or location of transactions.

The Administration is also concerned about possible moves by state and local tax authorities to target electronic commerce and Internet access

- *The system should be simple and transparent.* It should be capable of capturing the overwhelming majority of appropriate revenues, be easy to implement, and minimize burdensome record keeping and costs for all parties.

- *The system should be able to accommodate tax systems used by the United States and our international partners today.*

Wherever feasible, we should look to existing taxation concepts and principles to achieve these goals.

Any such taxation system will have to accomplish these goals in the context of the Internet's special characteristics—the potential anonymity of buyer and seller, the capacity for multiple small transactions, and the difficulty of associating online activities with physically defined locations.

To achieve global consensus on this approach, the United States, through the Treasury Department, is participating in discussions on the taxation of electronic commerce through the Organization for Economic Cooperation and Development (OECD), the primary forum for cooperation in international taxation.

The Administration is also concerned about possible moves by state and local tax authorities to target electronic commerce and Internet access. The uncertainties associated with such taxes and the inconsistencies among them could stifle the development of Internet commerce.

The Administration believes that the same broad principles applicable to international taxation, such as not hindering the growth of electronic commerce and neutrality between conventional and electronic commerce, should be applied to subfederal taxation. No new taxes should be applied to electronic commerce, and states should coordinate their allocation of income derived from electronic commerce. Of course, implementation of these principles may differ at the subfederal level where indirect taxation plays a larger role.

Before any further action is taken, states and local governments should cooperate to develop a uniform, simple approach to the taxation of electronic commerce, based on existing principles of taxation where feasible.

2   ELECTRONIC PAYMENT SYSTEMS

New technology has made it possible to pay for goods and services over the Internet. Some of the methods would link existing electronic banking and payment systems, including credit and debit card networks, with new retail interfaces via the Internet. Electronic money, based on stored-value, smart card, or other technologies, is also under development. Substantial private sector investment and competition is spurring an intense period of innovation that should benefit consumers and businesses wishing to engage in global electronic commerce.

At this early stage in the development of electronic payment systems, the commercial and technological environment is changing rapidly. It would be hard to develop policy that is both timely and appropriate. For these reasons, inflexible and highly prescriptive regulations and rules are inappropriate and potentially harmful. Rather, in the near term, case-by-case monitoring of electronic payment experiments is preferred.

From a longer term perspective, however, the marketplace and industry self-regulation alone may not fully address all issues. For example, government action may be necessary to ensure the safety and soundness of electronic payment systems, to protect consumers, or to respond to important law enforcement objectives.

The United States, through the Department of the Treasury, is working with other governments in international fora to study the global implications of emerging electronic payment systems. A number of organizations are already working on important aspects of electronic banking and payments. Their analyses will contribute to a better understanding of how electronic payment systems will affect global commerce and banking.

The Economic Communique issued at the Lyon Summit by the G-7 Heads of State called for a cooperative study of the implications of new, sophisticated retail electronic payment systems. In response, the G-10 deputies formed a

Government action may be necessary to ensure the safety and soundness of electronic payment systems, to protect consumers, or to respond to important law enforcement objectives

Working Party, with representation from finance ministries and central banks (in consultation with law enforcement authorities). The Working Party is chaired by a representative from the U.S. Treasury Department, and tasked to produce a report that identifies common policy objectives among the G-10 countries and analyzes the national approaches to electronic commerce taken to date.

As electronic payment systems develop, governments should work closely with the private sector to inform policy development, and ensure that governmental activities flexibly accommodate the needs of the emerging marketplace.

II Legal Issues

3 "UNIFORM COMMERCIAL CODE" FOR ELECTRONIC COMMERCE

In general, parties should be able to do business with each other on the Internet under whatever terms and conditions they agree upon.

Private enterprise and free markets have typically flourished, however, where there are predictable and widely accepted legal environments supporting commercial transactions. To encourage electronic commerce, the U.S. government should support the development of both a domestic and global uniform commercial legal framework that recognizes, facilitates, and enforces electronic transactions worldwide. Fully informed buyers and sellers could voluntarily agree to form a contract subject to this uniform legal framework, just as parties currently choose the body of law that will be used to interpret their contract.

Participants in the marketplace should define and articulate most of the rules that will govern electronic commerce. To enable private entities to perform this task and to fulfill their roles adequately, governments should encourage the development of simple and predictable domestic and international rules and norms that will serve as the legal foundation for commercial activities in cyberspace.

In the United States, every state government has adopted the Uniform Commercial Code (UCC), a codification of substantial portions of commercial law. The National Conference of Commissioners of Uniform State Law (NCCUSL) and the American Law Institute, domestic sponsors of the UCC, already are working to adapt the UCC to cyberspace. Private sector organizations, including the American Bar Association (ABA) along with other interest groups, are participants in this process. Work is also ongoing on a proposed electronic contracting and records act for transactions not covered by the UCC. The Administration supports the prompt consideration of these proposals, and the adoption of uniform legislation by all states. Of course, any such legislation will be designed to accommodate ongoing and possible future global initiatives.

Internationally, the United Nations Commission on International Trade Law (UNCITRAL) has completed work on a model law that supports the commercial use of international contracts in electronic commerce. This model law establishes rules and norms that validate and recognize contracts formed through electronic means, sets default rules for contract formation and governance of electronic contract performance, defines the characteristics of a valid electronic writing and an original document, provides for the acceptability of electronic signatures for legal and commercial purposes, and supports the admission of computer evidence in courts and arbitration proceedings.

The United States Government supports the adoption of principles along these lines by all nations as a start to defining an international set of uniform commercial principles for electronic commerce. We urge UNCITRAL, other appropriate international bodies, bar associations, and other private sector groups to continue their work in this area.

The following principles should, to the extent possible, guide the drafting of rules governing global electronic commerce:

- parties should be free to order the contractual relationship between themselves as they see fit;
- rules should be technology-neutral (i.e., the rules should neither require nor assume a particular technology) and forward looking (i.e., the rules should not hinder the use or development of technologies in the future);
- existing rules should be modified and new rules should be adopted only as necessary or substantially desirable to support the use of electronic technologies; and
- the process should involve the high-tech commercial sector as well as businesses that have not yet moved online.

With these principles in mind, UNCITRAL, UNIDROIT, and the International Chamber of Commerce (ICC), and others should develop additional model provisions and uniform fundamental principles designed to eliminate administrative and regulatory barriers and to facilitate electronic commerce by:

- encouraging governmental recognition, acceptance and facilitation of electronic communications (i.e., contracts, notarized documents, etc.);

- encouraging consistent international rules to support the acceptance of electronic signatures and other authentication procedures; and
- promoting the development of adequate, efficient, and effective alternate dispute resolution mechanisms for global commercial transactions.

The expansion of global electronic commerce also depends upon the participants, ability to achieve a reasonable degree of certainty regarding their exposure to liability for any damage or injury that might result from their actions. Inconsistent local tort laws, coupled with uncertainties regarding jurisdiction, could substantially increase litigation and create unnecessary costs that ultimately will be born by consumers. The U.S. should work closely with other nations to clarify applicable jurisdictional rules and to generally favor and enforce contract provisions that allow parties to select substantive rules governing liability.

Sellers must know that their intellectual property will not be stolen

Finally, the development of global electronic commerce provides an opportunity to create legal rules that allow business and consumers to take advantage of new technology to streamline and automate functions now accomplished manually. For example, consideration should be given to establishing electronic registries.

The Departments of Commerce and State will continue to organize U.S. participation in these areas with a goal of achieving substantive international agreement on model law within the next two years. NCCUSL and the American Law Institute, working with the American Bar Association and other interested groups, are urged to continue their work to develop complementary domestic and international efforts.

4   INTELLECTUAL PROPERTY PROTECTION

Commerce on the Internet often will involve the sale and licensing of intellectual property. To promote this commerce, sellers must know that their intellectual property will not be stolen and buyers must know that they are obtaining authentic products.

International agreements that establish clear and effective copyright, patent, and trademark protection are therefore necessary to prevent piracy and fraud. While technology, such as encryption, can help combat piracy, an adequate and effective legal framework also is necessary to deter fraud and the theft of intellectual property, and to provide effective legal recourse when these crimes occur. Increased public education about intellectual property in the information age will also contribute to the successful implementation and growth of the GII.

Copyrights

There are several treaties that establish international norms for the protection of copyrights, most notably the Berne Convention for the Protection of Literary and Artistic Works. These treaties link nearly all major trading nations and provide them with a means of protecting, under their own laws, each other's copyrighted works and sound recordings.

In December 1996, the World Intellectual Property Organization (WIPO) updated the Berne Convention and provided new protection for performers and producers of sound recordings by adopting two new treaties. The two treaties—the WIPO Copyright Treaty and the WIPO Performances and Phonograms Treaty—will greatly facilitate the commercial applications of online digital communications over the GII.

Both treaties include provisions relating to technological protection, copyright management information, and the right of communication to the public, all of which are indispensable for an efficient exercise of rights in the digital environment. The U.S. Government recognizes private sector efforts to develop international and domestic standards in these areas. The Administration understands the sensitivities associated with copyright management information and technological protection measures, and is working to tailor implementing legislation accordingly.

Both treaties also contain provisions that permit nations to provide for exceptions to rights in certain cases that do not conflict with a normal exploitation of the work and do not unreasonably prejudice the legitimate interests of the author (e.g., "fair use"). These provisions permit members to carry forward and appropriately extend into the digital environment limitations and exceptions in their national laws which have been considered acceptable under the Berne Convention. These provisions permit members to devise new exceptions and limitations that are appropriate in the digital network environment, but neither reduce nor extend the scope of applicability of the limitations and exceptions permitted by the Berne Convention.

The Administration is drafting legislation to implement the new WIPO treaties, and looks forward to working with the Senate on their ratification.

The two new WIPO treaties do not address issues of online service provider liability, leaving them to be determined by domestic legislation. The Administration looks

The Administration understands the sensitivities associated with copyright management information and technological protection measures

forward to working with Congress as these issues are addressed and supports efforts to achieve an equitable and balanced solution that is agreeable to interested parties and consistent with international copyright obligations.

The adoption of the two new WIPO treaties represents the attainment of one of the Administration's significant intellectual property objectives. The U.S. Government will continue to work for appropriate copyright protection for works disseminated electronically. The Administration's copyright-related objectives will include:

- encouraging countries to fully and immediately implement the obligations contained in the Agreement on Trade-Related Aspects of Intellectual Property (TRIPS);
- seeking immediate U.S. ratification and deposit of the instruments of accession to the two new WIPO treaties and implementation of the obligations in these treaties in a balanced and appropriate way as soon as possible;
- encouraging other countries to join the two new WIPO treaties and to implement fully the treaty obligations as soon as possible; and
- ensuring that U.S. trading partners establish laws and regulations that provide adequate and effective protection for copyrighted works, including motion pictures, computer software, and sound recordings, disseminated via the GII, and that these laws and regulations are fully implemented and actively enforced.

The United States will pursue these international objectives through bilateral discussions and multilateral discussions at WIPO and other appropriate fora and will encourage private sector participation in these discussions.

Sui Generis Protection of Databases

The December 1996 WIPO Conference in Geneva did not take up a proposed treaty to protect the non-original elements of databases. Instead, the Conference called for a meeting, subsequently held, to discuss preliminary steps to study proposals to establish sui generis database protection.

Based on the brief discussion of sui generis database protection that took place before and during the Diplomatic Conference, it is clear that more discussion of the need for and the nature of such protection is necessary domestically and internationally.

The Administration will seek additional input from, among others, the scientific, library, and academic communities and the commercial sector, in order to develop U.S. policy with respect to sui generis database protection.

Patents

Development of the GII will both depend upon and stimulate innovation in many fields of technology, including computer software, computer hardware, and telecommunications. An effectively functioning patent system that encourages and protects patentable innovations in these fields is important for the overall success of commerce over the Internet. Consistent with this objective, the U.S. Patent and Trademark Office (PTO) will (1) significantly enhance its collaboration with the private sector to assemble a larger, more complete collection of prior art (both patent and non-patent publications), and provide its patent examiners better access to prior art in GII-related technologies; (2) train its patent examiners in GII-related technologies to raise and maintain their level of technical expertise; and (3) support legislative proposals for early publication of pending patent applications, particularly in areas involving fast moving technology.

To create a reliable environment for electronic commerce, patent agreements should:

- prohibit member countries from authorizing parties to exploit patented inventions related to the GII without the patent owner's authority (i.e., disapproval of compulsory licensing of GII-related technology except to remedy a practice determined after judicial or administrative process to be anti-competitive);
- require member countries to provide adequate and effective protection for patentable subject matter important to the development and success of the GII; and
- establish international standards for determining the validity of a patent claim.

The United States will pursue these objectives internationally. Officials of the European, Japanese, and United States Patent Offices meet, for example, each year to foster cooperation on patent-related issues. The United States will recommend at the next meeting that a special committee be established within the next year to make recommendations on GII-related patent issues.

In a separate venue, one hundred countries and international intergovernmental organizations participate as members of WIPO's permanent committee on industrial property information (PCIPI). The United States will attempt to establish a working group of this organization to address GII-related patent issues.

Trademark and Domain Names

Trademark rights are national in scope and conflicts may arise where the same or similar trademarks for similar goods or services are owned by different parties in different countries. Countries may also apply different standards for determining infringement.

Conflicts have arisen on the GII where third parties have registered Internet domain names that are the same as, or similar to, registered or common law trademarks. An Internet domain name functions as a source identifier on the Internet. Ordinarily, source identifiers, like addresses, are not protected intellectual property (i.e., a trademark) per se. The use of domain names as source identifiers has burgeoned, however, and courts have begun to attribute intellectual property rights to them, while recognizing that misuse of a domain name could significantly infringe, dilute, and weaken valuable trademark rights.

Americans treasure privacy, linking it to our concept of personal freedom and well-being

To date, conflicts between trademark rights and domain names have been resolved through negotiations and/or litigation. It may be possible to create a contractually based self-regulatory regime that deals with potential conflicts between domain name usage and trademark laws on a global basis without the need to litigate. This could create a more stable business environment on the Internet. Accordingly, the United States will support efforts already underway to create domestic and international fora for discussion of Internet-related trademark issues. The Administration also plans to seek public input on the resolution of trademark disputes in the context of domain names.

Governance of the domain name system (DNS) raises other important issues unrelated to intellectual property. The Administration supports private efforts to address Internet governance issues including those related to domain names and has formed an interagency working group under the leadership of the Department of Commerce to study DNS issues. The working group will review various DNS proposals, consulting with interested private sector, consumer, professional, congressional and state government and international groups. The group will consider, in light of public input, (1) what contribution government might make, if any, to the development of a global competitive, market-based system to register Internet domain names, and (2) how best to foster bottom-up governance of the Internet.

5   PRIVACY

Americans treasure privacy, linking it to our concept of personal freedom and well-being. Unfortunately, the GII's great promise—that it facilitates the collection, re-use, and instantaneous transmission of information—can, if not managed carefully, diminish personal privacy. It is essential, therefore, to assure personal privacy in the networked environment if people are to feel comfortable doing business.

At the same time, fundamental and cherished principles like the First Amendment, which is an important hallmark of American democracy, protect the free flow of information. Commerce on the GII will thrive only if the privacy rights of individuals are balanced with the benefits associated with the free flow of information.

In June of 1995, the Privacy Working Group of the United States government Information Infrastructure Task Force (IITF) issued a report entitled *PRIVACY AND THE NATIONAL INFORMATION INFRASTRUCTURE: Principles for Providing and Using Personal Information*. The report recommends a set of principles (the "Privacy Principles") to govern the collection, processing, storage, and re-use of personal data in the information age.

These Privacy Principles, which build on the Organization for Economic Cooperation and Development's GUIDELINES GOVERNING THE PROTECTION OF PRIVACY AND TRANSBORDER DATA FLOW OF PERSONAL DATA and incorporate principles of fair information practices, rest on the fundamental precepts of awareness and choice:

An individual's reasonable expectation of privacy regarding access to and use of, his or her personal information should be assured

- Data-gatherers should inform consumers what information they are collecting, and how they intend to use such data; and

- Data-gatherers should provide consumers with a meaningful way to limit use and re-use of personal information.

Disclosure by data-gatherers is designed to stimulate market resolution of privacy concerns by empowering individuals to obtain relevant knowledge about why information is being collected, what the information will be used for, what steps will be taken to protect that information, the consequences of providing or withholding information, and any rights of redress that they may have. Such disclosure will enable consumers to make better judgments about the levels of privacy available and their willingness to participate.

In addition, the Privacy Principles identify three values to govern the way in which personal information is acquired, disclosed and used online—information privacy, information integrity, and information quality. First, an individual's reasonable expectation of privacy regarding access to and use of, his or her personal information should be assured. Second, personal information should not be improperly altered or destroyed. And, third, personal information should be accurate, timely, complete, and relevant for the purposes for which it is provided and used.

Under these principles, consumers are entitled to redress if they are harmed by improper use or disclosure of personal information or if decisions are based on inaccurate, outdated, incomplete, or irrelevant personal information.

In April, 1997, the Information Policy Committee of the IITF issued a draft paper entitled Options For Promoting Privacy on the National Information Infrastructure. The paper surveys information practices in the United States and solicits public comment on the best way to implement the Privacy Principles. The IITF goal is to find a way to balance the competing values of personal privacy and the free flow of information in a digital democratic society.

The Administration supports private sector efforts now underway to implement meaningful, consumer-friendly, self-regulatory privacy regimes

Meanwhile, other federal agencies have studied privacy issues in the context of specific industry sectors. In October 1995, for example, the National Telecommunications and Information Administration (NTIA) issued a report entitled Privacy and the NII: Safeguarding Telecommunications-Related Personal Information. It explores the application of the Privacy Principles in the context of telecommunications and online services and advocates a voluntary framework based on notice and consent. On January 6, 1997, the FTC issued a staff report entitled Public Workshop on Consumer Privacy on the Global Information Infrastructure. The report, which focuses on the direct marketing and advertising industries, concludes that notice, choice, security, and access are recognized as necessary elements of fair information practices online. In June of 1997, the FTC held four days of hearings on technology tools and industry self-regulation regimes designed to enhance personal privacy on the Internet.

The Administration supports private sector efforts now underway to implement meaningful, consumer-friendly, self-regulatory privacy regimes. These include mechanisms for facilitating awareness and the exercise of choice online, evaluating private sector adoption of and adherence to fair information practices, and dispute resolution.

The Administration also anticipates that technology will offer solutions to many privacy concerns in the online environment, including the appropriate use of anonymity. If privacy concerns are not addressed by industry through self-regulation and technology, the Administration will face increasing pressure to play a more direct role in safeguarding consumer choice regarding privacy online.

The Administration is particularly concerned about the use of information gathered from children, who may lack the cognitive ability to recognize and appreciate privacy concerns. Parents should be able to choose whether or not personally identifiable information is collected from or about their children. We urge industry, consumer, and child-advocacy groups working together to use a mix of technology, self-regulation, and education to provide solutions to the particular dangers arising in this area and to facilitate parental choice. This problem warrants prompt attention. Otherwise, government action may be required.

Privacy concerns are being raised in many countries around the world, and some countries have enacted laws, implemented industry self-regulation, or instituted administrative solutions designed to safeguard their citizens' privacy. Disparate policies could emerge that might disrupt transborder data flows. For example, the European Union (EU) has adopted a Directive that prohibits the transfer of personal data to countries that, in its view, do not extend adequate privacy protection to EU citizens.

If Internet users do not have confidence that their communications and data are safe from unauthorized access or modification, they will be unlikely to use the Internet on a routine basis for commerce

To ensure that differing privacy policies around the world do not impede the flow of data on the Internet, the United States will engage its key trading partners in discussions to build support for industry-developed solutions to privacy problems and for market driven mechanisms to assure customer satisfaction about how private data is handled.

The United States will continue policy discussions with the EU nations and the European Commission to increase understanding about the U.S. approach to privacy and to assure that the criteria they use for evaluating adequacy are sufficiently flexible to accommodate our approach. These discussions are led by the Department of Commerce, through NTIA, and the State Department, and include the Executive Office of the President, the Treasury Department, the Federal Trade Commission (FTC) and other relevant federal agencies. NTIA is also working with the private sector to assess the impact that the implementation of the EU Directive could have on the United States.

The United States also will enter into a dialogue with trading partners on these issues through existing bilateral fora as well as through regional fora such as the Asia Pacific Economic Cooperation (APEC) forum, the Summit of the Americas, the North American Free Trade Agreement (NAFTA), and the Inter-American Telecommunications

Commission (CITEL) of the Organization of American States, and broader multilateral organizations.

The Administration considers data protection critically important. We believe that private efforts of industry working in cooperation with consumer groups are preferable to government regulation, but if effective privacy protection cannot be provided in this way, we will reevaluate this policy.

6   SECURITY

The GII must be secure and reliable. If Internet users do not have confidence that their communications and data are safe from unauthorized access or modification, they will be unlikely to use the Internet on a routine basis for commerce. A secure GII requires:

Strong encryption is a double-edged sword

(1)   secure and reliable telecommunications networks;
(2)   effective means for protecting the information systems attached to those networks;
(3)   effective means for authenticating and ensuring confidentiality of electronic information to protect data from unauthorized use; and
(4)   well trained GII users who understand how to protect their systems and their data.

There is no single "magic" technology or technique that can ensure that the GII will be secure and reliable. Accomplishing that goal requires a range of technologies (encryption, authentication, password controls, firewalls, etc.) and effective, consistent use of those technologies, all supported globally by trustworthy key and security management infrastructures.

Of particular importance is the development of trusted certification services that support the digital signatures that will permit users to know whom they are communicating with on the Internet. Both signatures and confidentiality rely on the use of cryptographic keys. To promote the growth of a trusted electronic commerce environment, the Administration is encouraging the development of a voluntary, market-driven key management infrastructure that will support authentication, integrity, and confidentiality.

Encryption products protect the confidentiality of stored data and electronic communications by making them unreadable without a decryption key. But strong encryption is a double-edged sword. Law abiding citizens can use strong encryption to protect their trade secrets and personal records. But those trade secrets and personal records could be lost forever if the decrypt key is lost. Depending upon the value of the information, the loss could be quite substantial. Encryption can also be used by criminals and terrorists to reduce law enforcement capabilities to read their communications. Key recovery based encryption can help address some of these issues.

In promoting robust security needed for electronic commerce, the Administration has already taken steps that will enable trust in encryption and provide the safeguards that users and society will need. The Administration, in partnership with industry, is taking steps to promote the development of market-driven standards, public-key management infrastructure services and key recoverable encryption products. Additionally, the Administration has liberalized export controls for commercial encryption products while protecting public safety and national security interests.

The Administration is also working with Congress to ensure legislation is enacted that would facilitate develop ment of voluntary key management infrastructures and would govern the release of recovery information to law enforcement officials pursuant to lawful authority.

The U.S. government will work internationally to promote development of market-driven key management infrastructure with key recovery. Specifically, the U.S. has worked closely within the OECD to develop international guidelines for encryption policies and will continue to promote the development of policies to provide a predictable and secure environment for global electronic commerce.

III Market Access Issues

7 TELECOMMUNICATIONS INFRASTRUCTURE AND INFORMATION TECHNOLOGY

Global electronic commerce depends upon a modern, seamless, global telecommunications network and upon the computers and information appliances that connect to it. Unfortunately, in too many countries, telecommunications policies are hindering the development of advanced digital networks. Customers find that telecommunications services often are too expensive, bandwidth is too limited, and services are unavailable or unreliable. Likewise, many countries maintain trade barriers to imported information technology, making it hard for both merchants and customers to purchase the computers and information systems they need to participate in electronic commerce.

In order to spur the removal of barriers, in March 1994, Vice President Gore spoke to the World Telecommunications Development Conference in Buenos Aires. He articulated several principles that the U.S. believes should be the foundation for government policy, including:

(1) encouraging private sector investment by privatiz-

Customers find that telecommunications services often are too expensive, bandwidth is too limited, and services are unavailable or unreliable

ing government-controlled telecommunications companies;

(2) promoting and preserving competition by introducing competition to monopoly phone markets, ensuring interconnection at fair prices, opening markets to foreign investment, and enforcing anti-trust safeguards;

(3) guaranteeing open access to networks on a non-discriminatory basis, so that GII users have access to the broadest range of information and services; and

(4) implementing, by an independent regulator, pro-competitive and flexible regulation that keeps pace with technological development.

Domestically, the Administration recognizes that there are various constraints in the present network that may impede the evolution of services requiring higher bandwidth. Administration initiatives include Internet II, or Next Generation Internet. In addition, the FCC has undertaken several initiatives designed to stimulate bandwidth expansion, especially to residential and small/home office customers.

The goal of the United States will be to ensure that online service providers can reach end-users on reasonable and nondiscriminatory terms and conditions. Genuine market opening will lead to increased competition, improved telecommunications infrastructures, more customer choice, lower prices and increased and improved services.

Areas of concern include:

- *Leased lines:* Data networks of most online service providers are constructed with leased lines that must be obtained from national telephone companies, often monopolies or governmental entities. In the absence of effective competition, telephone companies may impose artificially inflated leased line prices and usage restrictions that impede the provision of service by online service providers.

- *Local loops pricing:* To reach their subscribers, online service providers often have no choice but to purchase local exchange services from monopoly or government-owned telephone companies. These services also are often priced at excessive rates, inflating the cost of data services to customers.

- *Interconnection and unbundling:* Online service providers must be able to interconnect with the networks of incumbent telecommunication companies so that information can pass seamlessly between all users of the network. Monopolies or dominant telephone companies often price interconnection well above cost, and refuse to interconnect because of alleged concerns about network compatibility or absence of need for other providers.

- *Attaching equipment to the network:* Over the years, some telecommunication providers have used their monopoly power to restrict the connection of communication or technology devices to the network. Even when the monopoly has been broken, a host of unnecessary burdensome "type acceptance" practices have been used to retard competition and make it difficult for consumers to connect.

- *Internet voice and multimedia:* Officials of some nations claim that "real time" services provided over the Internet are "like services" to traditionally regulated voice telephony and broadcasting, and therefore should be subject to the same regulatory restrictions that apply to those traditional services. In some countries, these providers must be licensed, as a way to control both the carriage and content offered. Such an approach could hinder the development of new technologies and new services.

In addition, countries have different levels of telecommunications infrastructure development, which may hinder the global provision and use of some Internet-based services. The Administration believes that the introduction of policies promoting foreign investment, competition, regulatory flexibility and open access will support infrastructure development and the creation of more data-friendly networks.

To address these issues, the Administration successfully concluded the WTO Basic Telecommunications negotiations, which will ensure global competition in the provision of basic telecommunication services and will address the many underlying issues affecting online service providers. During those negotiations, the U.S. succeeded in ensuring that new regulatory burdens would not be imposed upon online service providers that would stifle the deployment of new technologies and services.

As the WTO Agreement is implemented, the Administration will seek to ensure that new rules of competition in the global communications marketplace will be technology neutral and will not hinder the development of electronic commerce. In particular, rules for licensing new technologies and new services must be sufficiently flexible to accommodate the changing needs of consumers while allowing governments to protect important public interest objectives like universal service. In this context, rules to promote such public interest objectives should not fall disproportionately on any one segment of the telecommunications industry or on new entrants.

The Administration will also seek effective implementation of the Information Technology Agreement concluded by the members of the WTO in March 1997, which is designed to remove tariffs on almost all types of information technology. Building on this success, and with the encouragement of U.S. companies, the Administration is developing plans for ITA II, in which it will to seek to remove remaining tariffs on, and existing non-tariff barriers to, information technology goods and services. In addition, the Administration is committed to finding other ways to streamline requirements to demonstrate product conformity, including through Mutual Recognition Agreements (MRAs) that can eliminate the need for a single product to be certified by different standards laboratories across national borders.

The U.S. government supports the broadest possible free flow of information across international borders

Bilateral exchanges with individual foreign governments, regional fora such as APEC and CITEL, and multilateral fora such as the OECD and ITU, and various other fora (i.e., international alliances of private businesses, the International Organization of Standardization [ISO], the International Electrotechnical Commission [IEC]), also will be used for international discussions on telecommunication-related Internet issues and removing trade barriers that inhibit the export of information technology. These issues include the terms and conditions governing the exchange of online traffic, addressing, and reliability. In all fora, U.S. Government positions that might influence Internet pricing, service delivery options or technical standards will reflect the principles established in this paper and U.S. Government representatives will survey the work of their study groups to ensure that this is the case.

In addition, many Internet governance issues will best be dealt with by means of private, open standards processes and contracts involving participants from both government and the private sector. The U.S. government will support industry initiatives aimed at achieving the important goals outlined in this paper.

8   CONTENT

The U.S. government supports the broadest possible free flow of information across international borders. This includes most informational material now accessible and transmitted through the Internet, including through World Wide Web pages, news and other information services, virtual shopping malls, and entertainment features, such as audio and video products, and the arts. This principle extends to information created by commercial enterprises as well as by schools, libraries, governments and other non-profit entities.

In contrast to traditional broadcast media, the Internet promises users greater opportunity to shield themselves and their children from content they deem offensive or inappropriate. New technology, for example, may enable parents to block their children's access to sensitive information or confine their children to pre-approved Web sites.

To the extent, then, that effective filtering technology becomes available, content regulations traditionally imposed on radio and television would not need to be applied to the Internet. In fact, unnecessary regulation could cripple the growth and diversity of the Internet.

The Administration therefore supports industry self-regulation, adoption of competing ratings systems, and development of easy-to-use technical solutions (e.g., filtering technologies and age verification systems) to assist in screening information online.

There are four priority areas of concern:

Advertising will allow the new interactive media to offer more affordable products and services to a wider, global audience

- *Regulation of content.* Companies wishing to do business over the Internet, and to provide access to the Internet (including U.S. online service providers with foreign affiliates or joint ventures) are concerned about liability based on the different policies of every country through which their information may travel.

  Countries that are considering or have adopted laws to restrict access to certain types of content through the Internet emphasize different concerns as a result of cultural, social, and political difference. These different laws can impede electronic commerce in the global environment.

  The Administration is concerned about Internet regulation of this sort, and will develop an informal dialogue with key trading partners on public policy issues such as hate speech, violence, sedition, pornography and other content to ensure that differences in national regulation, especially those undertaken to foster cultural identity, do not serve as disguised trade barriers.

- *Foreign content quotas.* Some countries currently require that a specific proportion of traditional broadcast transmission time be devoted to "domestically produced" content. Problems could arise on the Internet if the definition of "broadcasting" is changed to extend these current regulations to "new services." Countries also might decide to regulate Internet content and establish restrictions under administrative authority, rather than under broadcast regulatory structures.

The Administration will pursue a dialogue with other nations on how to promote content diversity, including cultural and linguistic diversity, without limiting content. These discussions could consider promotion of cultural identity through subsidy programs that rely solely on general tax revenues and that are implemented in a nondiscriminatory manner.

- *Regulation of advertising.* Advertising will allow the new interactive media to offer more affordable products and services to a wider, global audience. Some countries stringently restrict the language, amount, frequency, duration, and type of tele-shopping and advertising spots used by advertisers. In principle, the United States does not favor such regulations. While recognizing legitimate cultural and social concerns, these concerns should not be invoked to justify unnecessarily burdensome regulation of the Internet.

There are laws in many countries around the world that require support for advertising claims. Advertising industry self-regulation also exists in many countries around the globe. Truthful and accurate advertising should be the cornerstone of advertising on all media, including the Internet.

A strong body of cognitive and behavioral research demonstrates that children are particularly vulnerable to advertising. As a result, the U.S. has well established rules (self-regulatory and otherwise) for protecting children from certain harmful advertising practices. The Administration will work with industry and children's advocates to ensure that these protections are translated to and implemented appropriately in the online media environment.

The rules of the "country-of-origin" should serve as the basis for controlling Internet advertising to alleviate national legislative roadblocks and trade barriers.

- *Regulation to prevent fraud.* Recently, there have been a number of cases where fraudulent information on companies and their stocks, and phony investment schemes have been broadcast on the Internet. The appropriate federal agencies (i.e., Federal Trade Commission and the Securities and Exchange Commission) are determin-

Consumers must have confidence that the goods and services offered are fairly represented, that they will get what they pay for, and that recourse or redress will be available if they do not

ing whether new regulations are needed to prevent fraud over the Internet.

In order to realize the commercial and cultural potential of the Internet, consumers must have confidence that the goods and services offered are fairly represented, that they will get what they pay for, and that recourse or redress will be available if they do not. This is an area where government action is appropriate.

The Administration will explore opportunities for international cooperation to protect consumers and to prosecute false, deceptive, and fraudulent commercial practices in cyberspace.

Federal agencies such as the Department of State, U.S. Trade Representative (USTR), the Commerce Department (NTIA), the FTC, the Office of Consumer Affairs and others have already engaged in efforts to promote such positions, through both bilateral and multilateral channels, including through the OECD, the G-7 Information Society and Development Conference, the Latin American Telecommunications Summits, and the Summit of the Americas process, as well as APEC Telecommunications Ministerials. All agencies participating in such fora will focus on pragmatic solutions based upon the principles in this paper to issues related to content control.

9   TECHNICAL STANDARDS

Standards are critical to the long term commercial success of the Internet as they can allow products and services from different vendors to work together. They also encourage competition and reduce uncertainty in the global marketplace. Premature standardization, however, can "lock in" outdated technology. Standards also can be employed as de facto non-tariff trade barriers, to "lock out" non-indigenous businesses from a particular national market.

The United States believes that the marketplace, not governments, should determine technical standards and other mechanisms for interoperability. Technology is moving rapidly and government attempts to establish technical standards to govern the Internet would only risk inhibiting technological innovation. The United States considers it unwise and unnecessary for governments to mandate standards for electronic commerce. Rather, we urge industry driven multilateral fora to consider technical standards in this area.

To ensure the growth of global electronic commerce over the Internet, standards will be needed to assure reliability, interoperability, ease of use and scalability in areas such as:

The prevalence of voluntary standards on the Internet, and the medium's consensus-based process of standards development and acceptance are stimulating its rapid growth

- electronic payments;
- security (confidentiality, authentication, data integrity, access control, non-repudiation);
- security services infrastructure (e.g., public key certificate authorities);
- electronic copyright management systems;
- video and data-conferencing;
- high-speed network technologies (e.g., Asynchronous Transfer Mode, Synchronous Digital Hierarchy); and
- digital object and data interchange.

There need not be one standard for every product or service associated with the GII, and technical standards need not be mandated. In some cases, multiple standards will compete for marketplace acceptance. In other cases, different standards will be used in different circumstances.

The success of electronic commerce will require an effective partnership between the private and public sectors, with the private sector in the lead

The prevalence of voluntary standards on the Internet, and the medium's consensus-based process of standards development and acceptance are stimulating its rapid growth. These standards flourish because of a non-bureaucratic system of development managed by technical practitioners working through various organizations. These organizations require demonstrated deployment of systems incorporating a given standard prior to formal acceptance, but the process facilitates rapid deployment of standards and can accommodate evolving standards as well. Only a handful of countries allow private sector standards development; most rely on government-mandated solutions, causing these nations to fall behind the technological cutting edge and creating non-tariff trade barriers.

Numerous private sector bodies have contributed to the process of developing voluntary standards that promote interoperability. The United States has encouraged the development of voluntary standards through private standards organizations, consortia, testbeds and R&D activities. The U.S. government also has adopted a set of principles to promote acceptance of domestic and international voluntary standards.

While no formal government-sponsored negotiations are called for at this time, the United States will use various fora (i.e., international alliances of private businesses, the International Organization for Standardization [ISO], the International Electrotechnical Commission [IEC], International Telecommunications Union [ITU], etc.) to discourage the use of standards to erect barriers to free trade on the developing GII. The private sector should assert global leadership to address standards setting needs. The United

States will work through intergovernmental organizations as needed to monitor and support private sector leadership.

A COORDINATED STRATEGY

The success of electronic commerce will require an effective partnership between the private and public sectors, with the private sector in the lead. Government participation must be coherent and cautious, avoiding the contradictions and confusions that can sometimes arise when different governmental agencies individually assert authority too vigorously and operate without coordination.

The variety of issues being raised, the interaction among them, and the disparate fora in which they are being addressed will necessitate a coordinated, targeted governmental approach to avoid inefficiencies and duplication in developing and reviewing policy.

An interagency team will continue to meet in order to monitor progress and update this strategy as events unfold. Sufficient resources will be committed to allow rapid and effective policy implementation.

The process of further developing and implementing the strategy set forth in this paper is as important as the content of the paper itself. The U.S. Government will consult openly and often, with groups representing industry, consumers and Internet users, Congress, state and local governments, foreign governments, and international organizations as we seek to update and implement this paper in the coming years.

Private sector leadership accounts for the explosive growth of the Internet today, and the success of electronic commerce will depend on continued private sector leadership. Accordingly, the Administration also will encourage the creation of private fora to take the lead in areas requiring self-regulation such as privacy, content ratings, and consumer protection and in areas such as standards development, commercial code, and fostering interoperability.

The strategy outlined in this paper will be updated and new releases will be issued as changes in technology and the marketplace teach us more about how to set the optimal environment in which electronic commerce and community can flourish.

There is a great opportunity for commercial activity on the Internet. If the private sector and governments act appropriately, this opportunity can be realized for the benefit of all people.

The Promise of One to One (A Love Story) [2]

Let us love you, Web sites first said to consumers in the fall of 1994, when I helped launch HotWired as one of the first of the commercially supported ventures. Let us love you, and we will love you back. Start by telling us your secrets. If you do, they promised, we will deliver everything you ever wanted— not just pizza (though that will satisfy the Homer Simpson in all of us), but every other consumer product and service you covet now, and others you can only dream of. Imagine it, if you can: the Ultimate Takeout Menu.

Join us, the Web sites whispered to marketers out of the other side of their mouths. If you give us your money, they promised, we will give you a more intimate knowledge of customers than has ever existed before. In fact, we'll give you so much more than those dinosaurs in print and broadcast can give you, we'll blow your minds. Because we'll vacuum up all those responses to the Ultimate Takeout Menu, repackage them, and spit them out the other end of the pipe. We'll give you the Ultimate Focus Group. (The Web sites also perhaps saw that the Ultimate Focus Group could distract marketers into ignoring the small fact—especially in 1994—that their audiences were infinitesimally smaller than the ones offered up by the dinosaurs.)

Delivering a happy convergence of these mirrored promises—the Ultimate Takeout Menu and the Ultimate Focus Group—would produce that Holy Grail of commercial relationships predicted by marketing gurus Don Peppers and Martha Rogers in their 1993 book *The One to One Future* even before the Web arrived in our lives.

The *One to One Future* was the title under the arm of nearly every publisher and marketer I ran into at Web conferences or read about in the trade press during the medium's earliest days. And their speeches and quotes were full of Peppers and Rogers mantras, like the ones the authors delivered in the February 1994 issue of this magazine ("Is Advertising Finally Dead?" *Wired* 2.02, page 71). Eight months before the commercial Web's debut, one-to-one's dynamic duo predicted that among the "new rules of engagement governing business competition" were "initiat-

---

ing, maintaining, and improving dialogs with individual consumers, abandoning the old fashioned advertising monologs of mass media."

An unspoken, and quite believable, premise of the one-to-one future is that as consumers in a service economy, we always want "more" and we reliably want that "more" to be ever easier to obtain. The Peppers and Rogers acolytes hauling around those dog-eared copies of the way new marketing bible understand. They've declared that the Web will offer personalization, customization, and unlimited choice a more perfect couch-potato experience. Filtering software, intelligent agents, and personal shoppers, they have said, will be at the beck and call of our digital alter egos (a declaration that merely extends a promise first offered, but not fulfilled, by companies like General Magic in the days before the Web took off)

The one-to-one disciples have also proclaimed that marketers, who always want to move more product, will now get instant feedback, near-perfect information, and deeper insights into the habits, feelings, likes, and dislikes of us, their often elusive customers. The Web will reverse the mistakes of the mass-market economy's unproductive commercial relationships, which were "based on guesswork on the part of the seller and frustration on the part of the buyer," as Firefly Network executive Saul Klein sardonically observes.

It is the perfect project for the decade's consumerist new economy society: finding, at long last, the one-to-one Shangri-La. The topic skimmed by one pundit or another at nearly every recent TED conference. The "Web lifestyle" Bill Gates says he now anticipates. And, since 1994, the target of dozens of companies in a race to build the growing set of tools—for consumers and marketers—alike that can make it real. Among the entrants are Firefly and Net Perceptions, which provide filtering and recommendation software for businesses; Excite and Yahoo!, with personalized services like My Excite Channel and My Yahoo!; MatchLogic, which sells marketers a service that centralizes management of advertising banners and measures the number of times consumers see and click on those ads; and RelevantKnowledge, Media Metrix, even Nielsen Media Research itself, which strive to build Web-ratings services that count and compare audiences—like the services Nielsen has offered for decades to the television industry.

These companies, and others, have adapted, altered, and reimagined the uses of technologies like Web-server logs, e-mail lists, and the once-innocuous, now-ubiquitous magic cookie in the quest for a true one-to-one experience. Some, like San Diego-based Aptex Software, are even performing an almost alchemical magic on surfing patterns, using technologies originally developed for the spooks of the national-security state.

The love story between consumers and marketers may at long last have a happy ending. The Ultimate Takeout Menu and the Ultimate Focus Group may actually be hovering within harmonious reach. Perhaps the promises were real, after all.

Or were they?

The love story between consumers and marketers may at long last have a happy ending

"The truth of the matter is that all this stuff is about optimization—optimizing your profits, optimizing your P&L—but most companies on the Web don't yet have a business to optimize," says Peter Rip, managing director of Knight-Ridder Ventures, the media company's venture capital arm. Before he joined K-R, Rip was a vice president and general manager at Infoseek, which has struggled to keep up with its rivals in a still-developing business niche.

Rip is right. A vast wealth of information is flowing through the system at every Web site—but take a look around the Net, and beyond Yahoo!, Lycos (barely), and one or two other players, the companies that should be leading the race to construct the Ultimate Takeout Menu and the Ultimate Focus Group have yet to earn a dime of profit. Most of them are more concerned with the immediate goal of survival, and haven't even entered the one-to-one contest. And although the market itself is nearly four years old, many of the companies trying to develop a business within it are far younger.

Mind you, since day one it's been easy for many Web sites to collect the most basic data about what their users are up to: how many times a page has been viewed, which domains visitors came from, the types of browsers they used, and which domains have linked to the site and driven traffic in its direction. But few commercial sites collect much beyond that basic information: ZIP code and area code are among the more prevalent requests; companies like Amazon.com don't even ask for your name until you make a purchase. Ironically, there's actually far less information available to marketers about consumer activity on the Web than they're able to gather elsewhere, particularly through credit-data companies such as Equifax or TRW.

Put bluntly, the information that marketers are gathering about consumers on the Web "pales by comparison with what marketers already have in their databases about purchase history," says Rex Briggs, who tracks and measures Web consumer patterns as a vice president at Millward Brown Interactive in San Francisco. (Briggs is also the former research director for HotWired.) Spend a bit of time talking to the operators of some leading sites on the Web and you discover why: Much of that data gets dumped into the black hole of a hard disk, where it may lie forever untouched and untapped. "In theory, any site can know a great deal about what its users are doing," says Donna Hoffman, a Vanderbilt University professor who, with husband and fellow faculty member Tom Novak, is a leader in the study of Internet marketing. "But in practice, very few sites have the technical expertise or the marketing expertise to know what to do with the data," Hoffman says. "They have not begun to mine the gold that's there."

At Excite—the Web-directory company generally acknowledged as Number Two in its category, behind Yahoo!—company cofounder and senior vice president Joe Kraus says the operation has been collecting data like age and ZIP code from visitors for more than two years now. But according to Kraus, Excite, which sold US$36 million of advertising in 1997, has yet to use that information even to better target its ads. Excite has had enough trouble just keeping up with its phenomenal growth: In February the company served 28 million pageviews each day, up from 4 million per day a year earlier. At this pace Excite collects 40 gigabytes of data in its log files every day. "If we tried to look at things at that level, we'd go insane—we'd drown in the information," says Craig Donato, Excite's vice president for product marketing.

Faced with such exponentially increasing volumes, Excite is trying, for the moment, merely to detect directional patterns in the data. If it's obvious, for example, that traffic is flowing to its horoscope pages, the company will pile on more horoscopes. "We know what people want by watching the logs," explains Kraus. This instant-gratification feedback loop can be fed until consumers are satiated. Then it's on to the next loop. The Drive-Thru Takeout Menu. News sites now employ it fervently: Witness their scandal-chasing coverage of Bill and Monica. Watching the traffic on Lewinsky stories rise through the roof, big news sites like Pathfinder, MSNBC, and washingtonpost.com briskly added special sections to the Menu, with more coverage serving to further feed the frenzy. It's this same phe-

This instant-gratification feedback loop can be fed until consumers are satiated

nomenon that for years has driven the traditional media to produce quickie books and magazine special issues but on the Web, for the first time, the continuously updated empirical evidence needed to assess those efforts is at hand.

At Excite, the logical extension of Drive-Thru was a new "personalized" front page, launched in April, that attempts to join many of the features of Excite's basic Web directory with those drawn from the My Excite service. My Excite (and similar services, such as My Yahoo!) allows you to customize features like news headlines, a portfolio of stock quotes, and weather reports. Excite's Craig Donato takes pains to emphasize the distinction between customization and personalization: "Customization is when you remember something for the user—like his stocks. With personalization, we're taking information about our relationship and using that to deliver a better experience for the user."

Now, when you use Excite services at www.excite.com, its server computers immediately try to personalize the exchange. If you've ever before divulged any basic personal information to Excite—even your ZIP code on a contest-entry form the servers locate it and, in the case of your ZIP code, trot out a local weather report with all the pride of a puppy delivering a slipper.

Hmm. It doesn't sound all that different from the techniques used for the "personalized" ink-jet messages you still find shoehorned into the hoariest junk-mail pitches filling your meatspace mailbox: "Congratulations, CHIP BAYERS! You and the members of the BAYERS household may have already won One Million Dollars!" Where's the one-to-one future? Where's the real Menu?

"One-to-one is a bit tricky," Donato allows.

To be fair, Excite is doing as well as, if not better than, its competitors at delivering on the promise. Nor are users unhappy with the kind of simulated personalization delivered via ZIP-code-based weather forecasts. "If you get users to commit data about themselves, they're far more likely to return frequently," Kraus says. He claims the key is to make the changes immediately noticeable to the user. If you're willing to "commit data," Excite will jump all over it. "Any active data we get, we put to instant use on the page."

"The trick is to use technology to achieve the same economies that you have in a mass-marketing model, while delivering some personalized messages to the consumer," says Rex Briggs of Millward Brown Interactive. A less visionary goal than one-to-one, surely, but far more realistic. It's called mass customization, and if you can get past the oxymoronic bounce, you can see that its possibilities are not lost on the consumer-products retailers who have carved out a market for themselves on the World Wide Web.

Brand-new companies like online bookseller Amazon.com, virtual record store CDnow, and N2K (which operates the Music Boulevard Web site) have ridden the strength of their rapid sales growth to successful IPOs and are already being credited with forcing fundamental changes in the retail categories they inhabit. PC manufacturer Dell's Web sales explosion—an average of $3 million per day in early 1998 has been so amazing that Apple, among other competitors, has been quick to copy it. And traditional catalog retailers like Lands' End and J.Crew are now trying to exploit the marketing and sales possibilities of the medium.

Amazon.com's phenomenal success has prompted recent visits to its virtual mountaintop by such seekers of the truth as Simon & Schuster consumer group president Jack Romanos and John Sargent, CEO of St. Martin's Press. The New York-based publishing executives, who still make most of their money pushing best-sellers through the major chain retailers like Barnes & Noble and Borders, have been drawn by the startling contrast between their business model and Amazon.com's.

"The thing they're responding to in particular," says David Risher, Amazon.com's senior vice president of product development, "is that very few of the books that Amazon.com sells are best-sellers. What the publishers get excited about is that we can revitalize a midlist or even backlist book by featuring it or by helping them target a book to a specialized audience."

In fact, Amazon.com has put traditional publishing into a state of delirium. This is, after all, the most anachronistic of the consumer-products industries, which for years has allowed retailers, constantly short on shelf space, to ship their unsold inventory back up the food chain. The publishers even pay for the privilege! As a result, publishers' warehouses are filled not only with copies of new books yet to be ordered and copies of evergreen classics like *A Tale of Two Cities*, but with millions of copies of books that languished at the Waldenbooks in your local mall when they were first released.

If you're a member of what Risher calls a "specialized audience," you like to buy as many books as possible on a given subject, but you're unlikely to find them all on the shelf. You're usually forced to endure a time-consuming special-order process, which requires several trips to the

Amazon.com has put traditional publishing into a state of delirium

bookstore and a good deal of waiting around. At Amazon.com, of course, if it's in print (and sometimes even when it isn't) it's always there—and deliverable to your doorstep in, for most transactions, two or three days. Great for you, great for Amazon.com, and great for the publishers. But one-to-one? Hardly.

"I'd say we're about 1 percent of the way there," Risher says of the company's ability to individually target customers. "There's a ton of work to be done to get there."

The problem is data glut. At the moment Amazon.com doesn't ask for much background on you, because it has no way to use that information. For most communications all you're asked to provide is your e-mail address. (If you post a book review, the site requests that you volunteer your city or town.) Even your name is optional. Then, when you order a book, Amazon.com asks only for your name, e-mail and mailing address, and credit card number. At this point, you are assigned a unique customer ID that, theoretically, allows the company to track all of your activities on the site: the pages you look at, the links you click, the recommendations you request. But Amazon.com execs will admit privately that the company's growth has outstripped its ability to warehouse, let alone mine, the data it collects. For the moment, most of that information—surprise!—simply disappears onto Amazon.com's hard disks.

Amazon.com execs will admit privately that the company's growth has outstripped its ability to warehouse, let alone mine, the data it collects

Mass customization is in evidence, however. "If you come tour the site and you bought a book before, you will see a message at the top of the screen that says 'Personal Recommendations'—a real-time lookup of other clients' most recent purchases," Risher says. "We change it every single day for the entire customer base. If every customer came every day, they'd be guaranteed to see a new book." Amazon.com is also integrating filtering software from Minneapolis-based Net Perceptions into a service called BookMatcher. Net Perceptions' software, like that of one of its chief competitors, Firefly, works best when you devote the time to answering series of questions about your likes and dislikes. Then it begins to recommend new selections to you, learning over time from your answers. But Risher, for one, has yet to be convinced of its utility.

"Basically, nobody yet—and this is not a slam at Net Perceptions—has figured out how to make this stuff work," he says. "One mistake is to make that Q&A session sound like an SAT. An even worse mistake is to make someone feel like all their answers are wrong! We've spent a lot of time figuring out what that list of questions should be."

The mass marketing continues, but the customization more or less ends right there. "We spend 98 percent of our energy right now doing things in aggregate," Risher acknowledges. Things like bulk e-mail. Once you sign up for an Amazon.com e-mail list, particularly one targeted at subject areas like cooking or science fiction, rest assured that you'll receive frequent updates about new titles. It's the sort of active-data response espoused by Excite's Joe Kraus. The company also periodically sends mass promotional e-mails to its entire customer list—a practice that has prompted some critics on the Usenet newsgroup news.admin.net-abuse.email to nickname it Spamazon.com. (Other large Web sites, including HotWired, have also been attacked from time to time for similar bulk mailings to member lists.) "Honestly, it's very frustrating for us, because we use e-mail as our primary communication with our customers," Risher says of the complaints.

But Amazon.com's experience also offers the paradox that one-to-one marketing on the Web may be unnecessary—or at least nonessential—depending on the product you're pushing. How else to explain the fact that the company has seen its repeat business grow even as its customer base has broadened? When Amazon.com filed for its IPO in March 1997 it claimed 340,000 customers, 40 percent of whom were repeat purchasers. By early this year 58 percent of its 1.5 million shoppers had purchased from Amazon.com before.

Amazon.com is now heading into new markets: The company already offers a limited selection of videos and CDs, and it has a major music effort under way that will bring it more directly into competition with CDnow and Music Boulevard. Its customer profiles—your profile—will become only more valuable to Amazon.com when the company can observe your buying habits across product categories. The relational possibilities (buy a Madonna album, receive a pitch for the Evita video, perhaps) are enticing from the marketer's perspective. Will they be a convenience, and an improvement, for you? Possibly. True one-to-one? Not necessarily.

While Amazon.com may not yet be getting much use from the data it collects, the site is gathering it using one of the most vilified—and most misunderstood—of Web tools. It's the magic cookie, or just plain cookie, a tiny tag of data inserted inside your browser files that can identify you—or, more accurately, your browser—as a unique entity every time you return to the site that issued it. If you're a moderate Web surfer, chances are that at this very moment your

If you're a moderate Web surfer, chances are that at this very moment your hard disk is host to about 200 cookies

hard disk is host to about 200 cookies placed there by the various sites you have visited to, say, get the latest news or conduct a search. On the Web, the cookie is becoming nearly ubiquitous at major commercial sites as a means of tracking user activity. (If you use Netscape, go into the Preferences menu and check the box next to the message "Warn me before accepting a cookie" to see just how prevalent it has become.)

Cookie and *magic cookie* are old Unix hacker terms. Eric Raymond's *New Hacker's Dictionary* defines a *magic cookie* as "something passed between routines or programs that enables the receiver to perform some operation; a capability ticket or opaque identifier....small data objects that contain data encoded in a strange or intrinsically machine-dependent way." *Cookie*, according to Raymond, means "a handle, transaction ID, or other token of agreement between cooperating programs. 'I give him a packet, he gives me back a cookie.' The claim check you get from a dry-cleaning shop is a perfect mundane example of a cookie; the only thing it's useful for is to relate a later transaction to this one (so you get the same clothes back)."

Lou Montulli is as surprised as anyone at the innovative uses found for one of his best-known hacks. The Netscape programmer is acknowledged by his peers as the Father of the Web Cookie—a somewhat dubious title, until you consider the alternatives: Montulli also gave the Web world the Netscape < blink > tag and The Amazing Fish Cam, one of the first computer-connected cameras aimed at a tank of saltwater fauna.

"The problem that sparked the idea was that we were trying to make an online-shopping application," Montulli recalls. "We had a newly formed application group that wanted to build a shopping cart."

It's harder than it sounds. Under hypertext transfer protocol, the language used by Web-browser software (your copy of Netscape) to communicate with Web-server software (like Wired's), a series of discrete connections open and close like a fluttering eyelid. In each of those connections, the browser software requests a specific piece of information, the server delivers it, and then the connection closes. Visiting a Web page with your Netscape or Internet Explorer browser sets off a cascade of such requests—one for each text, image, sound, and video file available on the page. Each time, the server knows only that a request has been made by a certain type of browser (say, Communicator 4.0) running on a certain type of machine (say, a PC running Windows 95) coming from a certain domain (like att.worldnet.com). Amidst all these connections, the server doesn't even try to identify a single browser as unique.

But if, like Montulli, you wanted to create a shopping basket that could be linked to an individual browser so that the user could fill the basket up with goods and pay for them, then the unique-identity problem had to be solved. Other programmers tried to solve the dilemma within the boundaries of HTML, the markup language riding atop HTTP, which describes the contents and structure of a Web page itself. HTML-based solutions, unfortunately, worked only within the individual site where they were tried. As soon as you moved out of the site, or even out of order—clicking on the back arrow was the easiest way to do it—the contents of any shopping basket described in HTML were easily lost.

Montulli's solution? Move the shopping-basket function from HTML to HTTP by sending a small data packet—the cookie—to a browser, which would store it in a file on the hard disk. The cookie could have a life span—years in length, if necessary, rather than the few seconds of an HTTP connection request. It could be updated on repeat visits. As a unique identifier, it could refer to information permanently stored in a database connected to a server. And the Web-server software could set a new cookie every time a browser connected to it.

Before Montulli's magic cookie saved the day, early Web publishers tried to track visitors by adapting a range of authentification tools. One tool originally created to restrict access to specific Web sites—by issuing each user a unique name and password—could be repurposed as an information-gathering device, for example. But authentication systems were a pain in the ass—people are always forgetting their login names and passwords—and they defeated the egalitarian, open nature of Web surfing, where each site was only one click away from another.

While marketers and publishers have gone crazy for cookies, some retailers still aren't sold on their ultimate usefulness

With the cookie, sites could store registration information for you. (Consumer convenience wins another round.) More important, the cookie could also be used to track even the browsers of those individuals who didn't register, providing publishers and advertisers with a wealth of new information about the traffic on their sites.

Ironically, while marketers and publishers have gone crazy for cookies, some retailers still aren't sold on their ultimate usefulness. "We use it for things like the shopping cart, where you can save things for 30 days. It's strictly a trade-off thing for convenience," says Amazon.com's David Risher. But in the future, Risher claims, the company may dispense with cookies altogether in favor of its own account-management tools. "Cookies are sort of complicated to track, and they're not very reliable," he says. "You don't want to build a marketing campaign around something affected by whether someone changes their browser or not."

Then there are the privacy concerns. The problem with all this cookie passing, some people complain, is that it occurs surreptitiously. Since you and I are basically lazy (how many people have netscape.com as their homepage because it's the browser's default setting?), we don't notice those little bits of code traveling onto our hard disks unless someone tells us. We don't know that we're being groomed for the Ultimate Focus Group.

It's difficult, in fact, to find a gung-ho endorsement for cookies, even from some of their biggest users

For nearly a year there's been a tug-of-war over the privacy and notification wording of the RFC 2109, the cookie standard being developed under the auspices of the Internet Engineering Task Force. Privacy advocates are demanding full disclosure, and marketers—particularly ad-network and ad-management companies like DoubleClick and Imgis (more on them later)—are lobbying for the status quo: the appearance of a pop-up window revealing that a cookie has been set only when a user alters his or her browser settings.

At least one marketer agrees that the lack of disclosure poses a serious privacy challenge. "I think cookies could be the death of the Internet," says Allen Olivo, Apple's senior director of worldwide marketing communications. "I think they're insidious. I realize the need for good, solid tracking information, and I have no problem with that. The problem is that they're hidden, and that's an invasion of electronic privacy."

It's difficult, in fact, to find a gung-ho endorsement for cookies, even from some of their biggest users. MatchLogic, a Web-marketing service company that Excite recently purchased for $89 million in stock, operates an ad-management service at Preferences.com that relies heavily on cookies to track ad views and clickthroughs across a range of Web sites. But MatchLogic executive vice president Ben Addoms—who also bears the title of president of MatchLogic's Digital 1:1 Division—says most cookie data isn't even being used in ways useful to advertisers: "If I look at the sites that can do geographic targeting, it's a pretty small number. I don't think the state of the art being used to target ads is very sophisticated right now."

Whether the use is sophisticated or not, when you look at the biggest users of cookies—ad-management networks one thing is apparent: They're a lot better at delivering on the promise of the Ultimate Focus Group for marketers than on the promise of the Ultimate Takeout Menu for you. Imgis, MatchLogic, and DoubleClick, for example, have set cookies inside millions of browsers visiting hundreds of sites. The benefit to you is less repetition of advertising when you surf the covered sites. The benefit to them is far greater: information on the behavior of millions of people using the sites.

In the future, not only will the cookie need to be more efficient to win the skeptics over, but data-mining techniques will need to keep pace with that smarter cookie. Addoms suggests that companies like Engage Technologies, a wholly owned subsidiary of CMG Information Services, may point the way. (CMG is a publicly traded holding company that owns, in addition to Engage, pieces of firms like Lycos, GeoCities, and Reel.com, among other properties.) Engage recently announced plans to create and rent access to a giant, anonymous database of user profiles—a sort of Penultimate Focus Group—called Engage.Knowledge, which will collect data from cookies delivered across multiple sites (including Lycos) and make it available for real-time lookups. Engage is calling the new service a "crystal ball" for marketers.

"You may be a 40-year-old white male, but you may act like a 16-year-old Hispanic woman"

"As far as on-the-edge or out-there technologies, there really isn't a lot," Addoms says. But who needs a lot when what's there is dripping with intrigue?

What we do is, we predict from behavior what their age, sex, and household income are," says Michael Thiemann from a car phone somewhere between Logan International Airport and downtown Boston. Thiemann, the CEO of Aptex Software, is explaining how the technology behind his company's SelectCast ad-targeting engine works.

"We can predict that you're straight or gay, whether you like sports, and a hundred other things. You may be a 40-year-old white male, but you may act like a 16-year-old Hispanic woman," says Thiemann.

This is not—trust me—the setup line for some horribly politically incorrect joke about a middle-aged cross-dresser who thinks he's Selena. Thiemann is serious. Aptex's SelectCast is a neural-network-based tool that constructs behaviorally based profiles of Web users. It then targets users with ads and personal promotions their behavior dictates they will like. Using Aptex, Thiemann claims, marketers can finally achieve the one-to-one future. His analogy—familiar to one-to-oneheads—is the friendly neighborhood shopkeeper during the halcyon days before mass marketing descended and doomed his existence. A man who knew his

customers by their habits, not by their demographic partic-
ulars. Of course, that shopkeeper also knew your name and
your face—Thiemann says that while SelectCast can certainly benefit from being linked to a name-based registration system, it can be just as effective working with
complete anonymity.

"Basically, your presence on any given site gives us a lot
of information that allows us to begin profiling you immediately," Thiemann explains. "If you're on a homepage, we
might use the general behavior-profile type for people at
that site, but once you start clicking beyond that homepage,
we are building—in real time—a personal profile."

That mathematical profile, or vector, is about a kilobyte in
size per user. According to Thiemann, while SelectCast processes gigabytes—perhaps terabytes—of data every day for
its customers in order to derive and improve the profiles
contained in its vectors, it is necessary only to pass that
data through its system. The system doesn't need to digest
it. "We don't keep it in some master relational database—
there's no massive database anywhere," he assures me.

Aptex's entry into the Web's advertising and marketing
game came courtesy of Infoseek, which first contacted
Aptex to discuss how its neural-network tools could be
applied to Infoseek's bread-and-butter business of Web cat-
egorizing and searching. Thiemann credits then Infoseek
CEO Robin Johnson for first suggesting that Aptex's technology could be used to target advertising.

"It's clustering based on interest to reach someone at a
certain psychographic stage," explains Peter Rip of Knight-
Ridder Ventures. (Rip was VP and general manager of Infoseek's network division when the company first began to
use Aptex's tools, and the white paper he wrote about the
success of the joint Infoseek-Aptex project has become part
of Aptex's standard marketing pitch.)

That project ultimately became Ultramatch, an Infoseek
service for ad buyers that targeted 22 user segments and
promised significantly higher clickthrough rates on all of
them. It worked in spectacular fashion, according to Rip,
and he believes that Aptex makes it possible for Web sites
to identify even smaller segments—say, webmasters looking for Java tools—for which advertisers would be willing
to pay four to five times the going rate for search-engine ad
inventory. In a market where the average ad can cost
between $20 and $40 per 1,000 impressions, "you could get
$200 CPMs on some microsegments," Rip says. SelectCast,
the outgrowth of the Ultramatch project, is now available to
any and all customers—or, at least, those that can afford its

base $100,000 price tag. But even the cost doesn't bother Aptex's most enthusiastic endorsers.

There's just one other problem with Aptex, besides the ungodly expense. And it's one that offers room for enough Big Brother fear and paranoia to stimulate an entire army of conspiracy nuts. "Do you know some of the biggest customers of neural networks?" Firefly's Saul Klein asked when I first mentioned Aptex to him. Of course, I answered. The CIA. The NSA. The spooks.

Thiemann is nonchalant about Aptex's history. The company is a spinoff of IINC, a longtime contractor for certain black-budget departments hidden in Uncle Sam's pockets. "Call it government intelligent agencies," says Thiemann, describing HNC's traditional customer base. In the early 1990s HNC won a bid to design the latest generation of research technology for those vaguely described government agencies—agencies that have a tendency to accumulate vast databases of information that needs constant and accurate sifting. "HNC has probably received more money for advanced analysis research than any other company around," Thiemann says. It appears HNC also had the sense to recognize that the Cold War cash cow that had fed it and other military-industrial contractors was drying up.

"In 1995 we were shipping our most advanced systems to the US government, and the Internet was taking off," Thiemann says. "We at HNC were saying, 'This was working so well at government operations—why not apply it in another high-information stream environment: the Internet?'" (As it happens, the generation of analysis technology used in certain government agencies before HNC won its contract was also being adapted to the Net at about the same time. That technology is now the core of the Verity search engine.)

Firefly's Klein—who can sound like Thiemann's twin when it comes to disparaging the more brain-dead approaches of traditional marketers on the Net—nevertheless says he's uncomfortable about what he labels Aptex's "stealth" approach to tracking.

"We as a company have no problem with behind-the-scenes filtering technologies," says Klein. "But we believe it is in the best economic interest of both the individual and the business to form consensual relationships. That's just my opinion." A few minutes later he launches into a more elaborate rant against the whole notion of tracking itself:

"My personal take on the whole tracking issue is, that's old media. That's what Nielsen people meters do. That's all about masquerading under the guise of 'customer first' and saying, 'OK, we're going to give you a better service, and we're not going to tell you how we do it, and we're going to set up all these video cameras to watch what you're doing, and we're going to make some assumptions based on analyses of what you do.'" All of this is, of course, a prelude to describing why the alternative offered by Klein and Firefly is a better option.

"What we're doing is giving people a tool that allows them to identify themselves to a business they want to do business with," Klein says about the Firefly Passport Web plug-in. Passport is part of Firefly's own proposal for jump-starting a one-to-one future, a proposal endorsed by both Microsoft and Netscape last year when they joined Firefly to promote the adoption of the Open Profiling Standard, a framework informing the World Wide Web Consortium's data-exchange proposal, P3P (Platform for Privacy Preferences Project). The standard has also attracted the attention and the praise of Clinton's Internet czar, Ira Magaziner, as well as representatives from the Federal Trade Commission.

Under OPS—and soon under P3P—you get to create a personal profile linked to your Web browser. This profile could contain everything from your name and e-mail address to credit card data and lifestyle information.

At each Web site you visit, you would choose how much of that information—if any—to make available. The Firefly Passport is the first OPS-compliant client; the company that made its name on collaborative filtering wants to follow the Netscape path and sprinkle free Passport clients far and wide, creating a critical mass for the servers it will then sell to Web-based businesses.

If there's one thing Michael Thiemann and Saul Klein can agree on, it's the need to clear out the undergrowth of traditional advertising and marketing before it wraps its tendrils around the Web and strangles it.

The problem, says Thiemann, is that training marketers in the advantages of systems like Aptex requires undoing their training in mass marketing. "We've all been trained in the Procter & Gamble School. We've been trained to make demographics stand in as proxies for what you build." Proxies like VALS, the Values and Lifestyles target-marketing spawn of the brains at SRI International, which attempted to divide Americans into eight categories based on personality types, including Actualizers, Achievers, Strivers, and Strugglers. (SRI also developed a Japanese edition of VALS.) And PRIZM—the Potential Rating Index by Zip Markets—developed at the Claritas Corporation in

1974, which purported to separate us all into 40 lifestyle clusters with names like Furs and Station Wagons, Back-Country Folks, Hard Scrabble, and Pools & Patios. "Tell me someone's ZIP code, and I can predict what they eat, drink, drive—even think," said Jonathan Robbin, who is *not* the Amazing Kreskin, but the PRIZM system's creator.

The goal of marketers using these systems—he nirvana of the mass marketing and advertising industries—was to identify an ideal customer profile for every product. Because ideal customers are loyal customers. Ideal customers are brand-friendly customers. Ideal customers are trusting customers. And ideal customers are, remember, the Ultimate Focus Group.

The two halves of the marketing brain that have transported themselves onto the Web—the direct marketers who send us junk mail and the advertisers who sponsor *Buffy the Vampire Slayer*—would very much like to transport these targeting categories with them. (Many, in fact, have—why else do you think they want to know your ZIP code?)

How primitive! But the old, impossibly monolithic mass-market approach still has one advantage over Web marketing: the consumer's trust.

"There's a big, big challenge, which I think has not been figured out yet, about how to develop trust with a brand online," suggests Klein. A point interactive-marketing researchers Donna Hoffman and Tom Novak recently verified in a paper they coauthored with colleague Marcos Peralta. Poring through the responses to two major consumer surveys on the Web the 1997 Internet Demographics Study, sponsored by Nielsen Media Research and CommerceNet, and the Seventh GVU WWW User Survey, conducted at Georgia Tech—the three discovered a gap in consumers' privacy concerns.

The Number One issue on the minds of Web surfers, the Number One issue that may be holding back the one-to-one future, is trust. More accurately, the lack of it

Call it the Trust Gap. It turns out that the Number One issue on the minds of Web surfers, the Number One issue that may be holding back the one-to-one future, is trust. More accurately, the lack of it.

"Consumers do not understand the relationship in an economic context," says Hoffman about the tarantella dance between Web buyer and Web seller. "Consumers want to be friends. They want a relationship. Now, how do you have a relationship? They want to be honest!" Codependent consumers no more. "Consumers want full disclosure, full consent, opt-in," concludes Hoffman. "But the best they get today is opt-out."

Absent trust, Web consumers seem to be more than willing to upset the marketing apple cart. They refuse to cooperate: Some 94 percent of them have declined to provide personal information at one time or another when asked for it. And they lie. Through their teeth! Forty percent have taken the time to *make shit up* when they actually do provide data on a Web form.

Absent trust, the confidence of the marketers themselves will eventually slip away. "If you don't trust me—I can have all the advanced technologies under the sun, but if you're putting bad information into my technology, it's useless," says Klein. "I might as well take out an ad on *Friends*. That's a trusted medium for communicating with people."

Ah, those two promises. Four years and countless magic cookies later, we know that at least one of them has largely been ignored. From the ad networks to Engage, the Focus Group has grown larger. The marketers are making out. Meanwhile, the consumer chasm (as well as the Trust Gap) detected by Hoffman and Novak still yawns, while a host of technological and organizational hurdles still block the path to fulfilling the pledge to consumers. Can Aptex and P3P and the marketers' soul-stirring testaments that a higher standard of privacy will live on the Web help bridge the gap and rebalance the two parties in this relationship? "Nirvana," says Saul Klein, "is balance."

Klein says equalization is coming, that the "serious" companies are rethinking the ways they deal with consumers. But the evidence of that, so far, is thin. And something Millward Brown Interactive's Rex Briggs said about mass customization sticks in my brain: It's all about using the trick of technology to deliver a personalized message that isn't really personal at all. Sites considering mass customization will ask whether it can help squeeze a little bit extra out of every customer. Improving incremental revenue, it's called. And if it's clear the little bit extra is there for the taking, Briggs suggests, you can bet sites will seize on the trick. The consumer, it is hoped, will perceive a one-to-one relationship; the truth will be somewhat different.

"I think the reality," Briggs says of the future, "is that technology is going to empower the producer far more than it empowers the consumer."

Promises, promises.

Old-Line Retailers Resist Online Life[3]

Executives at Saks Fifth Avenue were a bit dazzled in the fall of 1996 when Time Warner Inc. offered them space on an Internet "mall" for less than $100,000. It seemed like the right partner and the right time to try selling on the World Wide Web.

But once on Time Warner's Dreamshop site, Saks sold a $2,000 suit to one man and some candy. By last month, Dreamshop was no more, and Saks has shelved plans for another commerce site. The company will use the Internet to give investors information, but Saks executives have concluded that cyberspace is not conducive to selling the high-priced, high-touch goods they specialize in, like soft, silky scarves and buttery leather purses.

As an industry, online retailing may be picking up steam, reaching $3.7 billion in sales by the end of last year on the strength of books, music CD's, computers and other goods that buyers do not need to pick up or try on to decide what they want. But for Saks and many other traditional merchants, cyberspace is seeming downright inhospitable, a place without shelves or aisles—or revenues, in most cases.

And maybe most alienating to the old-line merchants, the online people do not even speak the language of retail.

"They talk in terms of hits," said Sheri Wilson-Gray, Saks's executive vice president of marketing. "But I don't know what that means in terms of the customer. I feel pretty confident in the judgment that there will not be major apparel transactions with a Saks customer in the short term there."

For the last two years, an avalanche of press releases, news reports and Zeitgeist buzz has proclaimed the Internet the great electronic bazaar that defines the future of commerce; any merchant left behind would surely perish.

But the truth is that American retail stores are struggling mightily to build a path onto the Net from the bricks and mortar that for the last century have defined their selling space. Few if any have made money on the Web, and many are still struggling to decide how to use the medium—or whether they belong online at all.

At the same time, they are hearing footsteps. Several large retailers—notably the bookseller Barnes & Noble—have

---

3. Article by Jennifer Steinhauer for the *New York Times*, D p1 Ap 20, '98 D p 1 +. Copyright © 1998 The New York Times Company. Reprinted with Permission.

already seen their turf invaded by Internet start-ups like Amazon.com. The start-ups usually have the advantages of knowing the quirks of electronic commerce, being small and agile enough to turn on a dime as online technologies and demographics shift. And they are free of the distractions of simultaneously competing in traditional retail.

"The Internet is a new channel, and they are all out there exploring it," said Don Gilbert, the senior vice president of information technology at the National Retail Federation. "But when you look at what people are buying now, in the grand scheme of things, it is not a significant part of their revenue stream."

Indeed, despite the seemingly impressive sales figures for electronic commerce so far, only 15 to 20 percent of those revenues went to the online sites of conventional retailers, according to Piper Jaffray Inc., a Minneapolis investment company. Most were rung up in the travel and financial services industries and in business-to-business sales.

The merchants finding the most success at selling online tend to be ones . . . that exist only online

The merchants finding the most success at selling online tend to be ones—again, like Amazon.com—that exist only online.

"Retailers are way back on the prairie, their wagon wheels are covered with mud, and they are not going anywhere," said Laura Berland, an executive vice president at ORB Digital Direct, an online commerce consulting firm. "It is very new technology, it is very expensive, and it wrenches at the heart of corporate culture."

To be sure, some of the frustrations retailers have encountered on the path to cyberspace are part of the medium's birth pains. But there are also other causes, including the industry's traditional unwillingness to spend money on untried technologies and the failure of many companies to define which managers' roles encompass electronic commerce or to understand the profoundly different ways that people shop online and in stores.

"The Internet scares the pants off of these guys," said Kate Dalhagen, a senior analyst at Forester Research in Boston.

Yet retailers who stay on the sidelines, she predicts, will almost certainly lose business to online enterprises.

Still, retailers' resistance is understandable. The Internet, for all its convenience, is still largely not a pleasant place to go shopping for things that require any sort of inspection, in part because of the low quality of images on the Web. Catalogues offer much better representations of clothing; colors, the textures of fabrics or the stitching details on a sweater are much clearer on glossy paper than they are on most computer screens.

What is more, unless a site is exceptionally well designed, clicking around to find items can be frustrating. And when Web traffic is high, as it often is on weekday afternoons and early evenings, online shopping can be slower than shopping in a store.

But what is trickiest about electronic retailing is learning how consumers shop online—almost the polar opposite of how they shop in a store. Many people who would browse in a department store and often buy on impulse go online with a specific product in mind, find it, buy it and log off. Hence the failure of Dreamshop and other online electronic malls that attempted to mimic the shopping patterns of real malls.

Nor are many retailers willing to spend the time and money needed to experiment with online sales.

For example, Sports Authority, the sporting goods superstore chain, has a consumer Web site, but it does little more than list store addresses. "We don't see a reason to make much of an investment in the Internet," said Jack Smith, Sports Authority's chief executive. "I don't really believe the Internet is the wave of the future for sporting goods."

Tell that to Brett Allsop, the president of Cedro Group Inc., which runs Sportsite.com, a compilation of dozens of specialized sporting goods catalogues whose merchandise is sold through one site. Since the site was begun in September, its sales have grown an average of 52 percent a month, Mr. Allsop said. Though he declined to disclose total revenue, he said that by the end of the year the site would be generating "seven figures" in sales.

Sportsite got its start through a joint venture with Yahoo, but will now finance its growth with venture capital and, eventually, an initial public offering, Mr. Allsop said.

Direct merchants like catalogue companies, including Lands' End, have had an easier transition to cyberspace than store-based retailers—except for chain stores with a history of investing in both technology and sophisticated inventory management. Wal-Mart Stores Inc., for instance, is commended by analysts for having one of the most sophisticated electronic commerce sites among traditional retailers.

Unlike most retailers' Web sites, the Wal-Mart site offers even more items online than it does in its giant stores. In fact, the site's best-selling products are Rolex watches and Nike T-shirts—items not even found in Wal-Mart stores.

What is trickiest about electronic retailing is learning how consumers shop online—almost the polar opposite of how they shop in a store

"The transition is not simple," said Phil Martz, the director of Wal-Mart Online. "It is a difficult task to track 1,000 orders a day from different homes and very different from shipping one case of something to a store and making sure it arrived."

No wonder, then, that some retailers have already given up on the idea of selling goods on the Web, and use it instead as a marketing medium to drive traffic to their stores.

Hillel Levin runs a company called Coolsavings.com, which distributes personalized coupons for retail stores and restaurants through the Internet. Clients include J. C. Penney, National Car Rental, Chuck E. Cheese and Blockbuster Video. It is not so much a capitulation, as a gradual realization about which kinds of consumer businesses lend themselves to online sales—and which do not.

"In the last year," Mr. Hillel said, "we have seen people who said, 'We believe the Internet has gone beyond the point of us having our own Web sites.'"

The American Way of Spam[4]

CHINO, Calif.—The life of a spammer is no bowl of cybercherries. Damien Melle, who makes a living sending huge amounts of e-mail advertising over the Internet, works out of his home in this hardscrabble Southern California suburb, in an office where the smell of fried food lingers like, say, unwanted e-mail in your In box.

On a recent afternoon, he fielded half a dozen hate calls. His Internet service provider canceled his account, again. And another Federal Express letter arrived from America Online's lawyers. They had subpoenaed his laptop from the shop where it was in for repairs.

On the bright side, no dog feces had come in the mail, as has happened at least once, and the anti-spammer vigilantes who had been tracking him seemed to have lost the scent somewhere in the ether. There was also the tally of the previous month's profits on the white board, the only wall covering except for a picture of the Virgin Mary. In March, Mr. Melle said, his company, which he runs with his brother Joe, cleared about $11,000.

"I made a lot of money last month, and I was at home," said Mr. Melle, 22, who manages, despite his travails, to make a daily delivery of about a half-million e-mail promotions. "I'll never work for a big company again. The Internet is an opportunity for people like us. That's why the big companies are nervous." Joe Melle, 31, who runs his part of the operation from Norristown, Pa., said, "We're just trying to put food on the table."

The brothers Melle are on the front lines of the spam wars, cyberspace's first all-out internecine conflict. Depending on which side you talk to, the stakes are, roughly, the future of capitalism, free expression and the American Way or the future of the Internet, individual privacy and the American Way.

"One of us has got to go off this Net, and it ain't going to be me," said Ron Guilmette, a software engineer in Sacramento, Calif., who is developing a program to block spam.

Like many aspiring electronic entrepreneurs, the Melles started a few years back by culling addresses by hand from the Web and e-mail discussion groups. Now computer programs with unrepentant names like Cyber Bomber and Stealth Mass Mailer help thousands of spammers keep their self-appointed rounds, with relative anonymity to boot.

---

4. Article by Amy Harmon for the *New York Times*, My 7, '98 G p 1 +. Copyright © 1998 The New York Times Company. Reprinted by Permission.

As a result, it has become essentially impossible to over-state just how much various Internet factions abhor those who send junk e-mail (although many are happy to try).

Internet access providers whose systems are clogged with commercial mail blame the spammers for slowing down the whole system. Subscribers revile them for sullying their mailboxes, and those of their Net-loving children, with offers of free hot sex, XXX photos, discount dental plans and tips on how they, too, might partake of the bulk-mail bounty from outfits like Money4you@dream-scometrue.com.

The war even has its own language. Spammers spoof headers (to hide their real e-mail addresses), relay-rape overseas mail servers (routing their mail through an unsus-pecting computer to avoid making their service providers suspicious) and shield their computers' whereabouts with cloaking programs.

Spam is a genu-inely troubling flash point for so many because it lays bare both the pros and cons of the Internet's unique brand of democratic expression

Anti-spammers retaliate with mail bombs (barraging their antagonists with a taste of their own medicine), computer code patches for security holes and the formidable Real-Time Black Hole List, part of a boycott campaign of provid-ers who service known spammers.

On the Spam-L list-serve, an online bastion of the spam-haters, members know their quarry by name: "Alex Chiu is back," one wrote. "Nuke him." (In an interview, the belea-guered Mr. Chiu, 27, said he had quit his job at a duty-free shop in San Francisco to market an anti-aging device he had invented. Now he sends out mail for clients, too, including sex-toy stores and individuals offering do-it-your-self business plans. Among his reasons for turning to spam: "I'm an environmentalist." Spam, of course, wastes no paper.)

Another spammer, Dan Hufnal, head of the Direct E-Mail Advertisers Association, said: "These people will go to any means to punish any company that would advertise this way or provide the connectivity for others who wish to do so. They're nothing short of terrorists. They don't act any different from the I.R.A."

Mr. Hufnal's attempts to provide Internet access for bulk e-mailers have been thwarted by a group of network engi-neers who identify spammers and shut them out of much of the Net.

Both sides display a tendency toward hyperbole that seems endemic to their chosen medium. But spam is a gen-uinely troubling flash point for so many because it lays bare both the pros and cons of the Internet's unique brand of democratic expression.

How to, Well, Eat Less Spam

You're used to junk mail. Without much thought, you toss out the shiny fliers from the local car dealer, the menus from the new Thai restaurant (free delivery), the assurances that YOUR NAME HERE may already be a millionaire. But junk e-mail is somehow different. You feel the privacy invasion more keenly when it shows up on your computer screen. You may have to pay to download it. And besides, a lot of it is raunchier than any solicitations you are likely to get in your snail-mail. There is no sure way to stop spam, but here are some tips on stemming the deluge.

USE FILTERS—The most commonly used e-mail programs, like Eudora Light and Outlook Express, allow users to specify which messages to automatically delete based on content. If the subject line contains "make money" or "!!!" for instance, you can direct the message to the Trash. Be sure to check it occasionally in case you have deleted something you would rather keep.

Dedicated antispam software like Spammer Slammer, which is free, adds another level of filtering. On America Online, mail controls and parental controls can be adjusted. To find out how to block AOL's pop-up ads, go to keyword "marketingprefs."

DON'T ASK TO BE REMOVED FROM A JUNK-MAIL LIST—Many bulk e-mail advertisers include an address to reply to for removal from their list. Some of them may actually remove you. But many more appear to simply take the reply as confirmation that they can continue to reach you there.

COMPLAIN TO YOUR SERVICE PROVIDER—Most Internet service providers don't want to deliver spam any more than you want to read it and want to be notified. Ask your provider for the best address to forward offending bulk mail (on AOL: TOSSpam@aol.com).

NOTIFY THE SPAMMER'S PROVIDER—Since junk e-mailers often forge their point of origin, deciphering the headers can require some detective work. For help, see How to Complain About Spam (weber.ucsd.edu/pagre/spam.html).

COMPLAIN TO THE FEDERAL TRADE COMMISSION—Although there are no Federal laws specifically for bulk e-mail, any e-mail that is fraudulent or obscene falls within existing statutes. The F.T.C. accepts complaints about unsolicited commercial e-mail at .

More information is available at these anti-spam Web sites:

THE E-MAIL ABUSE FAQ: member.aol.com/emailfaq/emailfaq.html
FIGHT SPAM ON THE INTERNET: spam.abuse.net
BLACKLIST OF INTERNET ADVERTISERS: math-www.uni-paderborn.de/axel/BL
FEDERAL AND STATE SPAM LAW SITE: www.jmls.edu/cyber/statutes/email
COALITION AGAINST UNSOLICITED COMMERCIAL E-MAIL: www.cauce.org
REALTIME BLACKHOLE LIST: maps.vix.com/rbl

The network's much-celebrated capacity to turn anyone with $20-a-month access into a publisher or entrepreneur is also what allows spammers to thrive. Yet anti-spam activists, or "anti-E-commerce radicals," as Mr. Hufnal calls them, insist that it is bulk e-mail itself that endangers electronic free speech. For proof, they point to the spam siege of Usenet, a portion of the Internet devoted to public bulletin boards where thousands of subjects are discussed.

Usenet newsgroups were the target of two notorious spam pioneers, Laurence Canter and Martha Siegel, immigration lawyers who in 1994 posted vast numbers of messages offering assistance in entering the green card lottery. Despite the efforts of software known as cancelbots and human "despammers," many of the newsgroups have since been overrun with junk messages.

Junk e-mail's bad rap is largely due to its tendency to promote get-rich-quick schemes or pornographic Web sites

"As someone who is very concerned with free speech on the Net, it certainly makes me anxious that this is the way the market is developing," said Dierdre Mulligan, staff counsel for the Center for Democracy and Technology, a public-interest group, and author of a report by the Federal Trade Commission's working group on spam that is scheduled for release this week. "But as someone who received three unsolicited political e-mails and 22 commercial e-mails today, I think the more we can let people tailor what they want to receive, the better."

The term spam, taken from the name of the spiced lunch meat relentlessly doled out in Army rations, morphed into an epithet when Internet denizens adopted it to refer to unsolicited promotional messages. So negative is the connotation that Hormel Foods, which holds the trademark for Spam, sent a cease-and-desist letter to one publicity-minded spammer who held a press conference surrounded by cans of the pink product.

Less clear is whether spam is universally undesirable or whether, as one spammer puts it, "one man's spam is another man's caviar." Junk e-mail's bad rap is largely due to its tendency to promote get-rich-quick schemes or pornographic Web sites. But there are already laws governing e-mail that is fraudulent or obscene. Spammers marketing legitimate products—they prefer to be called bulk e-mailers—insist that there are plenty of people who welcome their missives. Or how would they be making money?

Joel Theodore, 31, of Long Island, who promotes his company's computer systems via e-mail, responded to an Internet posting titled, "Repent, sinner!" by writing: "The truth is, most businesses are not repenting merely because of the fact that it is profitable. The reality is we are not just irresponsible people. We have done our best to target mail. We also have made sure no one will ever get another one if they do not want it. We also do not use any illegal practices. If you don't want to read it, hit delete!"

That's easy to say, retort the anti-spammers—they prefer to be called pro-privacy advocates—but consider the following: "If a spammer sends a million pieces of e-mail out for a worthless piece of merchandise, that means a million people are going to have to delete the e-mail or respond to it," said Jim Nitchals, a regular on the net-abuse.email Internet discussion group. "Add up the number of seconds, and we're talking days and months of human suffering and waste of energy and time."

And cash. Since it costs spammers about the same to send 10 million pieces of mail as it does to send 10, there is no natural barrier to entry. And unlike junk snail mail, spam haters contend, e-mail passes on the cost of the advertisement to the providers who transmit it and recipients who pay for connect time to download it. America Online, for instance, estimates that as much as 30 percent of the all the Internet mail it processes is junk mail, at a cost that may eventually pass on to users.

The nation's biggest online service, AOL, whose subscribers suffer the indignities of spam perhaps more than anyone else, has won several recent court victories over junk e-mailers, prohibiting them from sending unsolicited bulk e-mail to the service. The Melles are next on AOL's list. In a suit filed in Federal District Court in Alexandria, Va., AOL is seeking an injunction against the Melles' company, TSF Marketing, which earlier this year threatened to make public five million AOL subscriber addresses unless the company relaxed its restrictions on bulk mailers.

But spammers are fond of pointing out that AOL itself bombards users with infuriating pop-up advertisements touting such offers as "easy 1-step photo scanning" every time they log on. And as mainstream advertisers and non-profit and political organizations contemplate using bulk e-mail as a way to get their messages out, just what qualifies as spam becomes increasingly murky. The Democratic Party in California, for instance, plans to send e-mail to thousands of voters with a slate of endorsements and information on the party's candidates this year.

"It's hard to get a fixed definition of spam," Ms. Mulligan said. "You know it when you see it."

The war on spam is making an impact. Many Internet service providers have adopted subscriber contracts that

"Spammer"

Name: Damien Melle, 22.
Occupation: Commercial bulk e-mailer.
Spams sent: Roughly 15 million a month.
Internet accounts canceled: More than 100—about 5 to 8 times a month.
Philosophy of spam: "I made a lot of money last month. I'll never work for a big company again. The Internet is an opportunity for people like us."

"Anti-Spammer"

Name: Paul Vixie, 34.
Occupation: Programmer and administrator of Realtime Black Hole List.
Spams received: Roughly 600 a month.
Spammers silenced (if only for a while): About 75.
Philosophy of spam: "This is just not O.K. with me. All Internet communications should be consensual."

prohibit sending bulk e-mail, and even "bulk friendly" providers have been hounded into changing their policies. Sanford Wallace, known as the Spam King—at his peak, he was sending 25 million pieces of mail a day—said last month that he was retiring from the trade.

Now Congress is considering three anti-spam bills, one of which would hold junk e-mail to the same standard as junk faxes. Courts have found some spammers liable for trespassing, and Internet users are adopting a host of new technological defenses. The new version of Microsoft's e-mail software, for instance, includes a feature—based on an analysis of 2,000 pieces of spam—that automatically blocks messages containing phrases like "for free!" or whose subject line contains both an exclamation point and a question mark.

Such measures do not impress Paul Vixie, the administrator of the Realtime Black Hole List, into which spammers have been known to disappear forever. Mr. Vixie, who wrote one of the programs that makes the Internet run, remembers the days when the network was spam-free. Now he gets spam about 100 times a day. So he is fighting back.

With a posse of volunteers, Mr. Vixie tracks each piece of junk mail he receives to its source—or as close as he can get. He then informs the spammer's service provider that it is harboring a Net transgressor. The provider has a choice: ditch the spammer or suffer the consequences. If a provider fails to take action, it is dropped into the abyss of the Black Hole List, which means that none of its subscribers can send e-mail to other providers who support Mr. Vixie's efforts. Mr. Vixie estimates that about one-fifth of the service providers on the Net support such e-mail boycotts.

"See, it's raising the hair on the back of my neck," he told a visitor recently as he hunched over his computer in his Silicon Valley office and stalked his prey. "This is just not O.K. with me. Fundamentally, this is an abuse of a privilege. All Internet communications should be consensual."

The Black Hole List maintainers realize that their tactics punish some innocent victims. But they are adamant about their right to refuse traffic from any Internet providers friendly to spam.

"It's heartbreaking for me to get e-mail from somebody's mother who can't send mail to her son at college because the school subscribes to the Black Hole List," Mr. Vixie said. "But I write them back and say: 'I'm sorry you're being inconvenienced. But your provider is spamming me. And they won't stop.'"

Why Web Warriors Might Worry[5]

Part of the pleasure and excitement of online journalism is smashing antique rules, overturning taboos, and rethinking the very idea of news. Part of the danger is that some of those antique rules still make sense and some of those taboos can still keep us from eating our mothers—or our standards. In the brave but chaotic new world of online journalism, rethinking the news doesn't always mean improving it.

Even some optimistic observers have several areas of concern:

INTERACTIVITY. This is supposed to be the most distinctive contribution of online journalism. Webheads see interactivity as a way to draw millions of mouse potatoes together in a virtual community, to engage and involve them in the news, and to stimulate public debate. Well, sometimes.

Take, for example, the CNN-*Time* Web site AllPolitics, which runs the gamut of interactive devices and gimmicks: free-form bulletin boards, instant "Take a Stand" polls ("Is FDR the greatest president of the 20th century?"), an e-mail forum called "Voter's Voice" on the issue of the day (late-term abortion, the budget), and a daily trivia quiz that can earn you a totebag and your name in lights, or at least in HTML. Throughout 1996 the site offered a riot of campaign-theme games, including a post-election single-elimination tournament called "Pitfalls" designed to predict Bill Clinton's biggest second-term problem. (Campaign fundraising beat out Hillary and Bosnia, among others.)

Bulletin boards and e-mail may make for discussions as feisty as anything that iconic old town square ever saw—but much of this famous "interactivity" is closer in spirit to Jeopardy than to a C-SPAN call-in. Why should a Web site's instant poll on FDR's status be hailed as constructive engagement when the networks' overnight tracking polls on Bob Dole's status were routinely denounced as shallow or undemocratic? Why is sitting alone pondering a trivia question about Millie, the former First Dog, more communitarian than sitting alone heaving your shoe at the television set?

Some new-media mavens also boast how much more accessible—and thus accountable—online journalists are

---

5. Article by Andie Tucher. Reprinted from the *Columbia Journalism Review* v36 p35-6 Jl/Ag '97. Copyright © 1998 by *Columbia Journalism Review*.

than traditional newspeople. But while reader feedback can help keep reporters honest, some new-media journalists are toying with another use of reader opinion that skates close to an abdication of their editorial judgment. MSNBC, for instance, invites you to rate the stories you read on a scale of one to seven according to how highly you would recommend each one to other "viewers," as MSNBC calls them. After you submit your rating, you're whisked to a page that lists the Top Ten stories of the minute with their scores.

According to Merrill Brown, editor-in-chief of MSNBC Interactive, the goal of the ranking is "principally and almost solely" to help people "share good ideas about interesting stuff they found in a deep, rich news environment that can be difficult to navigate, and also to give us some clues about what people are interested in." He insists that the rankings play no role in editorial decision-making. "In the hands of Rupert Murdoch it would turn out that way," he says, "but we're pretty serious about this enterprise." Serious or not, it's hard not to notice how many health stories land in the Top Ten—and how many new health stories crowd the MSNBC site every day.

On the Web, journalism, parajournalism, and pseudojournalism don't just coexist; they invade each other

CREDIBILITY AND AUTHORITY. On the Web, journalism, parajournalism, and pseudojournalism don't just coexist; they invade each other, through the handy online device of the hypertext link. While a newspaper editor can—theoretically, anyway—maintain iron control over the content of her four sections' worth of newsprint, no online journalist, no matter how scrupulous his own standards, can predict where his readers might daisy-chain their way. Even the most respectable news site has the potential to launch the unwary surfer straight through the looking glass.

The Web browser interested in the JonBenet Ramsey case, for instance—the Christmas-night murder of the children's-beauty-pageant queen in Colorado—might logically choose to start with the perfectly credible Denver Post, a local paper that has devoted extensive coverage to the crime. But the Post Web site includes a link to the home page of the Boulder sheriff's office. The sheriff's page links to a resource called "Law Enforcement Sites." And that site can take you to something blandly entitled "JonBenet Ramsey Homicide Web Sites," a page, maintained by one Ken Polzin, Jr., of links to some four dozen other Web sites pertaining to the case.

Polzin's standard for inclusion is clearly "relevance," not accuracy or even sanity. His page can take you to MSNBC's search engine, transcripts of press conferences, or a redacted version of the official autopsy report. Or you can just as easily surf right into the "Reverse Speech" site and listen for yourself to the "smoking gun" in the case: snippets from the audiotape of the Ramsey parents' CNN interview played backwards, supplemented with helpful transcripts in case you can't quite make out on your own that John Ramsey's tergiversated voice is in fact saying "I done it. It's a show you're running."

You can almost make a Six-Degrees-of-Kevin-Bacon game of it: how many links does it take to get from the home page of The *New York Times* to, say, a news release announcing authoritatively that "Pressure is growing on Capitol Hill for immediate impeachment hearings on President Clinton and Vice President Gore"? (Or so says the Committee to Impeach the President, which has just doubled its roster of supporters in Congress—to two.) How about a guide to the "hanky code" used by gay men to signal their preferences? (I made each connection in eight links.) But the question remains: how many rushed or inattentive surfers will end up wondering whether The Denver Post also has new evidence that Paul McCartney is dead?

CHURCH AND STATE. The rules seem to be different for online advertising, too. A survey by the Newspaper Association of America points to a disturbing trend: while no decent newspaper would dream of assigning its metro reporter to write headlines for its advertisers, most of the newspapers with separate new-media staffs routinely ask editorial employees to design or produce banner ads for their Web sites.

Chris McKenna, a producer for *Time* Online, says that while her own organization has never asked her to do any business-side work, there does seem to be a sense among many news organizations that all standards are a bit looser online. "Some print media don't seem to take their online sites quite as seriously," she says. "They don't give them enough resources; they might expect a producer, say, to be a researcher and fact-checker and editor, too. It's as if they're saying 'Hey, we can compromise a bit, it's not our flagship product.'"

Basic Internet Tips[6]

- **Do business with companies you know and trust.** Be sure you know who the company is and where it is physically located. Businesses operating in cyberspace may be in another part of the country or in another part of the world. Resolving problems with companies that are unfamiliar can be more complicated in long-distance or cross-border transactions.

- **Understand the offer.** Look carefully at the information about the products or services the company is offering, and ask for more information, if needed. A legitimate company will be glad to provide it; a fraudulent marketer won't. Be sure you know what is being sold, the total price, the delivery date, the return and cancellation policy, and the terms of any guaranty. The federal telephone and mail order rule, which also covers orders by computer, requires goods or services to be delivered by the promised time or, if none was stated, within thirty days. Print out the information so that you have documentation if you need it.

- **Check out the company's track record.** Ask your state or local consumer protection agency if the company has to be licensed or registered, and with whom, and check to see if it is. You can also ask consumer agencies and the Better Business Bureau in your area about the company's complaint record. But keep in mind that fraudulent companies can appear and disappear quickly, especially in cyberspace, so lack of a complaint record is no guarantee that a company is legitimate.

- **Be careful to whom you give your financial or other personal information.** Don't provide your bank account numbers, credit card numbers, social security number or other personal information unless you know the company is legitimate and the information is necessary for the transaction. Even with partial information, con artists can make unauthorized charges, deduct money from your account, and impersonate you to get credit in your name.

- **Take your time to decide.** While there may be time limits for special offers, high-pressure sales tactics are often danger signs of fraud.

---

6. This document appeared on the Internet Fraud Watch Web site www.fraud.org/internet/inttip/basint.htm. Internet Fraud Watch is a program of the National Consumers League.

- **Be aware that there are differences between private sales and sales by a business.** All sorts of goods and services are sold or traded by individuals through unsolicited e-mails, newsgroups postings, chat room discussions, web auctions and online classified advertisements. While most people are honest, your legal rights against the seller may not be the same as with a business, and you could have difficulty pursuing your complaint if the merchandise is misrepresented, defective or never delivered.

- **You may be better off paying by credit card than with a check, cash or money order, as long as you know with whom you're doing business.** When you use your credit card for a purchase and there is a problem, you have the right to notify your card issuer that you are disputing the charge, and you don't have to pay it while your dispute is being investigated. It's easier to resolve a problem if you haven't already paid. Also, unless you are purchasing through a secured site (preferably using the new Secured Encryption Technology), it may be safer to provide your payment information by phone or mail rather than online.

- **Don't judge reliability by how nice or flashy a Web site may seem.** Anyone can create, register and promote a Web site; it's relatively easy and inexpensive. And just like any other forms of advertising, you can't assume that someone has screened and approved it.

- **Know that people in cyberspace may not always be what they seem.** Someone who is sharing a "friendly" tip about a money-making scheme or great bargain in a chat room or on a bulletin board may have an ulterior motive: to make money. And sometimes those friendly people turn out to be crooks!

- **Know that unsolicited e-mail violates computer etiquette and is often used by con artists.** It also violates most agreements for Internet service. Report "spamming," as unsolicited e-mail is called, to your online or Internet service provider.

- **Don't download programs to see pictures, hear music, or get other features from Web sites you're not familiar with.** You could unwittingly download a virus that wipes out your computer files or even hijacks your Internet service, reconnecting you to the Net through an international phone number, resulting in enormous phone charges.

If you need advice about an Internet or online solicitation, or you want to report a possible scam, use the Online Reporting Form or Online Question & Suggestion Form features on this Web site or call the NFIC hotline at 1-800-876-7060.

III. The Internet and Society

Editor's Introduction

The Internet seems to have become a vital part of our world, but is it really having any concrete effects on society? Is the proliferation of information on the Internet really bringing about more equality? Is the free-flow of ideas through the Internet into authoritarian countries going to be the trigger that brings about freedom for repressed peoples? Is the presence of pornography on the Internet truly corrupting children? Is the Internet giving governments and businesses means of prying into our private lives? Can we trust anything we read online? Is there anything that can be done to ensure that the Internet takes the path of improving society?

As indicated by the articles in this chapter, which examines the way our society is being altered by the Internet, the answer to each of those questions is yes, and no, and maybe, depending on who is answering the question.

This chapter begins with four articles analyzing the multicultural nature of the Internet, representing four different perspectives. "The Web Reflects a Wider World" looks at how the Web is rapidly taking on a more international flavor, allowing people to overcome geographic barriers to communicate with others in their native language, whatever that may be. That is followed by an article describing the "Cyberghetto" that is forming, essentially adding another barrier for minorities to overcome when it comes to competing in today's job market. "Indonesia Revolt Was Net Driven" tells of the role that the Internet played in the recent revolt in Indonesia, in which the long serving president, Suharto, was forced to step down. The last of this group, "Bringing the Internet to the Developing World," tells of the progress being made in bringing this new technology to the less technologically advanced nations, and explains some of the obstacles that are faced in making the Internet available to everyone worldwide.

We then turn to more personal, and controversial, issues: children online, privacy, and censorship.

"The Keyboard Kids" examines ways in which some children are using the Internet. It also looks at how actively their parents oversee their time online and discusses some of the tools parents can use in making sure that their children aren't misbehaving online. The next four articles tackle the touchy topics of privacy and censorship, with discussions on the technical tools available to give individuals control over their own privacy and access to adult information, and government attempts to set policies concerning these topics. Privacy and censorship are quite possibly the most hotly debated issues related to the Internet, and to make matters more difficult, there are few other issues that don't in some ways involve these topics. In that vein, the articles on these topics are the most unabashedly opinionated in this book. For each opinion expressed in these articles, there are groups with equally heartfelt disagreements.

"Protecting Our Children from Internet Smut" is an analysis of how Internet pornography became a heavily publicized topic, making the covers of the major weekly news magazines. Taking an adamantly anti-censorship approach, the author argues that the issue was blown out of proportion by the media and politicians who were basing their arguments on sloppy scholarship.

Every time a person visits a Web site, the site can gather certain information about that person, and when a person makes a purchase or registers for a Web site, personal information is falling into the hands of people who very likely wish to make money from that information by using it to market products effectively or by selling that information to others. "No Telling" looks at this loss of privacy, and argues that government cures will be much worse than original problem.

Encryption is an issue that may seem arcane to some people, but to ensure the security of online credit-card purchases or bank transactions, data must be sent in a manner that allows only the intended recipient to read it. Powerful encryption is what will make online purchases safe and reliable. Encryption may also afford an equal level of secrecy to terrorists to communicate with one another, regardless of their physical location, without the worry of law enforcement agencies being able to read their messages. This situation has businesses (wishing to make online commerce as safe as possible) and civil libertarians (wanting to ensure that government cannot read the private correspondense that passes over the Internet), pitted against the government (wanting the power to read any message, once given court-approved permission, to try to ensure our safety) over the freedom to use powerful encryption. "Clipping Encryption" is an argument against the government's need to limit encryption.

The "Filtering FAQ" is a close look at the various tools, both technical and governmental, that may be answers to the issues of privacy and undesirable content. As in the previous chapter, we are ending this chapter with what may be a lesson in common sense. There is much information on the Internet: some totally reliable, some completely untrue. Taking a teacher's perspective, Carol Caruso offers suggestions for weeding the bad information from the good.

The Web Reflects a Wider World[1]

For Becky Juarez, a chatty teenager who recently graduated from high school, the Internet is a juicy electronic grapevine virtually crammed with information she wants, like gossip about her favorite movie stars, no-nonsense descriptions of courses offered by the college she plans to attend in the fall and tidbits about bittersweet teen-age life, exchanged in scads of E-mail messages and in online chat rooms.

Like millions of others who went on line in the 90's, Ms. Juarez, who is 18, says she cannot imagine life without her daily dose of sitting at her family's computer and surfing the electronic universe.

But in the last year, she has discovered that her reach on the World Wide Web has been extended because thousands of Web sites now speak her language, Spanish.

Ms. Juarez, who is a native of Puerto Rico and lives in San Juan, is fluent in English and French but has Spanish as her first language. "I think it's cool a lot of people in Latin America, especially those who speak only Spanish, can feel good to be in a site that is in our own language," Ms. Juarez said, speaking of the Internet. Since its birth 19 years ago in the United States, the Net has been dominated by the English language and North American culture.

"Now they have an opportunity to do what they want to do on the Internet and be more comfortable about it." Ms. Juarez said in flawless English in a recent telephone interview. "I like it a lot."

It is not only the Spanish language, however, that is showing up more often on the Internet. There have also been marked increases in the use of Portuguese, German, Japanese, Chinese and Scandinavian languages, among others, on the Internet, say officials of some of the largest Internet companies based in the United States.

Speakers with a first language other than English are the fastest-growing group of new Internet users; the total number of people on line is about 107 million. According to an Internet research group, Emarketer, the number of Internet users from outside the United States will begin to outnumber those inside the country by the end of this year.

The fastest-growing Internet markets are in China and India, whose combined populations represent a third of the

---

1. Article by Michel Marriott for the *New York Times*, Je 18, '98 G p 1 +. Copyright © 1998 The New York Times Company. Reprinted with Permission.

world's six billion people. Vital Signs 1998, an annual statistical snapshot of the world compiled by the World Watch Institute, a nonprofit public policy group, projects that the number of Chinese and Indians on line will multiply 15-fold, to 5.5 million users, by 2000. (While many Indians speak English, many have said that they prefer to use their native languages on line.)

The increase in the number of people preferring to use languages other than English on line could have profound implications for how the Internet is used and developed, some analysts say. If the Internet in the next century becomes more of a global mass medium, the way commerce, news, research and entertainment are presented on the Internet will have to be rethought.

The increase in the number of people preferring to use languages other than English on line could have profound implications for how the Internet is used and developed

In fact, the popularity of other languages on the Web has prompted major search engines like Yahoo and Excite to offer their services in multiple languages. Just this month, Netscape Communications announced a partnership with the leading Latin American Internet service, Star Media Network, for a free Internet guide in Spanish and Portuguese.

Many analysts predict that the Internet might soon begin to resemble international television, where audiences expect to view programs, even American imports like reruns of *Seinfeld* and *Star Trek*, in their own languages.

"English is the dominant language of the Internet, but it is only a matter of time when the non-English speakers catch up to that level," said L. Jasmine Kim, international marketing manager for Yahoo. "I see the speed they are leapfrogging."

She explained that part of that leapfrogging—skipping over the Internet technology and practices of more developed Internet nations—was being fueled by the transformation of the Internet in the rest of the world into more of a mass medium, rather than being primarily a tool for members of a highly educated, high-income elite, like the first wave of Internet adopters in the United States. That suggests that the average overseas Internet user will increasingly be less like Becky Juarez, a multilingual, upper-middle-class teen-ager, and will more likely be people with moderate incomes who speak their native language primarily or exclusively.

A wider range of languages on the Internet, Ms. Kim said, may mean that a wider range of ideas will be exchanged in cyberspace and a greater diversity of goods and products will be offered for sale over the Internet—in other words, the long-promised global village.

But as the profile of the average Internet user changes, what the new users tend to want and do on the Internet remains fairly consistent with the preferences of Internet users in the United States. Jack C. Chen, co-founder and president of Star Media, the Latin American Internet service, which is free, said that while there are regional variations across Latin America, e-mail and chat rooms are very popular. "Cybersexo" is a popular topic in Latin American chat rooms, just as cybersex draws a crowd as a topic in American chat rooms.

Local news and weather are also very popular in [other] countries on the Internet, said Mark VanHern, a founder of Excite and the product manager in charge of its Chinese version, and people certainly prefer those types of information in their own language. Even though the number of the world's native English speakers is second only to the number of people speaking Chinese, he said, in China, for instance, "Joe Schmoe does not speak English, and he doesn't want to. For him, the World Wide Web will mostly be in Chinese with some English."

Catching Up to English

Non-English speakers make up the fastest-growing group of Internet users today. There are now an estimated 55.7 million people worldwide who use a language other than English on the Internet. Among that number, here are the most popular languages used on the Web.

Spanish—24.2%
Japanese—22%
German—13%
French—10.4%
Chinese—5.6%
Swedish—4.3%
Italian—3.7%
Dutch—3.6%
Portuguese—2.3%
Finnish—2.2%
Korean—1.6%
Other—7.1%

(Source: Euro-Marketing Associates)

Currently, more than half of the Internet's users—62 million people—live in the United States

One result of the shift in language could be a crack in American hegemony over Internet culture. Currently, more than half of the Internet's users—62 million people—live in the United States, but the rate of online growth has slowed there. Some Internet users complain that while the Internet is awash in information, almost all of it flows in one direction: from the United States to the rest of the increasingly wired world.

"Eighty-five percent of what I see on the Internet is in English only," said Oscar Ruben Batista Gaxiola, who lives in Mexicali, Mexico, near the California border. While he can read and speak English, he said: "I would rather go to Spanish sites. Basically, it is more comfortable for me."

Paulo Mello, a 50-year-old Brazilian businessman who works in Rio de Janeiro, said he felt much the same way. He mostly uses the Internet, through Star Media, for sports and news in Portuguese. As the National Basketball Association finals wound down last week and World Cup soccer heated up in France, Web sites featuring soccer players were vastly more popular among non-English speakers on the Internet.

"I would hope that as the Internet emerges as a new industry and as a new medium, people would realize early in the game that the entire world does not speak our language," said Steve Horen, a senior research analyst on Internet issues for Nationsbanc Montgomery Securities in San Francisco.

Yet many people, like Michel Eckersley, the owner of Digital Design, a computer design house based in New York, say they believe that English will long continue to be the standard language of cyberspace, much as English is the international language of aviation.

Mr. Eckersley, a British man who was born in Malaysia and speaks several languages, said English had practically become the default language of business. In a world of many languages and dialects, where many different tongues are often used even in a single country, English is the common language of commerce, he said.

For that reason, the language will deepen its hold on the world as more people go on line, reinforcing the highly influential cultural might of American film, television, music and life styles, Mr. Eckersley said.

"English language is the dominant language of the world," he said. "I think it will be the dominant language of the Internet, of computers, as more and more people learn English."

Brett Renwick, the Internet site project manager in the marketing department of Great Brands of Europe, which includes Web sites for French brands like Evian and Dannon, said even the French, famously fastidious about guarding their language against dilution by foreign words and phrases, had been forced to surrender to American vernacular on Internet matters.

"Did you know that the French have no word for Internet?" Mr. Renwick asked. "They don't." And it is not unusual for French-language Web sites to direct users to more detailed English-language sites on the same subjects or products, he said.

But Fernando J. Espuelas and Jack Chen, the partners who founded Star Media, say the dominance of English on the Internet is being challenged, at least in Latin America.

Mr. Espuelas and Mr. Chen, childhood friends in the United States, began the production version of Star Media, the first service of its kind, in early 1997, and the response was swift.

Star Media's site already attracts one million visits each month, said Mr. Espuelas, the company's chief executive and chairman. Star Media (www.starmedia.com) gets about 50 million page views a day, Mr. Espuelas said, and he expects that number to reach 60 million by the end of the year.

Like any mainstream Internet service, Star Media provides a flashy offering of world and regional news, weather, stock listings, E-mail, chat rooms, Internet access and more, all in Spanish and Portuguese and tailored to the 18 Latin American countries the company serves. One of the more popular features is a soccer trivia game timed to the World Cup.

"We are only in Spanish and Portuguese, and we believe that is where the market will be," said Mr. Espuelas, who moved from his native Uruguay to Connecticut when he was 9 years old. "There is an expectation that everyone will eventually become American. I don't think so."

Mr. Espuelas, who is fluent in Spanish and English and lives in the United States, said he recognized English's popularity. And he conceded that the growth in the number of people learning English as a secondary language was unlikely to slow.

"But that doesn't take away the reality that your mother tongue is your mother tongue," Mr. Espuelas said. "Especially on the Internet."

Cyberghetto: Blacks Are Falling through the Net[2]

I left journalism last year and started working for an Internet development firm because I was scared. While many of my crypto-Luddite friends ("I find e-mail so impersonal") have decided that the Web is the work of the devil and is being monitored by the NSA, CIA, FBI, and the IRS, I began to have horrible dreams that sixteen-year-old punks were going to take over publishing in the next century because they knew how to write good computer code. I'd have to answer to some kid with two earrings, who will make fun of me because I have one earring and didn't study computer science in my spare time.

You laugh, but one of the best web developers in the country is a teenager who has written a very sound book on web design and programming. He's still in his prime learning years, and he's got a staff.

What should worry me more is that I am one of the few African Americans in this country who has a computer at home, uses one at work, and can use a lot of different kinds of software on multiple platforms. According to those in the know, I'm going to remain part of that very small group for quite some time.

The journal *Science* published a study on April 17 which found that, in households with annual incomes below $40,000, whites were six times more likely than blacks to have used the World Wide Web in the last week. Low-income white households were twice as likely to have a home computer as low-income black homes. Even as computers become more central to our society, minorities are falling through the Net.

The situation is actually considerably worse than the editors of *Science* made it seem. Some 18 percent of African American households don't even have phones, as Philip Bereano, a professor of technical communications at the University of Washington, pointed out in a letter to the *New York Times*. Since the researchers who published their study in *Science* relied on a telephone survey to gather their data, Bereano explains, the study was skewed—it only included people who had at least caught up to the Twentieth Century.

---

2. Article by Frederick L. McKissack Jr. from *The Progressive* p. 20-2 Je '98. Copyright © 1998 *The Progressive*. Reprinted with permission.

About 30 percent of American homes have computers, with the bulk of those users being predominantly white, upper-middle-class households. Minorities are much worse off: Only about 15 percent have a terminal at home.

The gulf between technological haves and have-nots is the difference between living the good life and surviving in what many technologists and social critics term a "cyberghetto." Professor Michio Kaku, a professor of theoretical physics at City University of New York, wrote in his book *Visions: How Science Will Revolutionize the Twenty-first Century*, of the emergence of "information ghettos."

"The fact is, each time society made an abrupt leap to a new level of production, there were losers and winners," Kaku wrote. "It may well be that the computer revolution will exacerbate the existing fault lines of society."

The term "cyberghetto" suggests that minorities have barely passable equipment to participate in tech culture. But most minorities aren't even doing that well.

Before everybody goes "duh," just think what this means down the line. Government officials are using the Web more often to disseminate information. Political parties are holding major online events. And companies are using the Web for making job announcements and collecting résumés. Classes, especially continuing-education classes, are being offered more and more on the Web. In politics, commerce, and education, the web is leaving minorities behind.

The disparity between the techno-rich and techno-poor comes to a head with this statistic: A person who is able to use a computer at work earns 15 percent more than someone in the same position who lacks computer skills.

"The equitable distribution of technology has always been the real moral issue about computers," Jon Katz, who writes the "Rants and Raves" column for *Wired* online, wrote in a recent e-mail. "The poor can't afford them. Thus they will be shut out of the booming hi-tech job market and forced to do the culture's menial jobs."

This technological gap, not Internet pornography, should be the public's main concern with the Web.

"Politicians and journalists have suggested frightening parents into limiting children's access to the Internet, but the fact is they have profoundly screwed the poor, who need access to this technology if they are to compete and prosper," Katz said. "I think the culture avoids the complex and expensive issues by focusing on the silly ones. In twenty-five years, when the underclass wakes up to discover it is doing all the muscle jobs while everybody else is

The gulf between technological haves and have-nots is the difference between living the good life and surviving in what many technologists and social critics term a "cyberghetto."

in neat, clean offices with high-paying jobs, they'll go berserk. We don't want to spend the money to avoid this problem, so we worry about Johnny going to the *Playboy* web site. It's sick."

In his 1996 State of the Union address, President Clinton challenged Congress to hook up schools to the Internet.

"We are working with the telecommunications industry, educators, and parents to connect ... every classroom and every library in the entire United States by the year 2000," Clinton said. "I ask Congress to support this educational technology initiative so that we can make sure the national partnership succeeds."

The national average is approximately ten students for every one computer in the public schools. According to a study by the consulting firm McKinsey & Co., the President's plan—a ratio of one computer to every five students—would cost approximately $11 billion per year over the next ten years.

Some government and business leaders, worried about a technologically illiterate work force in the twenty-first century, recognize the need for increased spending. "AT&T and the Commerce Department have suggested wiring up schools at a 4:1 ratio for $6 or $7 billion," says Katz.

But according to the U.S. Department of Education, only 1.3 percent of elementary and secondary education expenditures are allocated to technology. That figure would have to be increased to 3.9 percent. Given the tightness of urban school district budgets, a tripling of expenditures seems unlikely.

Then there's the question of whether computers in the schools are even desirable. Writer Todd Oppenheimer, in a July 1997 article for *Atlantic Monthly* entitled "The Computer Delusion," argued that there is no hard evidence that computers in the classroom enhance learning. In fact, he took the opposite tack: that computers are partially responsible for the decline of education.

Proponents of computers in the classroom struck back. "On the issue of whether or not technology can benefit education, the good news is that it is not—nor should be—an all-or-nothing proposition," writes Wendy Richard Bollentin, editor of *On The Internet* magazine, in an essay for *Educom Review*.

There is an unreal quality about this debate, though, since computer literacy is an indispensable part of the education process for many affluent, white schoolchildren.

Consumers are beginning to see a decline in prices for home computers. Several PC manufacturers have already introduced sub-$1,000 systems, and there is talk of $600 systems appearing on the market by the fall. Oracle has spent a great deal of money on Network Computers, cheap hardware where software and files are located on large networks. The price is in the sub-$300 range. And, of course, there is WebTV, which allows you to browse on a regular home television set with special hardware.

Despite the trend to more "affordable" computers, a Markle Foundation-Bellcore Labs study shows that this may not be enough to help minorities merge onto the Information Superhighway. There is "evidence of a digital divide," the study said, with "Internet users being generally wealthier and more highly educated, and blacks and Hispanics disproportionately unaware of the Internet."

So, what now?

"For every black family to become empowered, they need to have computers," journalist Tony Brown told the *Detroit News*. "There is no way the black community is going to catch up with white society under the current system. But with a computer, you can take any person from poverty to the middle class."

This is the general line for enlightened blacks and community leaders. But having a computer won't bridge the racial and economic divide. Even if there is a 1:1 ratio of students to computers in urban schools, will students' interest be piqued when they don't have access to computers at home? One out of every forty-nine computer-science professors in the United States is black. Will this inhibit black students from learning how to use them? And even if every black student had a computer at home and at school, would that obliterate all racial obstacles to success?

Empowerment is not just a question of being able to find your way around the Web. But depriving minorities of access to the technology won't help matters any. We need to make sure the glass ceiling isn't replaced by a silicon ceiling.

Bringing the Internet to the Developing World[3]

On September 20, 1997, the government of Mali launched its national Internet gateway at the country's first Exposition of Information Technologies. Mali thus became the first country in Africa to benefit from the assistance of the Leland Initiative, a five-year, $15-million effort of the U.S. Agency for International Development (USAID) to provide 21 African countries with support for national-level Internet connectivity. The program provides developing countries with training and equipment for establishing satellite links and helps resolve any policy issues that might restrict Internet growth.

By early 1998, Mali had four private-sector Internet service providers serving about 1,000 accounts, and the number is growing daily. With the Leland Initiative's help, Mali is working hard to provide Internet service in rural areas. However, as a developing country, it faces a host of challenging problems—an unreliable telephone system, low literacy, an exorbitant cost for telephone calls, customs duties on computers, and a relative lack of equipment and trained technical staff in the schools.

Global Access Barriers

- African nations face high costs and literacy challenges.
- Latin American sites must route through U.S.
- In China, Net surfers must register with police.
- A poor infrastructure hinders the Czech republic.

"Mali realizes that providing free and easy access to, and availability of, information is the key to its economic development, and so it really can't miss the opportunity of connecting to the Internet," explained Christine Deschamps, president of the International Federation of Library Associations and Institutions (IFLA).

In February, Deschamps attended a policy seminar in Accra, Ghana, sponsored by the British Council and funded

3. Article by Ron Chepesiuk from *American Libraries* p 55 + Se '98. Copyright © 1998 Ron Chepesiuk. Reprinted with permission.

by the World Bank, that led to the establishment of a regional network—the West African Network for the Information Society (WANIS). At the seminar, West African countries agreed to work through WANIS to develop common policies that would spur Internet growth in their region.

The widening gap

West Africa, like the world's other developing regions, is struggling to hitch its future to the promise of the Internet in an attempt to close the information gap that separates the world's industrialized nations from the poorer ones. "The lack of Internet access in many developing countries certainly threatens to widen the information gap between the have and have-not nations," said Hwa-Wei Lee, dean of the university libraries at Ohio University in Athens, who has taught library science courses in China for the past 15 years. "But it should be pointed out that this situation is quickly improving in some parts of the world, as computers become more affordable for local populations and countries begin to expand and refine their telecommunications networks and Internet connectivity."

The California-based Computer Industry Almanac, which publishes the Internet Industry Almanac, reported in January that the United States leads the world in Internet connectivity with 54.68 million users (54.7% of the world total). The United States market share was about 65% in 1994, but it is expected to drop to 40% by 2001. As more and more of the world becomes Internet capable, populous developing countries like China and Russia will surpass many smaller industrialized nations in number of Internet users.

A surge in Internet access

"Many developing countries are adopting a competitive attitude," said David Kohl, dean and university librarian at the University of Cincinnati. "They realize that when the rules of the game change, the one who figures out the new rules the fastest wins."

Kohl has had the chance to observe firsthand the library systems of China, Turkey, and other developing countries as an Association of Research Libraries delegate to several international conferences. He noted that in his travels to

TELECOMMUNICATIONS INDICATORS

The 21 Countries of the Leland Initiative	Lines per 100	Waiting List	Cost of 3-min. Call US$
Benin	1.0	5,246	.07
Botswana	3.5	11,484	.11
Cote d'Ivoire	1.0	55,600	.06
Eritrea	n/a	39,680	0
Ethiopia	<1.0	178,992	0
Ghana	<1.0	28,349	.10
Guinea-Bissau	1.0	742	1.70
Guinea-Conakry	<1.0	2,122	.11
Kenya	1.0	70,581	.04
Madagascar	<1.0	9,969	.12
Malawi	<1.0	24,886	n/a
Mali	<1.0	n/a	.09
Mozambique	1.0	6,172	.22
Namibia	5.0	7,383	0
Rwanda	<1.0	5,000	n/a
Senegal	1.0	14,448	.05
South Africa	9.0	136,600	0
Tanzania	<1.0	117,980	.06
Uganda	<1.0	5,045	.20
Zambia	0.9	34,362	.10
Zimbabwe	1.2	101,933	.04

< Less than

Source: USAID and International Telecommunication Union data, 1995

remote parts of China, he was surprised to find many libraries with Web sites in both English and Chinese.

At first China feared that a strong Internet presence would make it difficult for the country's centralized Communist government to control the flow and content of information, but the country changed its position in 1994. A recent report by *China Daily,* an online version of China's English-language newspaper, stated that in mid-1995 the number of Internet subscribers in China was about 40,000, but by the end of 1997 that figure had grown to 620,000.

"China now has 100 Internet service providers in operation, and in many Southeast Asian countries the Internet penetration is even greater," Lee revealed.

The developing countries of East and Southeast Asia—most notably Korea and Taiwan, and to a lesser extent the second-tier industrializing economies of Malaysia, Thailand, Indonesia, and the coastal provinces of China—are certainly narrowing the information gap, but it's proving to be no easy, straightforward task. In addition to technological handicaps, numerous political, socioeconomic, legal, and cultural barriers must be hurdled if equity is to be achieved.

In addition to technological handicaps, numerous political, socioeconomic, legal, and cultural barriers must be hurdled if equity is to be achieved

The overriding technical problems involve cost and infrastructure. Today in Latin America, well over a million people surf the Net regularly, and the number of residential and business connections has skyrocketed in many countries, particularly Chile, Brazil, Mexico, and Argentina, the most important markets. However, nearly all Internet traffic in Latin America currently must be routed through a network access point in Virginia, making transmission slow and costly.

In Brazil, for example, Internet provider Embratel charges a monthly fee of U.S. $48 for 15 hours of online time plus $3 per additional hour, compared to an average of $19.95 a month in the United States. Fortunately, the situation is changing. A service known as Latin Internet Exchange (LIX) recently established the first network access point in the Dominican Republic, a development that is expected to significantly reduce connect time and costs.

Meanwhile, far away in the Czech Republic, the problem is not distance but slow telephone lines. Ales Brozek of the State Scientific Library at Usti nad Labem noted that 40 Czech libraries, including 26 public libraries, have Internet-accessible OPACs, but he added that poor infrastructure and telecommunications quality make providing that service difficult.

"The budgets of many Czech libraries right now are tighter than in previous years, so one can expect the management of these libraries to prefer the acquisition of books and periodicals to the leasing of quick and expensive telephone lines," Brozek explained.

Andrew Lass, associate professor of anthropology at Mount Holyoke College in South Hadley, Massachusetts—who has been responsible since 1993 for coordinating a library automation project known as CASLIN (Czech and Slovak Library Information Network)—said the former Czechoslovakia is a good example of why it's important for industrialized countries like the United States to lobby the governments of developing nations and wake them up to the importance of supporting projects that provide high-speed and cost-effective Internet connectivity. In many developing nations "governments have mainly focused on short-term problem solving and so have lost sight of the more costly long-term goals, among which 'libraries without walls' belong," he explained.

Generating worldwide access to the Internet requires large investments, not only in equipment and infrastructure, but also in education and training

Large investments required

The long-term goals may seem costly, but bringing library collections to an acceptable standard requires an unrealistic expenditure of money to purchase books and other materials. "Library collections in developing countries are small and inadequate and often built of gift collections of a haphazard kind," said Niels Mark, director of the Statsbiblioteket in Denmark. "They woefully lack current periodicals and cannot keep subscriptions complete or afford to buy recently published material. The electronic library is the real future of libraries in the Third World, particularly for university and research libraries."

Mark points out that generating worldwide access to the Internet requires large investments, not only in equipment and infrastructure, but also in education and training. "Upgrading the level of technological skill is certainly going to be an important contribution in bridging the gap between north and south, but is it realistic to believe that poor underdeveloped countries can afford this and become part of the worldwide electronic library?" he asked.

To bridge the gap in technology and training, IFLA has stepped forward and offered its assistance. At its 1993 conference in Barcelona, IFLA's section on Document Delivery and Interlending voted to launch a project on interlibrary lending and document delivery in developing countries.

The goal was to establish regional and global electronic links and improve the skills of local library staffs in operating interlibrary-loan and document-delivery systems. Today IFLA, with the help of the Norwegian and Danish governments, provides financial and technical support to several African countries to help them buy the necessary equipment and establish links.

"It is encouraging to see the enthusiasm and expectations of the management and staff in both the universities and libraries of participating African countries, to note that government bodies are accepting their responsibility for the project, and to see that commercial communications companies are interested in supporting it," Mark said.

In addition to costs, inadequate training, and poor telecommunications infrastructure, libraries in developing countries face other formidable obstacles. Electricity is often unreliable. "In some countries in Africa, libraries can't rely on a steady supply of cheap, electrical power," noted Vice-president of OCLC's Sales and International Division Phyllis B. Spies. "When it's available, libraries may only get a few hours daily."

A different kind of filtering

In some countries, governments have installed proxy servers that censor information delivered online or they have developed policies that restrict its flow

Then there is information filtering. In some countries, governments have installed proxy servers that censor information delivered online or they have developed policies that restrict its flow. In China, for instance, Internet users are required to register with the police and sign an agreement promising to do no damage to the country or anything illegal such as transmitting state secrets or information deemed harmful to state security. Meanwhile, the Arab countries in the Middle East are concerned about the Internet's profound cultural and social impact on their society; as one writer noted, "Once the Internet is viable, even filters have little control over such activity."

But according to Lee, attempts at censorship of the Internet by restricting so called harmful information have "not been as effective, despite government threats of criminal punishment and fines for violators."

International library leaders would like to see Western nations offer more assistance to libraries in developing countries. Among their suggestions:

- IBM and other major corporations could donate more equipment;
- Ameritech and other vendors could help by reducing

their rates;

- OCLC could become a major player by opening its databases at a nominal fee for a few years;
- Sprint, AT&T, and other telephone companies could be encouraged to reduce their rates; and
- major library institutions and organizations such as IFLA and the Library of Congress could continue to provide training and share information resources.

As Deschamps noted, "Libraries in developing countries have a difficult enough time affording the costs of connection, the hardware, and the registration or license fees that servers charge, let alone paying for the copyright charges. So is there a way that the World Intellectual Property Organization could make copyright cheaper or free of charge for developing countries?"

No doubt the Internet will revolutionize how the global community learns, interacts, conducts business, and seeks and exchanges information. The challenge will be how to ensure that all countries, industrialized and developing, rich and poor, benefit from this exciting technology.

"The bottom line is that a team effort is needed by the Western industrialized countries to help libraries in the developing world connect to the Information Superhighway," said Ravi Sharma, director of the West Virginia State College Library in Institute and publisher of *Library Times International*. "Otherwise the world library community will never take 'local touch, global reach' a reality."

Indesia Revolt Was Net Driven[4]

WASHINGTON—As rebellions broke out across Indonesia this month, protesters did not have tanks or guns. But they had a powerful tool that wasn't available during the country's previous uprisings: the Internet.

Bypassing the government-controlled television and radio stations, dissidents shared information about protests by e-mail, inundated news groups with stories of President Suharto's corruption, and used chat groups to exchange tips about resisting troops. In a country made up of thousands of islands, where phone calls are expensive, the electronic messages reached key organizers.

"This was the first revolution using the Internet," said W. Scott Thompson, an associate professor of international politics at the Fletcher School of Law and Diplomacy at Tufts University. Thompson, like many academics who follow Indonesia, kept track of the dissidents' communications with one another from thousands of miles away.

New technologies have changed the ways the world learns about a fast-changing political crisis. As Chinese troops quashed a democracy movement in Tiananmen Square in 1989, the dissidents communicated with the outside world by fax, and TV networks used satellites to send out chilling footage. The same year, thanks to West German television, many East Germans learned that the Berlin Wall was being toppled.

Details of a Russian coup in 1991 spread by fax and a primitive version of the Internet, and a year later CNN sent images of a military uprising in Thailand around the world.

Thanks to the Internet, Thompson said, Indonesian activists circumvented press censorship. In one chat group, he said, participants circulated inspiring accounts of the 1986 "peoples' power" rebellion in the Philippines.

Some of the messages simply gave encouragement. Last week, in an America Online chat group about Asia, a correspondent nicknamed "Asia Son" urged Indonesians to keep denouncing President Suharto's corruption and cronyism. "One or two people saying that [are] easily dragged away and silenced," Asia Son wrote. "One or two million doing it is not so easy."

The same day, in broken English, another correspondent urged looters not to pick on Indonesia's ethnic Chinese minority: "Why are they always the victim when there is a

4. Article by David L. Marcus from *The Boston Globe* p 1 + My 23 '98. Copyright © 1998 *The Boston Globe*. Reprinted with permission.

riot? . . . All they do is make a honest living. They work hard and when you worked hard you deserve success."

As Indonesia heated up this week, Abigail Abrash, an Asia specialist at the Robert E. Kennedy Memorial Center for Human Rights in Washington, stayed in constant touch with friends in Jakarta and other Indonesian cities. She sent them summaries of the American news coverage of the uprisings. Abrash received front-line reports from students occupying Indonesia's Parliament building. From what she read, it seemed that someone brought a laptop inside and went on line while surrounded by armed troops.

"In a country that's as far-flung as Indonesia, the Net has meant that people have been able to communicate at a time like this," she said.

It seemed that someone brought a laptop inside and went online while surrounded by armed troops

In Indonesia, with more than 17,000 islands, calling from one place to another costs as much as $1.50 a minute, a considerable amount in a country reeling from a recession. The Internet often costs much less. On a trip by boat two years ago, Abash was amazed to find that even remote towns in Indonesian Borneo were "wired."

In the past few years, dissidents in Burma, Nigeria, Cuba, China, and other countries have relied on the Internet, but access there is restricted to relatively few professors, researchers, high-level government workers, and employees of multinational businesses. In Indonesia, the Internet is especially popular among students—the group that took to the streets and was instrumental in forcing Suharto to resign Thursday.

"With the Internet, people in the country can get information out for support, and they can also use the network to communicate with each other in the country and build a body of knowledge about activities in the country," said Stephen Hansen, a human-rights specialist for the American Association for the Advancement of Science in Washington.

Diana Lady Dougan, chairwoman of International Communications Studies at the Brookings Institution in Washington, said some of the Internet's advocates tend to overemphasize its significance in Indonesia. "The Net was an escalating factor there, but I don't think it changed the outcome," she said. "It fast-forwarded things."

Indonesian activists suspect that their phones are tapped, and some worry that their e-mail is monitored, too. Several have developed systems of encryption with their American colleagues, but they refused to describe their methods.

On Thursday, the Internet enabled human-rights groups in Indonesia to warn colleagues in Europe and the United

States that military troops threatened to imprison Muchtar Pakpahan, a hospitalized dissident.

The US groups contacted Capitol Hill, where Representative Bernard Sanders, a Vermont Independent; Barney Frank, a Massachusetts Democrat; Christopher Smith, a New Jersey Republican; and seven others wrote to Secretary of State Madeleine K. Albright asking for help.

Soon after, the U.S. Embassy in Jakarta sent a representative to Pakpahan's hospital room as a signal of support. "The responsiveness is unbelievable—we have people on the ground who e-mail information, then we can react right away," said Brendan Smith, a legislative aide to Sanders.

Yesterday, troops took away Pakpahan, but at least the US Embassy was a witness, Smith said. Congressmen are continuing to protest.

Radio Free Asia, which the US government has used to broadcast pro-democracy messages, can be heard in China, Laos, Vietnam, and Burma, but not in Indonesia, long regarded as pro-American. Catharin Dalpino, who was the State Department's top officer for democracy, said the US government needs to more aggressively use interactive technologies such as the Internet while relying less on traditional media such as radio.

"Nowadays, a so-called democracy program should lead to something instead of people just sitting in their living rooms saying, 'Oh, that's interesting,'" said Dalpino.

The Keyboard Kids[5]

Ah summer, those lazy afternoons with the hot sun streaming down, the gentle winds, the honeyed song of birds and the sound of children playing ... indoors on computers.

Yup, we've raised a generation of keyboard kids, and they're e-mailing more, chatting more, making more long-distance friends and generally getting into more trouble online than ever before. As usual, it's up to their beleaguered parents to maintain a watchful eye—the same parents, of course, who in school hallways are widely considered as clueless about the Internet as they are about Portishead (a band). Wired children, particularly in the formative years from about 10 to 14, are eager for their first taste of independence, intrigued by the propinquity of naughty stuff and finding in the online world a means to navigate the minefield of adolescent insecurities. "You can open up more and say what you want," says one 12-year-old America Online user. "I feel more comfortable saying things to [unseen] people."

According to a recent study by the research group Find/SVP, more than 9.8 million children are using the Internet, a number projected to triple in the next four years. Aggressive marketer AOL now gets 52 percent of the 12-to-17 audience, says Web research firm PC Meter. Some of these numbers are coming at the expense of television. In a recent poll by CNN and *USA Today*, 28 percent of teens said they could live without their TV, but only 23 percent said they could get by without a computer. Perhaps the most sobering statistic of all: at the peak of *Titanic* mania, AOL says, there was a message posted about Leonardo DiCaprio every 10 seconds.

Twelve-year-old Liz contributed to that collective feat. The Westchester County, N.Y., seventh grader comes home every day from school, jumps on AOL and meets up with, of all people, her schoolmates. She chats with them in invite-only private chat rooms and sends Instant Messages to the 101 friends she keeps on her Buddy List, the AOL function that alerts her when they sign on. She's also a publisher, working with two friends to send an e-mail newsletter on teen topics to 1,000 subscribers. The five hours a day she spends on AOL replaces time spent watching television and using the phone. Her mother doesn't use

---

the parental controls that AOL provides to block off adult areas. If she wanted to, Liz says compassionately, "I would let her, but she is not very computer-literate."

Liz's mother is not alone. AOL says 52 percent of parents don't use the controls, even though they have improved in the past year. Last December AOL recognized that younger teens are a distinct species and instituted separate options that can keep kids from the private chat rooms (which monitors can't penetrate) and can hide the lascivious material on AOL and the Web. Parents can also specify exactly who their children can get e-mail from and block the trashy, unsolicited messages called "spam" that pour into users' mailboxes. AOL vice president Katherine Borsecnik acknowledges the service has a responsibility to protect children but says parents must play a role: "Neither of us is going to get very far without the other ensuring this environment is safe."

The kids, of course, think they can take care of themselves. Nearly an entire class of eighth graders at the Thomas Jefferson Middle School in Fair Lawn, N.J., raised their hands when asked if they were connected at home. About half said their parents tried to control their online time, but all agreed it's easy to go to a friend's house where the parents aren't as strict.

Playing online games, chatting and doing homework research were volunteered as the most popular activities, along with, especially, socializing with the opposite sex. "It's just easier to talk to girls online," said one boy. "You have no awkward body movements."

YO! TALK TO ME!

Some common online terms of the chattering classes:

Buddy List: A feature on AOL that notifies you as soon as a friend signs on to the service

IM: Short for Instant Message. A one-on-one chat, usually with a Buddy List friend—but beware of IMs from strangers.

Private chat room: A place where groups can chat simultaneously, by invitation only

Punting: Using special programs to mischievously cause another user's screen to freeze, forcing him to log off

Scrolling: Rapidly repeating phrases or gibberish to disrupt a discussion

Whasayc: 'Write back as soon as you can'

"It's just easier to talk to girls online," said one boy. "You have no awkward body movements."

Online love doesn't seem to be that easy, though. Asked what she talks about in chat rooms, one girl says, "We flirt with boys, mess with their minds, then sign off abruptly." The students also admit to a bit of role-playing. "I say I'm 17, in college and own a convertible," says one 14-year-old girl. "I'm 18 and six feet tall," says a 12-year-old boy.

The problem, says Parry Aftab, a mother of two and author of "A Parents' Guide to the Internet," is that children's "technological abilities far exceed their judgment." Despite the horror stories you hear on the news, most Internet misadventures end innocuously. Atlanta 13-year-old Jessica meets her friends after school in Yahoo!'s chat rooms on the Web, and once gave out her address for a free Hanson newsletter. Instead, she received a pile of magazines that she didn't want, along with the bills for them. "We learned that once you give out your home address, you have to be prepared for the consequences," says her mom. Jessica now needs permission to make an online purchase, and uses her mother's post-office box. Or consider New Jersey 14-year-old John, whose dad found the pornographic pictures he had downloaded to his computer. In exchange for a promise to avoid the stuff, John's father bought him a year's subscription to Playboy. "I was curious, too, at that age," says the sympathetic dad. As it turns out, John's almost too busy to read the magazine—he runs his own music and skating sites on the Web and gets hundreds of e-mails a day from his readers.

Kids can avoid most serious problems on the Net by following some simple, well-published rules. Get a parent's permission before giving out personal information like a credit-card number or address, and never meet a new online friend in person without an adult present. Parents can also turn to more orderly Web-based communities like theglobe.com and Talk City. Inspired by AOL's success but eschewing all the chaos of spam and the wild, unregulated chat rooms, they offer supervised discussions and programs like online summer camps.

Finally, filtering software like Cyber Patrol, installed on the computer's hard drive, can provide parents with the ability to screen out parts of the Web they consider inappropriate.

Still, after listening to young teens speak about the Internet, you have to believe they are still going to flirt, test the rules and find ways to investigate adult sites. In the end, the most effective thing parents can do is put the computer in a common room and occasionally supervise—just as they would if the kids were playing outside.

Protecting Our Children from Internet Smut: Moral Duty or Moral Panic?[6]

The term moral panic is one of the more useful concepts to have emerged from sociology in recent years. A moral panic is characterized by a wave of public concern, anxiety, and fervor about something, usually perceived as a threat to society. The distinguishing factors are a level of interest totally out of proportion to the real importance of the subject, some individuals building personal careers from the pursuit and magnification of the issue, and the replacement of reasoned debate with witchhunts and hysteria.

Moral panics of recent memory include the Joseph McCarthy anti-communist witchhunts of the 1950s and the satanic ritual abuse allegations of the 1980s. And, more recently, we have witnessed a full-blown moral panic about pornography on the Internet. Sparked by the July 3, 1995, *Time* cover article "On a Screen Near You: Cyberporn," this moral panic has been perpetuated and intensified by a raft of subsequent media reports. As a result, there is now a widely held belief that pornography is easily accessible to all children using the Internet. This was also the judgment of Congress, which, proclaiming to be "protecting the children," voted overwhelmingly in 1996 for legislation to make it a criminal offense to send "indecent" material over the Internet into people's computers.

The original *Time* article was based on its exclusive access to Marty Rimm's Georgetown University Law Journal paper, "Marketing Pornography on the Information Superhighway." Although published, the article had not received peer review and was based on an undergraduate research project concerning descriptions of images on adult bulletin board systems in the United States. Using the information in this paper, *Time* discussed the type of pornography available online, such as "pedophilia (nude pictures of children), hebephelia (youths) and ... images of bondage, sadomasochism, urination, defecation, and sex acts with a barnyard full of animals." The article proposed that pornography of this nature is readily available to anyone who is even remotely computer literate and raised the stakes by offering quotes from worried parents who feared for their children's safety. It also presented the possibility that pornographic material could be mailed to children without their parents' knowledge. *Time*'s example was of a ten-year-old boy who supposedly received pornographic images in his e-mail showing "10 thumbnail size pictures

---

6. Article by Julia Wilkins for *The Humanist* p4-7 S/O '97. Copyright © 1998 *The Humanist*. Reprinted by permission.

showing couples engaged in various acts of sodomy, heterosexual intercourse and lesbian sex." Naturally, the boy's mother was shocked and concerned, saying, "Children should not be subject to these images." *Time* also quoted another mother who said that she wanted her children to benefit from the vast amount of knowledge available on the Internet but was inclined not to allow access, fearing that her children could be "bombarded with X-rated pornography and [she] would know nothing about it."

From the outset, Rimm's report generated a lot of excitement—not only because it was reportedly the first published study of online pornography but also because of the secrecy involved in the research and publication of the article. In fact, the *New York Times* reported on July 24, 1995, that Marty Rimm was being investigated by his university, Carnegie Mellon, for unethical research and, as a result, would not be giving testimony to a Senate hearing on Internet pornography. Two experts from *Time* reportedly discovered serious flaws in Rimm's study involving gross misrepresentation and erroneous methodology. His work was soon deemed flawed and inaccurate, and *Time* recanted in public. With Rimm's claims now apologetically retracted, his original suggestion that 83.5 percent of Internet graphics are pornographic was quietly withdrawn in favor of a figure less than 1 percent.

Time admitted that grievous errors had slipped past their editorial staff, as their normally thorough research succumbed to a combination of deadline pressure and exclusivity agreements that barred them from showing the unpublished study to possible critics. But, by then, the damage had been done: the study had found its way to the Senate.

Government Intervention

Senator Charles Grassley (Republican—Iowa) jumped on the pornography bandwagon by proposing a bill that would make it a criminal offense to supply or permit the supply of "indecent" material to minors over the Internet. Grassley introduced the entire *Time* article into the congressional record, despite the fact that the conceptual, logical, and methodological flaws in the report had already been acknowledged by the magazine.

On the Senate floor, Grassley referred to Marty Rimm's undergraduate research as "a remarkable study conducted by researchers at Carnegie Mellon University" and went on to say:

> The university surveyed 900,000 computer images. Of these 900,000 images, 83.5 percent of all computerized photographs available on the Internet are porno-

graphic.... With so many graphic images available on computer networks, I believe Congress must act and do so in a constitutional manner to help parents who are under assault in this day and age.

Under the Grassley bill, later known as the Protection of Children from Pornography Act of 1995, it would have been illegal for anyone to knowingly or recklessly transmit indecent material to minors. This bill marked the beginning of a stream of Internet censorship legislation at various levels of government in the United States and abroad.

The most extreme and fiercely opposed of these was the Communications Decency Act, sponsored by former Senator James Exon (Democrat—Nebraska) and Senator Dan Coats (Republican—Indiana). The CDA labeled the transmission of "obscene, lewd, lascivious, filthy, indecent, or patently offensive" pornography over the Internet a crime. It was attached to the Telecommunications Reform Act of 1996, which was then passed by Congress on February 1, 1996. One week later, it was signed into law by President Clinton. On the same day, the American Civil Liberties Union filed suit in Philadelphia against the U.S. Department of Justice and Attorney General Janet Reno, arguing that the statute would ban free speech protected by the First Amendment and subject Internet users to far greater restrictions than exist in any other medium. Later that month, the Citizens Internet Empowerment Coalition initiated a second legal challenge to the CDA, which formally consolidated with ACLU v. Reno. Government lawyers agreed not to prosecute "indecent" or "patently offensive" material until the three-judge court in Philadelphia ruled on the case.

Although the purpose of the CDA was to protect young children from accessing and viewing material of sexually explicit content on the Internet, the wording of the act was so broad and poorly defined that it could have deprived many adults of information they needed in the areas of health, art, news, and literature—information that is legal in print form. Specifically, certain medical information available on the Internet includes descriptions of sexual organs and activities which might have been considered "indecent" or "patently offensive" under the act—for example, information on breastfeeding, birth control, AIDS, and gynecological and urinological information. Also, many museums and art galleries now have Web sites. Under the act, displaying art like the Sistine Chapel nudes could be cause for criminal prosecution. Online newspapers would not be permitted to report the same information as is available in the print media. Reports on combatants in war, at the scenes of crime, in the political arena, and outside abortion clinics often provoke images or language that could be constituted "offensive" and therefore illegal on the net. Furthermore, the CDA provided a legal basis for banning books which had been ruled unconstitutional to ban from school libraries. These include many of the classics as well as modern literature containing words that may be considered "indecent."

The act also expanded potential liability for employers, service providers, and carriers that transmit or otherwise make available restricted communications. According to the CDA, "knowingly" allowing obscene material to pass through one's computer system was a criminal offense. Given the nature of the Internet, however, making service providers responsible for the content of the traffic they pass on to other Internet nodes is equivalent to holding a telephone carrier responsible for the content of the conversations going over that carrier's lines. So, under the terms of the act, if someone sent an indecent electronic comment from a workstation, the employer, the e-mail service provider, and the carrier all could be potentially held liable and subject to up to $100,000 in fines or two years in prison.

The court determined that "there is no evidence that sexually oriented material is the primary type of content on this new medium"

On June 12, 1996, after experiencing live tours of the Internet and hearing arguments about the technical and economical infeasibility of complying with the censorship law, the three federal judges in Philadelphia granted the request for a preliminary injunction against the CDA. The court determined that "there is no evidence that sexually oriented material is the primary type of content on this new medium" and proposed that "communications over the Internet do not 'invade' an individual's home or appear on one's computer screen unbidden. Users seldom encounter content 'by accident.'" In a unanimous decision, the judges ruled that the Communications Decency Act would unconstitutionally restrict free speech on the Internet.

The government appealed the judges' decision and, on March 19, 1997, the U.S. Supreme Court heard oral arguments in the legal challenge to the CDA, now known as Reno v. ACLU. Finally, on June 26, the decision came down. The Court voted unanimously that the act violated the First Amendment guarantee of freedom of speech and would have threatened "to torch a large segment of the Internet community."

Is the panic therefore over? Far from it. The July 7, 1997, *Newsweek*, picking up the frenzy where *Time* left off, reported the Supreme Court decision in a provocatively

illustrated article featuring a color photo of a woman lick-
ing her lips and a warning message taken from the Web site
of the House of Sin. Entitled "On the Net, Anything Goes,"
the opening words by Steven Levy read, "Born of a hysteria
triggered by a genuine problem—the ease with which
wired-up teenagers can get hold of nasty pictures on the
Internet—the Communications Decency Act (CDA) was
never really destined to be a companion piece to the Bill of
Rights." At the announcement of the Court's decision, anti-
porn protesters were on the street outside brandishing signs
which read, "Child Molesters Are Looking for Victims on
the Internet."

Meanwhile, government talk has shifted to the development of a universal Internet rating system and widespread
hardware and software filtering. Referring to the latter,
White House Senior Adviser Rahm Emanuel declared,
"We're going to get the V-chip for the Internet. Same goal,
different means."

But it is important to bear in mind that children are still a
minority of Internet users. A contract with an Internet service provider typically needs to be paid for by credit card or
direct debit, therefore requiring the intervention of an
adult. Children are also unlikely to be able to view any kind
of porn online without a credit card.

In addition to this, there have been a variety of measures
developed to protect children on the Internet. The National
Center for Missing and Exploited Children has outlined pro-
tective guidelines for parents and children in its pamphlet,
Child Safety on the Information Superhighway. A number
of companies now sell Internet newsfeeds and web proxy
accesses that are vetted in accordance with a list of forbidden topics. And, of course, there remain those blunt software instruments that block access to sexually oriented
sites by looking for keywords such as sex, erotic, and X-
rated. But one of the easiest solutions is to keep the family
computer in a well-traveled space, like a living room, so
that parents can monitor what their children download.

There have been a variety of measures developed to protect children on the Internet

Fact or Media Fiction?

In her 1995 CMC magazine article, "Journey to the Centre
of Cybersmut," Lisa Schmeiser discusses her research into
online pornography. After an exhaustive search, she was
unable to find any pornography, apart from the occasional
commercial site (requiring a credit card for access), and
concluded that one would have to undertake extensive
searching to find quantities of explicit pornography. She
suggested that, if children were accessing pornography

online, they would not have been doing it by accident. Schmeiser writes: "There will be children who circumvent passwords, Surfwatch software, and seemingly innocuous links to find the 'adult' material. But these are the same kids who would visit every convenience store in a five-mile radius to find the one stocking *Playboy*." Her argument is simply that, while there is a certain amount of pornography online, it is not freely and readily available. Contrary to what the media often report, pornography is not that easy to find.

There is pornography in cyberspace (including images, pictures, movies, sounds, and sex discussions) and several ways of receiving pornographic material on the Internet (such as through private bulletin board systems, the World Wide Web, newsgroups, and e-mail). However, many sites just contain reproduced images from hardcore magazines and videos available from other outlets, and registration fee restrictions make them inaccessible to children. And for the more contentious issue of pedophilia, a recent investigation by the Guardian newspaper in Britain revealed that the majority of pedophilic images distributed on the Internet are simply electronic reproductions of the small output of legitimate pedophile magazines, such as Lolita, published in the 1970s.

Clearly the issue of pornography on the Internet is a moral panic

Clearly the issue of pornography on the Internet is a moral panic—an issue perpetuated by a sensationalistic style of reporting and misleading content in newspaper and magazine articles. And probably the text from which to base any examination of the possible link between media reporting and moral panics is Stanley Cohen's 1972 book, Folk Devils and Moral Panic, in which he proposes that the mass media are ultimately responsible for the creation of such panics. Cohen describes a moral panic as occurring when "a condition, episode, person or group of persons emerges to become a threat to societal values and interests; ... the moral barricades are manned by editors ... politicians and other 'right thinking' people." He feels that, while problematical elements of society can pose a threat to others, this threat is realistically far less than the perceived image generated by mass media reporting.

Cohen describes how the news we read is not necessarily the truth; editors have papers to sell, targets to meet, and competition from other publishers. It is in their interest to make the story "a good read"—the sensationalist approach sells newspapers. The average person is likely to be drawn in with the promise of scandal and intrigue. This can be seen in the reporting of the National Enquirer and People, with their splashy pictures and sensationalistic headlines, helping them become two of the largest circulation magazines in the United States.

Cohen discusses the "inventory" as the set of criteria inherent in any reporting that may be deemed as fueling a moral panic. This inventory consists of the following:

Exaggeration in Reporting. Facts are often overblown to give the story a greater edge. Figures that are not necessarily incorrect but have been quoted out of context, or have been used incorrectly to shock, are two forms of this exaggeration.

Looking back at the original *Time* cover article, "On a Screen Near You: Cyberporn," this type of exaggeration is apparent. Headlines such as "The Carnegie Mellon researchers found 917,410 sexually explicit pictures, short stories and film clips online" make the reader think that there really is a problem with the quantity of pornography in cyberspace. It takes the reader a great deal of further exploration to find out how this figure was calculated. Also, standing alone and out of context, the oftquoted figure that 83.5 percent of images found on Usenet Newsgroups are pornographic could be seen as cause for concern. However, if one looks at the math associated with this figure, one would find that this is a sampled percentage with a research leaning toward known areas of pornography.

The Repetition of Fallacies. This occurs when a writer reports information that seems perfectly believable to the general public, even though those who know the subject are aware it is wildly incorrect. In the case of pornography, the common fallacy is that the Internet is awash with nothing but pornography and that all you need to obtain it is a computer and a modem. Such misinformation is integral to the fueling of moral panics.

Take, for example, the October 18, 1995, Scotland on Sunday, which reports that, to obtain pornographic material, "all you need is a personal computer, a phone line with a modem attached and a connection via a specialist provider to the Internet." What the article fails to mention is that the majority of pornography is found on specific Usenet sites not readily available from the major Internet providers, such as America Online and Compuserve. It also fails to mention that this pornography needs to be downloaded and converted into a viewable form, which requires certain skills and can take considerable time.

Misleading Pictures and Snappy Titles. Media representation often exaggerates a story through provocative titles and flashy pictorials—all in the name of drawing in the reader.

The common fallacy is that the Internet is awash with nothing but pornography and that all you need to obtain it is a computer and a modem

The titles set the tone for the rest of the article; the headline is the most noticeable and important part of any news item, attracting the reader's initial attention. The recent *Newsweek* article is a perfect example. Even if the headline has little relevance to the article, it sways the reader's perception of the topic. The symbolization of images further increases the impact of the story. *Time*'s own images in its original coverage—showing a shocked little boy on the cover and, inside, a naked man hunched over a computer monitor—added to the article's ability to shock and to draw the reader into the story.

Through sensationalized reporting, certain forms of behavior become classified as deviant. Specifically, those who put pornography online or those who download it are seen as being deviant in nature. This style of reporting benefits the publication or broadcast by giving it the aura of "moral guardian" to the rest of society. It also increases revenue.

By classifying a subject and its relevant activities as deviant, they can stand as crusaders for moral decency, championing the cause of "normal" people

In exposing deviant behavior, newspapers and magazines have the ability to push for reform. So, by classifying a subject and its relevant activities as deviant, they can stand as crusaders for moral decency, championing the cause of "normal" people. They can report the subject and call for something to be done about it, but this power is easily abused. The *Time* cyberporn article called for reform on the basis of Rimm's findings, proclaiming, "A new study shows us how pervasive and wild [pornography on the Internet] really is. Can we protect our kids—and free speech?" These cries to protect our children affected the likes of Senators James Exon and Robert Dole, who took the *Time* article with its "shocking" revelations (as well as a sample of pornographic images) to the Senate floor, appealing for changes to the law. From this response it is clear how powerful a magazine article can be, regardless of the integrity and accuracy of its reporting.

The *Time* article had all of Cohen's elements relating to the fueling of a moral panic: exaggeration, fallacies, and misleading pictures and titles. Because certain publications are highly regarded and enjoy an important role in society, anything printed in their pages is consumed and believed by a large audience. People accept what they read because, to the best of their knowledge, it is the truth. So, even though the *Time* article was based on a report by an undergraduate student passing as "a research team from Carnegie Mellon," the status of the magazine was great enough to launch a panic that continues unabated—from the halls of Congress to the pulpits of churches, from public schools to the offices of software developers, from local communities to the global village.

No Telling[7]

The Push for Internet Privacy Controls Combines a Bad Theory with a Dangerous Agenda.

Over the past week, I received about two dozen unsolicited mass e-mails, otherwise known as "spam." About half were devoted to sex, including six messages promoting a new Web site and one paradoxically promising a site "SO HOT WE CANT SHOW IT ON THE WEB." Most of the rest advertised the stuff of late-night TV commercials and dubious classified ads: "LUXURY CARS FOR UNDER $1000" from government auctions, family histories and coats of arms ("All Nationalities,"), credit cards for people with lousy credit records, a psychic hotline. One offered to teach me how to become a spammer myself. The most reputable-seeming message promoted a site for golf-related classified ads.

I wasn't interested in any of them. None of the spammers had bothered to find out the most obvious facts about me—*Hustler* is not known for its appeal to women—much less to determine, for instance, that I have an excellent credit record and don't play golf.

Spam costs virtually nothing to send, and it bothers the people who receive it. That upsets "privacy advocates" and their friends in Congress: "No one—from the consumer to the small businesses who run servers—should be forced to pay for unsolicited advertisements," said Rep. Chris Smith (R-N.J.) when he announced a bill to ban spam. Smith is too easily outraged. A week's worth of junk costs me maybe a quarter, hardly the sort of expense that justifies congressional action.

The cost to Internet service providers can indeed be substantial, and suits by America Online, Earthlink, and other ISPs have already forced big-time spammers to pay large damages for violating the ISPs' terms of service. But for consumers, spam should be of no more public concern than grocery lines, Sunday drivers, or squirming children in restaurants; it is simply part of living with other people, and the solution is as close as the delete key. To demand legal action every time something annoys you is the surest way to end up living in a conflict-filled society ruled by intrusive regulation and constant litigation. Telling people to hit "delete" or let their ISP know they're being bothered won't attract TV cameras, however. For that you need a crisis and a bill.

Cyberspace is full of "crises" these days, many involving "privacy rights," and Congress is full of bills to address them, 32 by one count. What really has privacy advocates riled isn't spam but its exact opposite: targeted marketing information. Cyberspace offers people the chance to easily find others with similar interests—hence the flourishing of specialized Web sites and Usenet groups. That same efficient search, enhanced by sorting software, has commercial applications. Web sites can collect data from the people who visit them and either display individually tailored advertising or send visitors product information later. Or they may not be interested in individual information at all but in general patterns and aggregates: What is the average age of our audience? Which parts of our site are most popular? Where do our visitors come from?

Cyberspace is full of "crises" these days, many involving "privacy rights," and Congress is full of bills to address them

The answer to the burning question, How is anyone ever going to make money on the Web?, probably lies in collecting and efficiently using such information. Eventually commercial sites must pay for themselves, and one of the most promising ways to do so is to use them to find customers for other products and services.

Absent a single, government-imposed rule for what information can be gathered and how it can be used, commercial Web sites have taken many different approaches: Some let individuals choose exactly what to reveal about themselves and how to let the information be used. Others tell visitors how they intend to use information and leave it to each visitor to decide whether to stick around. Still others say nothing at all, letting the surfer beware. (Common sense goes a long way in those cases: If a site asks your name, address, and telephone number, chances are the company may someday try to sell you something, and it may also rent or sell the information to others.) Meanwhile, software has been developed that gives Web browsers more control over what information can be automatically collected about them. And many people surf anonymously.

This laissez faire regime not only allows different strokes for different folks. It also lets bootstrapped Web sites grow without immediately creating complex systems for managing information from visitors. It allows small operations to informally poll people without violating federal laws. It permits experimentation and learning. It fits the flexible, diverse, entrepreneurial, sometimes-amateurish world of the Web.

Very little of this commercial activity has hostile intent, unless you consider advertising assault. But it displeases people for whom "privacy" is an absolute. Under pressure from privacy lobbyists, the Federal Trade Commission is out trolling the Web, looking for sites that dare to collect information from visitors without posting a "voluntary" privacy policy. But privacy policies, voluntary or not, won't satisfy advocates who are determined to impose a single standard on everyone.

Testifying before a House subcommittee in late March, Marc Rotenberg, the director of the Electronic Privacy Information Center, condemned the variety and gradual evolution of privacy standards. "Where once individual *consent* was central to the disclosure of personal information, now the focus is on individual *choice* for a range of disclosures," he said. "Where privacy techniques focused on the means to protect identity, now the focus is on means to obtain information. Many of the techniques that are put forward as 'technical solutions'...will make it easier, not more difficult, to obtain information from individuals using the Internet. Something is clearly amiss."

Rotenberg is infuriated by the very idea of "self-regulation." Debating how to give Web surfers choices, he maintains, detracts from the urgent need to adopt a single, technocratic standard for everyone. All this choice is too disorderly and out of control. It does not produce the outcome Rotenberg wants. "[S]elf-regulation has not helped protect privacy on the Internet," he says. "It has in fact made it harder for us to focus on the larger questions of a coherent privacy policy. It has also led to erosion in our basic understanding of privacy protection." Self-regulation has permitted diversity and allowed people to disagree. If you believe that "privacy" is an inalienable right, that is an intolerable situation.

Very little of this commercial activity has hostile intent, unless you consider advertising assault

By their nature, new communications technologies make it harder to keep secrets: "We shall soon be nothing but transparent heaps of jelly to each other," worried a London writer in 1897, concerned about the telephone. And there is no question that the general public is anxious about protecting privacy in cyberspace. They've heard lots of scary stories about stalkers, child molesters, con artists, and credit card fraud. They've read George Orwell. They're easily persuaded that every corner of the Web is filled with vicious evil people. "Privacy advocates" like Rotenberg tap into that generalized fear—much of it a fear of totalitarian government—to justify a broad agenda of commercial regulation, based on dangerous assumptions about the nature of information and identity.

True to our technocratic political culture, people are unwilling when asked about the subject to be patient. A much-cited *Business Week* poll found that 53 percent of respondents said that "government should pass laws now for how personal information can be collected and used on the Internet," while 23 percent said that "government should recommend privacy standards for the Internet but not pass laws at this time." Only 19 percent said that "government should let groups develop voluntary privacy standards but not take any action now unless real problems arise." As David Medine, the FTC's point man on the issue, told *Business Week*, "This is the last year for industry to demonstrate effective self-regulation."

Before we rush to replace diverse and voluntary standards with a single, inflexible approach, however, it's worth considering the many different issues subsumed under the label "privacy" and "personal information." The stakes are much higher than advocates like Rotenberg often admit: In the name of privacy, activists are pushing serious restrictions on the freedom to gather and disseminate truthful information—otherwise known as freedom of speech and the press. They are demanding that businesses provide valuable information without reaping anything in return. They are seeking to impose today's preferences, technologies, and limited imagination on the unknown and evolving future. And the world of stifled speech they want to create is not limited to a few big players in a well-defined (and implicitly suspect) "industry." It includes everyone who sells anything or collects any information in cyberspace: from Time Warner and Yahoo! to startup entrepreneurs working out of their spare bedrooms and teenagers gathering e-mail addresses of fellow Leonardo DiCaprio fans.

Privacy advocates begin with the assumption that you own your "identity"—all the disparate information about yourself—and therefore have the right to control which information is available to others. That's what Rotenberg means when he refers to "consent." Such activists want to require that before someone can tell someone else a fact about you, the teller should have to get your permission; you exclusively own the facts about your life, your personal information."

But this premise simply isn't true. The other party in any relationship—whether your former landlord, your boss, your ex-girlfriend, or Amazon.com—owns information about you as surely as you do. Gathering and sharing such information is as old as gossip and is absolutely essential to a free society. Neither speech nor commerce can function if such communication is illegal. Privacy advocates want to outlaw not only journalism but reputation.

If we are in fact worried about what happens to electronic information about our lives, well-established systems of contract and criticism can control who says what to whom, with whose permission. The very systems Rotenberg scorns for emphasizing "choice" over "consent" allow parties to agree in advance which information, if any, will stay private. Breaking such an agreement would violate contract law. And just making the deal leads Web sites to invest the time and effort to create systems that will honor it. That's what "privacy policies" are all about.

Nor is contract the only check on un wanted information sharing. Criticism works too, especially when directed at companies that must compete for customers. Faced with outraged clients, America Online reversed its decision to let telemarketers use members' phone numbers, a practice that wasn't specifically forbidden in its terms of service. Amazon has been careful to protect the information it collects about customers' book-buying habits, using it internally but not offering it to outsiders; that information could be quite valuable to other direct marketers (including *REASON*), but its sale would create an enormous controversy. (The obvious way around such controversy, of course, is to offer lists only of customers who have agreed to be on them—a contractual solution.)

Neither contract nor criticism is perfect. Leaks happen at private organizations, just as they do with grand juries, the Internal Revenue Service, and prosecutors' offices; they just happen somewhat less frequently, and the legal consequences for the leaker are swifter and more severe. Earlier this year, an AOL employee blatantly violated the company's contract with customers by telling a caller which AOL member had a particular screen name. That information led the Navy to begin discharge proceedings against a decorated, 17-year-veteran sailor for being gay. The sailor successfully sued the Navy on the grounds that its investigation violated the "don't ask, don't tell" policy, but his career was seriously disrupted. Clearly AOL should be liable for breaking its contract in a particularly damaging fashion. And the company has come in for stinging criticism, forcing it to take very public steps to reassure customers that such problems won't happen again.

Lawsuits and ostracism aren't good enough for Rotenberg. The AOL case, he says, "shows the shortcomings of contractual solutions. Even with a very clear contract provision detailing when personal information may be disclosed, the Navy investigator was still able to obtain personal information." It's not clear what new federal law—short of a change in the policy against gays in the military—would have prevented a rogue AOL employee's harmful attempt at "customer service." The AOL case proves only that contract is not foolproof, which makes it no worse than any other legal system.

To Rotenberg, however, that horror story is a convenient prop to justify restricting the sale of marketing information—a completely unrelated matter—and establishing a federal privacy agency. Instead of permitting diversity, choice, and enforceable contracts, he and other "privacy advocates" demand that we trust our privacy to the very federal government whose investigator convinced an AOL employee to violate company rules and whose policy forces gay service members to assume false public identities.

In his House testimony, Rotenberg tried to wrap his notion of "privacy" in American constitutional law, by quoting a famous dissent by Supreme Court Justice Louis Brandeis. Rotenberg wanted to suggest that spammers, marketing databases, and customized Web ads somehow violate fundamental rights. But Brandeis was making quite a different point. The Constitution's Framers, he wrote, "sought to protect Americans in their beliefs, their thoughts, their emotions and their sensations. They conferred, as against the Government, the right to be let alone—the most comprehensive of all rights and the right most valued by civilized men."

This right, however, has absolutely nothing to do with infringing other people's freedom to communicate. It is quite explicitly a right *against the government*, enshrined in the Fourth Amendment's protections against search and seizure. It says not that you own every fact about yourself but that the government cannot invade your home, your papers, or your life without giving an awfully good reason.

There are serious privacy issues in cyberspace, issues that go to the heart of such constitutional guarantees; they involve government actions such as wide-ranging subpoenas of database information, misuse of IRS files, or warrantless seizure of private "papers" located not in someone's house or office but on a third party's server. In contrast to commercial transactions, all this information is obtained through coercion, and the government's intentions are not benign. If privacy advocates really want to assuage public fears of Big Brother, they should concentrate on curbing the government's police power, which is exercised without the check of competition, rather than working to suppress commercial speech.

Instead, to achieve their idea of "privacy," activists want to obliterate the freedom to gather information, to communicate, and to contract. They demand "a coherent privacy policy," a single best way for everyone. To enforce this goal, they would give the government greater power over cyberspace—power that will be backed by subpoenas and interrogations, searches and seizures, power that will demand trials and punishment. That is a very strange way to protect the right to be left alone.

Clipping Encryption[8]

The White House wants the keys to your computer

President Clinton raised a few eyebrows when he announced his support for the Internet Tax Freedom Act, a bill that would place a six-year moratorium on new taxes that apply only to the Internet. The National Governors Association had stridently attacked the bill, and the group assumed its old colleague from Arkansas would follow suit.

Clinton cited the "remarkable growth" of commerce on the Internet and his desire to help "further its growth" as reasons for supporting the tax moratorium. And the president is right to be concerned that the nation's 30,000 state and local taxing authorities could strangle electronic trade with new levies. But there's another set of policies the Clinton administration supports that has shackled the development of Internet commerce and hampered the Net's use as a communications tool: controls on data encryption.

Encryption programs are mathematical formulas that scramble messages sent over data networks. Effective encryption could make any electronic message—e-mail, cell-phone call, or wire transfer—indecipherable to anyone except the sender and the intended recipient. As more people rely on computers, the demand for security in cyberspace will skyrocket.

In an online world, encryption can be an effective way for people to enhance their security. And the Fourth Amendment to the Constitution affirms the right of all individuals to "be secure in their persons, houses, papers, and effects against unreasonable searches and seizures." But the Clinton administration and its allies in law enforcement don't want your communications to be private. With this in mind, the Department of Commerce recently established the President's Export Council Subcommittee on Encryption, a 20-member panel with representatives from law enforcement agencies, high-tech companies, and financial institutions that will advise the White House. This group won't be debating the merits of strong encryption; instead, it will merely rubber-stamp proposals to compromise your

---

8. Article by Rick Henderson. Reprinted, with permission, from the June 1998 issue of *Reason Magazine.* Copyright © 1998 by the Reason Foundation, 3415 S. Sepulveda Blvd., Suite 400, Los Angeles, CA 90034. www.reason.com.

privacy that the administration has been hawking unsuccessfully for six years.

Whenever possible, the Clinton administration has conducted discussions about encryption policy away from public scrutiny. The panel will continue that practice. The Web site operated by the Department of Commerce (www.doc.gov) doesn't list the subcommittee, its mission, or its members; nor does the main White House Web site (www.whitehouse.gov). An article in the CyberWire Dispatch newsletter notes that "all members have received security clearances, and some future meetings will be closed to the public."

Despite the importance of the subcommittee's work, it has garnered little attention from the mainstream press. One week after the panel's first public meeting on February 23, a Nexis search listed only three references to the group: a press release issued by one of the corporate members and two notices of the meeting in a federal daybook for reporters. No major news service covered it.

If encryption policy is set behind closed doors, the privacy of every law-abiding American will be left to the whims of regulators, cops, and spooks

But if encryption policy is set behind closed doors, the privacy of every law-abiding American will be left to the whims of regulators, cops, and spooks. Current controls date back to the Cold War, when encryption was treated like a weapon. The Department of Commerce now regulates encryption, and it has relaxed some controls. But the restrictions have frozen a fast-moving technology in place, making it vulnerable to hacker attacks. And the feds aren't interested in loosening their grip on encryption without a struggle.

Consider key recovery, the Clinton administration's latest plan to monitor the communications of anyone who uses online services or wireless phones. Users of key recovery software would have to deposit the "keys" that scramble and unscramble their messages with a "trusted third party" (something resembling an escrow agency) which the government could approach if it wanted to intercept private transmissions.

Buying key recovery software to protect your cell phone or your e-mail would be no different from giving government agents the key to your house and trusting that they will never drop by unannounced. It's an invitation for law enforcement agencies (including tax collectors) to monitor anyone who uses encryption.

And if you think constitutional guarantees would protect your privacy as long as you keep your nose clean, you haven't been reading the key recovery proposals Congress is considering. One bill would allow the cops to acquire your keys if they obtained an easy-to-get subpoena, rather than the search warrant typically required to tap a telephone conversation or bug a location for sound. Another would make the mere possession of encryption software that doesn't contain key recovery features (such as the readily available Pretty Good Privacy programs) a criminal offense. The National Sheriffs Association, whose president is a member of the new encryption panel, wants the cops to have access to encrypted messages at any time, without having to go through the inconvenient process of getting a search warrant, or even a subpoena. FBI Director Louis Freeh has testified frequently before Congress, saying that the administration would demand key recovery provisions as part of any new encryption law.

Law enforcement officials claim that allowing strong encryption will prevent them from stopping terrorists, drug dealers, and pedophiles. But criminals won't apply for export licenses—and they won't hand their encryption keys over to a government-friendly third party. Secure encryption can help make sure that the Fourth Amendment remains as important in the online world as it was in the days of quill pens and inkwells.

Computer Professionals for Social Responsibility Filtering FAQ[9]

Introduction

Seen by some as a powerful tool for protecting children from online pornography and by others as "censorware," Internet content filters have generated much controversy, debate, and confusion.

This document attempts to describe the concerns and issues raised by the various types of filtering software. It is hoped that these questions and answers will help parents, libraries, schools, and others understand the software that they may be considering (or using).

Additions, clarifications, and corrections regarding the content of this document will be most graciously accepted: please send e-mail to hhochheiser@cpsr.org.

1)   Basics

1.1)   What is a content filter?

A content filter is one or more pieces of software that work together to prevent users from viewing material found on the Internet. This process has two components.

Rating: Value judgments are used to categorize web sites based on their content. These ratings could use simple allowed/disallowed distinctions like those found in programs like CyberSitter or NetNanny, or they can have many values, as seen in ratings systems based on Platform for Internet Content Selection (PICS, see question 3.0).

Filtering: With each request for information, the filtering software examines the resource that the user has requested. If the resource is on the "not allowed" list, or if it does not have the proper PICS rating, the filtering software tells the user that access has been denied and the browser does not display the contents of the web site.

The first content filters were stand-alone systems consisting of mechanisms for determining which sites should be blocked, along with software to do the filtering, all provided by a single vendor.

The other type of content filter is protocol-based. These systems consist of software that uses established standards

---

9. This document was composed by Harry Hochheiser, Director at Large of the Computer Professionals for Social Responsibility. The document can be found at www.cpsr.org/filters/faq.html, where it is periodically updated. Reprinted with permission.

for communicating ratings information across the Internet. Unlike stand-alone systems, protocol-based systems do not contain any information regarding which sites (or types of sites) should be blocked. Protocol-based systems simply know how to find this information on the Internet, and how to interpret it.

1.2)   Why do many people want filtering?

The Internet contains a wide range of materials, some of which may be offensive or even illegal in many countries. Unlike traditional media, the Internet does not have any obvious tools for segregating material based on content. While pornographic magazines can be placed behind the counter of a store, and strip-tease joints restricted to certain parts of town, the Internet provides everything through the same medium.

Filters and ratings systems are seen as tools that would provide the cyberspace equivalent of the physical separations that are used to limit access to "adult" materials. In rating a site as objectionable, and refusing to display it on the user's computer screen, filters and ratings systems can be used to prevent children from seeing material that their parents find objectionable. In preventing access, the software acts as an automated version of the convenience-store clerk who refuses to sell adult magazines to high-school students.

Some products include a feature that will capture the list of all Internet sites that have been visited from your computer

Filters are also used by businesses to prevent employees from accessing Internet resources that are either not work related or otherwise deemed inappropriate.

1.3)   Can filtering programs be turned off?

It is assumed that parents or other authoritative users who install filtering programs would control the passwords that allow the programs to be disabled. This means that parents can enable the filter for their children but disable it for themselves. As with all other areas of computer security, these programs are vulnerable to attack by clever computer users who may be able to guess the password or to disable the program by other means.

1.4)   I don't want to filter, but I do want to know what my child is viewing. Is that possible?

Some products include a feature that will capture the list of all Internet sites that have been visited from your computer. This allows a parent to see what sites their child has viewed, albeit after the fact. Similar software allows employers to monitor the Internet use of their employees. Users of these systems will not know that their Internet use is being watched unless they are explicitly told.

Whether used in homes or workplaces, these tools raise serious privacy concerns.

1.5) What is the scope of Internet content filtering? Do filters cover the WWW? Newsgroups? IRC? E-mail?

While some stand-alone systems claim to filter other parts of the Internet, most content filters are focused on the World-Wide-Web. Given the varied technical nature of the protocols involved, it's likely that filtering tools will do well with some of these, and poorly with others. For example, filtering software can easily block access to newsgroups with names like "alt.sex". However, current technology cannot identify the presence of explicit photos in a file that's being transferred via FTP. PICS-based systems currently only filter web sites.

Currently available filtering tools use some combination of two approaches to evaluate content: lists of unacceptable (or acceptable) sites, and keyword searches

2   Stand-alone Systems

2.1) What is a stand-alone system?

A stand-alone filtering system is a complete filtering solution provided by a single vendor. These filters block sites based on criteria provided by the software vendor, thus "locking in" users. If a customer does not like the vendor's selection of sites that are to be blocked, she must switch to a different software product.

2.2) Who decides what gets blocked and what doesn't?

This is the biggest practical difference between stand-alone systems and protocol-based systems. Stand-alone systems limit users to decisions made by the software vendor, although some let the parents or installers remove sites. Protocol-based systems provide users with a choice between alternative ratings systems, which publishers and third parties can use to develop ratings for content. See question 3.2 for more information.

2.3) How do stand-alone programs determine what should be blocked?

Currently available filtering tools use some combination of two approaches to evaluate content: lists of unacceptable (or acceptable) sites, and keyword searches.

List-based blocking works by explicitly enumerating sites that should either be blocked or allowed. These lists are generally provided by filter vendors, who search for sites that meet criteria for being classified as either "objectionable" or "family-friendly".

Filtering software vendors vary greatly in the amount of information and control they make available to users. Most vendors do not allow users to see the actual list of blocked sites, as it is considered to be a kind of trade secret. However, some vendors provide detailed descriptions of the criteria used to determine which sites should be blocked. Some vendors might allow users to add sites to the list, either in their own software or by sending sites to the vendor for review.

Stand-alone filtering tools also vary in the extent to which they can be configured by users. Some software packages allow users to make selections from a list of the categories they would like blocked. For example, a parent may wish to block explicit sex but not discussions of homosexuality as a life-style. Others might allow users to choose from a range of choices in any given topic area. For example, instead of simply blocking all nudity, these tools might allow users to chose to allow partial nudity while blocking full nudity.

Keyword-based blocking uses text searches to categorize sites. If a site contains objectionable words or phrases, it will be blocked.

2.4) What's wrong with list-based filtering?

There are several problems with filtering based on lists of sites to be blocked.

First, these lists are incomplete. Due to the decentralized nature of the Internet, it's practically impossible to definitively search all Internet sites for "objectionable" material. Even with a paid staff searching for sites to block, software vendors cannot hope to identify all sites that meet their blocking criteria. Furthermore, since new web sites are constantly appearing, even regular updates from the software vendor will not block out all adult web sites. Each updated list will be obsolete as soon as it is released, as any site that appears after the update will not be on the list, and will not be blocked. The volatility of individual sites is yet another potential cause of trouble. Adult material might be added to (or removed from) a site soon after the site is added to (or removed from) a list of blocked sites.

Blocking lists also raise problems by withholding information from users

Blocking lists also raise problems by withholding information from users, who may or may not have access to information describing the criteria used to block web sites. While some vendors provide descriptions of their blocking criteria, this information is often vague or incomplete. Several vendors have extended blocking beyond merely "objectionable" materials. In some instances, political sites and sites that criticize blocking software have been blocked.

This obscurity is compounded by practices used to protect these lists of blocked sites. Vendors often consider these lists to be proprietary intellectual property, which they protect through mathematical encryption, which renders the lists incomprehensible to end users. As a result, users are unable to examine which sites are blocked and why. This arbitrary behavior demeans the user's role as an active, thoughtful participant in their use of the Internet.

2.5) What's wrong with filtering based on keyword searches?

Keyword searching is a crude and inflexible approach that is likely to block sites that should not be blocked while letting "adult" sites pass through unblocked. These problems are tied to two shortcomings of this approach:

Keyword searches cannot use contextual information. While searches can identify the presence of certain words in a text, they cannot evaluate the context in which those words are used. For example, a search might find the word "breast" on a web page, but it cannot determine whether that word was used in a chicken recipe, an erotic story, or in some other manner. In one notable incident, America Online's keyword searches blocked a breast cancer support group.

Keyword searches cannot interpret graphics. It is not currently possible to "search" the contents of a picture. Therefore, a page containing sexually explicit pictures will be blocked only if the text on that page contains one or more words from the list of words to be blocked.

3 The Platform for Internet Content Selection (PICS)

3.1) What is PICS?

The Platform for Internet Content Selection (PICS) was developed by the W3 Consortium—the guiding force behind the World-Wide-Web—as a protocol for the exchange of rating information. Paul Resnick—University of Michigan professor and the creator of PICS—described PICS in a *Scientific American* (March 1997) article:

> The Massachusetts Institute of Technology's World Wide Web Consortium has developed a set of technical standards called PICS (Platform for Internet Content Selection) so that people can electronically distribute descriptions of digital works in a simple, computer-readable form. Computers can process these labels in the background, automatically shielding users from undesirable material or directing their attention to sites of particular interest. The original impetus for PICS was to allow parents and teachers to screen materials they felt were inappropriate for children using the Net. Rather than censoring what is distributed, as the Communications Decency Act and other legislative initiatives have tried to do, PICS enables users to control what they receive.

There are two components involved in the practical use of PICS: ratings systems, and software that uses ratings systems to filter content.

3.2) How does PICS-based filtering differ from stand-alone systems?

Stand-alone filtering products generally include lists of sites to be filtered and explicit filtering criteria. Purchasers of these products are tied to the filtering decisions made by the software vendor.

PICS-based software uses an alternative approach based on distributed sharing of ratings information. Instead of using blocking lists or keyword searches, programs that use PICS use standardized "ratings systems" to determine which sites should be blocked. Available from software vendors or from Internet sites, these ratings systems are used to describe the content of Internet sites (see question 3.7 for a description of how PICS works in practice). Users of PICS-based software are usually given the ability to choose which ratings system they would like to use.

Users of PICS-based software are usually given the ability to choose which ratings system they would like to use

As an open standard, PICS can be used for a wide range of applications. In addition to providing a means for blocking content deemed unsuitable for children, PICS might also be used for describing content in terms of its educational content, potential for violations of privacy, or any other criteria that involve rating of Internet sites.

In some senses, programs that use PICS are much more flexible than stand-alone filtering software. Users of PICS software are not tied to the judgments of the software vendor, and the descriptions of the criteria used by the ratings systems are publicly available. However, users are currently limited to choosing between a small number of ratings systems, each of which has its own biases and viewpoints. Users that disagree with the popular ratings systems may be unable to use PICS in a manner that fits their needs and viewpoints.

3.3) What is a ratings system?

A *ratings system* is a series of categories and gradations within those categories that can be used to classify content. The categories that are used are chosen by the developer of the ratings system, and may include topics such as such as "sexual content," "race," or "privacy." Each of these categories would be described along different levels of content, such as "Romance; no sex," "Explicit sexual activity," or somewhere in between. Prominent ratings systems currently in use include RSACi, SafeSurf, and NetShepherd.

A *rating* is a description of some particular Internet content, using the terms and vocabulary of some ratings system.

3.4)   How are ratings systems developed?

The PICS developers and the W3 Consortium built PICS to be an open standard, so anyone can create a ratings system. Individuals and groups can develop ratings systems by defining categories and describing ratings within those categories. Once a ratings system is developed, it must be publicized to users and publishers.

3.5)   Who rates sites?

The PICS standard describes two approaches to the rating of sites:

Self-Rating: Web site publishers can evaluate their own content and put PICS rating information directly into their web pages. Currently, this evaluation can be done through Web pages provided by developers of the major ratings services.

Third-Party Ratings: Interested third parties can use PICS ratings systems to evaluate web sites and publish their own ratings for these sites. Educational groups, religious groups, or individuals can rate sites and publish these ratings on the Internet for users to access.

3.6)   What PICS-based ratings systems can I use?

From a technical perspective, you can use any PICS-based ratings system. However, your practical options are somewhat more limited. While you might configure your browser to use "Joe's Internet Ratings," it's unlikely that many sites have ratings for Joe's system, so it wouldn't be of very much use.

Your browser software may influence choice of ratings service. If you use Microsoft's Internet Explorer, you only have one choice (RSACi) built in to the initial distribution. To use other ratings services, IE users must download files from the Net and install them on their PCs.

Currently (as of September 1997), there are three PICS services that are being widely used or promoted:

RSACi: Sponsored by the Recreational Software Advisory Council (known for ratings on video games), RSACi is probably the most widely used PICS ratings system in use today. RSACi's ratings categories include violence, nudity, sex, and language, with 5 ratings within each category. As of September 1997, RSACi claims to have over 43,000 sites rated.

SafeSurf: Developed by the SafeSurf corporation, this system's categories include "Age Range," "Profanity," "Heterosexual Themes," "Homosexual Themes," "Nudity," "Violence," "Sex, Violence, and Profanity," "Intolerance," "Glorifying Drug Use," "Other Adult Themes," and "Gambling," with 9 distinctions for each category.

SafeSurf and RSACi both rely on self-rating of Internet sites by web publishers.

NetShepherd: Based in Calgary, Net Shepherd rates sites based on quality levels (1-5 stars). Unlike SafeSurf and RSACi, NetShepherd conducts third-party ratings of web sites. They claim to have rated over 300,000 sites. NetShepherd has also announced partnerships with firms such as Altavista and Catholic Telecom, Inc.

3.7)   How do I use PICS?

To use PICS, users start by configuring their browsers or PICS software to use a ratings system (such as RSACi or SafeSurf). Once the ratings system is chosen, users must examine each of the categories in order to choose a preferred level of information for that category. In practical terms, this means deciding how much they are willing to allow. For example, one ratings system's choices for nudity include "none," "revealing attire," "partial nudity," "frontal nudity," and "explicit."

Once these choices have been made, the browser software uses them to filter sites. When an Internet site is requested, the browser compares the site's rating with the user's selection. If the site has ratings for the chosen system and those ratings fit within the parameters chosen by the user, it is displayed as usual. If the appropriate ratings fall outside of those parameters (perhaps the site has "frontal nudity," while the user was only willing to accept "partial nudity"), access to the site is prohibited, and the user is shown a message indicating that the site is blocked.

Since most web sites are not currently rated, most software provides users with the option of blocking out sites that do not contain PICS ratings.

In order to prevent mischievous children from changing ratings or disabling PICS altogether, most browsers can be configured to require a password before disabling PICS.

3.8)   Should I rate my site?

The answer to this question will depend upon who's being asked.

RSACi, SafeSurf, and other proponents of ratings would obviously like everyone to rate their sites, while civil libertarians and opponents of ratings argue against any ratings.

Publishers of family-oriented sites or those who are trying to reach audiences concerned with Internet content might

In order to prevent mischievous children from changing ratings or disabling PICS altogether, most browsers can be configured to require a password before disabling PICS

consider rating. Similarly, purveyors of adult material might rate their sites in order to be "good citizens".

3.9)   What should a publisher consider before self-rating?

Web site publishers must decide which (if any) ratings systems to use. Since each ratings system requires a separate valuation process, and separate modifications to web pages, it may not be practical for web-site publishers to use all of the popularly available ratings.

In evaluating ratings systems, publishers may want to examine the categories used by each system and the distinctions used by those categories. Different systems will classify ratings systems in different ways, some of which may misrepresent the content of web sites. For example, sites discussing safe sex might not want to be placed in the same category with pornographic sites.

Web site publishers might also consider the popularity of the ratings services. Currently (as of September 1997), there are only a few major ratings services. Publishers are free to user other ratings, but these may not be useful to the Internet users who rely upon the popular systems. This presents a dilemma for some publishers, who can either accept the ratings of the popular systems, even if those ratings misrepresent their material, or refuse to rate their sites, knowing that this might cause their sites to be unavailable to some users.

Versions of Microsoft's Internet Explorer have provided an extreme example of this problem. Although IE allows users to use any PICS ratings system, RSACi is the only system that is built in to the selection list. Since Internet Explorer is the most widely-used PICS-capable browser (as of fall 1997, Netscape's Navigator does not support PICS), it seems likely that many PICS users will be relying upon RSACi. For publishers interested in reaching a wide audience, this market force may determine their choice of ratings system.

Finally, philosophical concerns may cause some people to decide not to rate. Web-site publishers who are not comfortable with the general content of available ratings systems, or who object to the concept of ratings, may choose not to rate their own sites.

MSNBC's troubles with ratings provide an ironic illustration of this possibility. Displeased with the RSACi ratings that would be necessary, MSNBC management removed all rating information from the site. MSNBC and other news organizations briefly discussed the possibility of creating a new ratings system specifically for news reporting.

While this proposal was eventually rejected, it illustrates some of the problems with content ratings. Well-funded publishers like MSNBC might be able to effectively create ratings systems that meet their needs, but smaller publishers who want to rate their sites may be forced to accept unsatisfactory ratings.

3.10)   What concerns are raised by third-party ratings?

Since third-party ratings aren't validated by any technical means, third-party ratings can be easily misused. Just as stand-alone filtering software can block sites for political or business reasons (even if those sites do not contain adult content), third-party raters might apply inaccurate labels to web sites in order to make sure that they would be blocked by PICS-compliant software.

To make matters worse, third-party rating does not require the consent or even notification of a web site publisher. Since third-party ratings are distributed by third-party "label bureaus," a web-site publisher may not know if her pages have been rated, or what the ratings said.

Third-party ratings also present significant technical challenges that may discourage their development. Unlike self-ratings, third-party PICS ratings do not reside on publisher's web pages. Instead, they must be distributed to users using one of two methods:

- File Transfer: Users could download ratings from the web sites provided by third-party services. For ratings services that cover any significant portion of the Internet, this could easily amount to megabytes of data, which could be cumbersome to download using slow modems. Furthermore, these lists would quickly become obsolete, and would therefore require regular updates.

- Label Bureaus: Third-party raters (or others) might establish servers that would provide ratings information. In this model, users of a rating service would retrieve a rating from the rating service, and this rating would be used to determine whether or not the site should be blocked. For a widely-used ratings system, this would require computing power and Internet bandwidth capable of handling constant streams of requests for ratings. This might be cost-prohibitive for many potential ratings services.

3.11)   What about sites that aren't rated? What if someone puts the wrong rating on a site?

PICS ratings can be truly useful for parents only if a significant percentage of the Internet's web sites are accu-

PICS ratings can be truly useful for parents only if a significant percentage of the Internet's web sites are accurately rated

rately rated. Currently, this is not the case. The 40,000 sites that have self-rated with RSACi, or even the 300,000 sites rated by NetShepherd, represent a small fraction of the total number of web sites available.

Some software, such as Microsoft's Internet Explorer, provides users with the option of blocking out any site that does not have a rating. This choice may be appropriate for some, but it severely restricts the available options. By blocking out most of the Web (including possibly some sites designed for younger users), this approach presents children with a severely restricted view of the world.

The accuracy of PICS ratings is obviously a concern. For example, unscrupulous purveyors of adult material might attempt to use an inaccurate rating in an attempt to slip through PICS filters. In RSACi's terms of use, the RSAC reserves the right to audit sites in order to guarantee accuracy of ratings. SafeSurf takes this one step further. The proposed *Online Cooperative Publishing Act* calls for legal penalties for sites that label inaccurately, or refuse to rate. In June 1997, Sen. Patty Murray (D-Washington) proposed the Child-safe Internet Act of 1997, which called for similar penalties. While these legislative suggestions might be effective in promoting the use of ratings, they raise serious concerns in terms of first-amendment rights and possibilities for overly aggressive enforcement. Question 4.1 discusses these possibilities in more depth. There are currently no quality controls on third-party ratings.

These issues of quality and accountability would become even trickier if numerous schemes were to come into use. If there were dozens of PICS ratings schemes to choose from, publishers would not know which to choose, and users might not know which to trust.

3.12)   What if I don't like the ratings systems that are available? Can individuals and organizations start new ratings systems?

Currently, there are two choices for individuals and organizations that are uncomfortable with the existing ratings systems.

The first—and currently the only viable alternative—is to avoid use of PICS for self-rating, and in Internet browsers.

The second approach would be to develop a new ratings vocabulary, as an alternative to RSACi, SafeSurf, or other currently available ratings systems. This involves several steps:

The first step is generation of a ratings system, including categories that would be discussed and distinctions within those categories. This would require a discussion of the values that will be represented in the ratings system, and how these values should be expressed.

Once the system has been developed, sites must be rated. This can be done in one of two ways:

- The developers of the ratings system could convince web-site publishers to self-rate. This would require significant resources, as raising awareness of the new ratings system through advertising, press contacts, and other means can be quite expensive. Of course, this new ratings system would raise "chicken-and-the-egg" concerns. Why should publishers use this system for self-rating unless they know that it's being used? And, conversely, why should users choose a ratings system that doesn't have very many sites rated?

- The new ratings system can create third-party ratings for the Web. This would also require significant human resources to generate these ratings. If we assume that workers could generate these ratings at a rate of 1/ minute, or 480 over the course of an 8-hour day, it would take 8 people working 40-hour weeks roughly an entire year to rate one million web sites. Of course, the Internet already has more than one million sites, and it will have grown significantly before those 8 people finish their year of ratings work. Furthermore, workers rating web sites at this rate would probably make more than a few mistakes in their choice of ratings. As described in question 3.10, distribution of third-party ratings also presents significant technical challenges and expenses.

Once the ratings have been generated for the web sites, the new ratings system must be publicized to potential users. As described above, this could be expensive and difficult.

Given the significant resources that will be needed to effectively deploy a new ratings system, it seems unlikely that there will be a large number of PICS alternatives available in the near future. The developers of PICS are trying to change this through the PICS Incubator project, which offers resources to organizations interested in developing new ratings systems.

3.13) What's wrong with PICS and Internet ratings in general?

In theory, there are many useful applications of rating information.

Book reviews and movie ratings are only two examples of the many ways in which we use information filters. Used in conjunction with other information sources—including advertising and word-of-mouth—these ratings provide a basis for making informed decisions regarding information.

Unfortunately, PICS does not currently provide users with the contextual information and range of choices necessary for informed decision making. When deciding which movies to see, we have access to reviews, advertisements and trailers which provide information regarding the content. These details help us choose intelligently based on our values and preferences. On the other hand, PICS-based systems do not provide any contextual detail: users are simply told that access to a site is denied because the site's rating exceeds a certain value on the rating scale.

Ratings systems also fail to account for the global nature of the Internet.

Furthermore, the limited range of currently available PICS ratings system does not provide users with a meaningful choice between alternatives. Parents who are not comfortable with any of the current ratings systems may not find PICS to be a viable alternative.

Continuing with our analogies to other media, consider book reviews in a world where only two or three publications reviewed books. This might work very well for people who agree with the opinions of these reviewers (and, of course, for the reviewers themselves!), but it would work very poorly for those who have differing viewpoints.

Some might argue that the "success" of a single set of movie ratings offers a model for PICS. However, ratings are generally applied only to movies made for entertainment by major producers. Documentaries and educational films are generally not rated, but similar web sites could be rated under PICS.

Movie ratings also provide a cautionary lesson that should be considered with respect to the Internet. Unrated movies, or movies with certain ratings, often have a difficult time reaching audiences, as they may not be shown in certain theaters or carried by large video chains. This has led to self-censorship, as directors trim explicit scenes in order to avoid NC-17 ratings. This may be appropriate for commercially-oriented entertainment, but it could be dangerous when applied to safe-sex information on the Internet.

Ratings systems also fail to account for the global nature of the Internet. Legal or practical pressures aimed at convincing Internet publishers to rate their own sites will have little effect, as these businesses or individuals have the option of simply moving their material to a foreign country.

Furthermore, the existing ratings systems are of limited value to those in countries that do not share western values.

Concerns about unrated international material or differing cultural values could be addressed through direct censorship. For example, governments might use PICS ratings or proprietary filtering software to implement "national firewalls" which would screen out objectionable material. Alternatively, ratings might be used to "punish" inappropriate speech. If search engines chose to block sites with certain ratings (or unrated sites), or if browsers blocked certain ratings (or lack of ratings) by default, these sites might never be seen.

It is possible that a wide range of PICS ratings system could come into use, providing families with a real opportunity to choose ratings that meet their values. The utility of PICS might also be increased by use of new technologies like "metadata" (data about data, used to describe the content of web pages and other information resources), which might be used to provide contextual information along with PICS ratings. However, these tools may not be available for general use for some time, if at all.

Some people confuse ratings with the topical organization that is used in libraries and Web sites like Yahoo. While no system of organization of information is neutral, topical schemes attempt to describe what a resource is "about." Rating rarely helps us find information resources topically and is usually too narrowly focused on a few criteria to be useful for information retrieval.

4   Alternatives

4.1)   Can anything work?

The answer to this question will depend largely on the perspective of the asker.

If this question is taken to mean: "Are there any solutions that would provide children with the ability to use the Internet without ever seeing material that is explicit or "adult," the answer is probably yes. This would require a combination of three factors:

Legislation requiring "accurate" ratings and specifying penalties for those who do not comply.

Technical measures to prevent the transmission of unlabeled material, or any material from foreign sites (which would not be subject to US laws).

Mandatory use of filtering software, using mandated settings.

The obvious legal, political, and practical problems with this scenario would certainly doom it to failure. While mandated standards have been suggested by some groups, it is quite likely that they would be found unconstitutional and in violation of the Supreme Court's Reno v. ACLU decision that overturned key provisions of the Communications Decency Act. Furthermore, the accuracy of content ratings is a matter of judgment that would not easily be legislated. Practically, laws requiring the use of filtering software would be virtually unenforceable. Finally, if efforts aimed at "sanitizing" the Internet somehow managed to survive legal challenges, they would have a chilling effect upon speech on the Internet.

If the question is interpreted as meaning: "Are there any solutions that provide some protection from adult or objectionable material without restricting free speech?" the answer is much less clear. Stand-alone systems clearly don't meet these criteria, as they place users at the whims of software vendors, who may block sites for arbitrary reasons. In theory, PICS might fit this role, but the lack of a meaningful choice between substantially different ratings systems leaves parents and publishers with the choice of using ratings that they may not agree with, or that fail to adequately describe their needs or materials.

Describing speech as "adult" or "appropriate for children" is inherently a tricky and value-laden process

Describing speech as "adult" or "appropriate for children" is inherently a tricky and value-laden process. In the U.S., many people have attempted to prevent schools and libraries from using everyday publications like *Huckleberry Finn* and descriptions of gay/lesbian lifestyles. The fierce debates over these efforts show that no consensus can be reached. Increased use of filtering software would likely be the beginning, rather than the end, of debates regarding what Internet materials are "appropriate" for children, and who gets to make that decision.

4.2)   I understand that there are many problems with filters and ratings. What can I do to protect my children?

The first thing that parents should do is to consider the extent of the problem. While some news reports might leave parents with the impression that the Internet is nothing but pornography, this is far from the case. In fact, it's unlikely that children would randomly stumble across pornographic material. Furthermore, many adult sites have explicit warnings or require payment by credit card, which further decrease the chances of children "accidentally" finding pornography.

Secondly, parents should play an active role and show interest in their children's use of the Internet. For some children this might mean restricting Internet use to closely supervised sessions. Other children might be able to work with clearly defined rules and guidelines. To discourage unsupervised use of the Internet, parents might consider measures such as placing the family computer in a common space in the home and retaining adult control over any passwords required for Internet access.

Parents should also work to educate children regarding proper use of the Internet. Just as parents teach children not to talk to strangers on the street, parents might discourage children from visiting certain web sites, divulging personal or family information, or participating in inappropriate chats.

Some parents might consider using filtering software, despite all of the potential drawbacks. Parents considering this route should closely examine their options, in order to understand their options and the implications of any choice.

Much of the "adult" content on the Internet can be found on cable TV, at local video stores, or in movie theaters

For stand-alone filtering systems, this means investigating the criteria used in developing blocking lists and/or news reports describing the software. If possible, parents might try to find stand-alone systems that allow users to view and edit the lists of blocked sites.

Parents considering the use of PICS systems should investigate the categories used by the various ratings systems, in order to find one that meets their needs. Information about PICS-based systems can be found at the home pages of the respective ratings systems.

In general, the use of a filtering product involves an implicit acceptance of the criteria used to generate the ratings involved. Before making this decision, parents should take care to insure that the values behind the ratings are compatible with their beliefs.

Finally, parents should realize that the Internet is just a reflection of society in general. Much of the "adult" content on the Internet can be found on cable TV, at local video stores, or in movie theaters. Since other media fail to shield children from violence or sexual content, restrictions on the Internet will always be incomplete.

4.3)   What roles can ISPs play?

Some have called upon ISPs to play a greater role in helping parents filter the Net for their children. There are two ways that ISPs might participate in these efforts:

ISP-Based Filtering: ISPs might do the filtering themselves, preventing their customers from accessing objectionable materials, even if those customers do not have their own filtering software. This requires the use of a *proxy server*, which would serve as a broker between the ISP's customers and remote web sites. When a customer of a filtering ISP wants to see a web site, his request goes to the proxy server operated by the ISP. The proxy server will then check to see if the site should be blocked. If the site is allowable, the proxy server retrieves the web page and returns it to the customer.

This approach is technically feasible. In fact, it's currently used by many corporations, and some ISPs that offer this service. However, proxying requires significant computational resources that may be beyond the means of smaller ISPs. Even if the ISP can afford the computers and Internet bandwidth needed, this approach is still far from ideal. In order to do the filtering, proxy servers would have to use stand-alone or PICS-based systems, so they would be subject to the limitations of these technologies (see 2.4, 2.5, and 3.13). The shortcomings of existing filtering systems may prove particularly troublesome for ISPs that advertise filtering services, as these firms could be embarrassed or worse if their filters fail to block adult material. Finally, ISPs that filter material may lose customers who are interested in unfiltered access to the Internet.

Providing Filtering Software: Others have suggested that ISPs should be required to provide users with filtering software. While this might be welcome by parents who are thinking about getting on to the Net (and by software vendors!) it could present a serious financial burden for smaller ISPs.

4.4) What about Internet access in libraries?

Internet access in public libraries has been a contentious area of discussion. Claiming concern for children using library computers to access the Internet, numerous municipalities have installed, or are considering installing filtering software on publicly-accessible Internet terminals. However, as cyberspace lawyer, publisher, and free-speech activist Jonathan Wallace has pointed out, the use of blocking software in public libraries may be unconstitutional:

> Most advocates of the use of blocking software by libraries have forgotten that the public library is a branch of government, and therefore subject to First Amendment rules which prohibit content-based censorship of speech. These rules apply to the acquisition or the removal of Internet content by a library. Secondly, government rules classifying speech by the acceptability of content (in libraries or elsewhere) are inherently suspect, may not be vague or overbroad, and must conform to existing legal parameters laid out by the

Supreme Court. Third, a library may not delegate to a private organization, such as the publisher of blocking software, the discretion to determine what library users may see. Fourth, forcing patrons to ask a librarian to turn off blocking software has a chilling effect under the First Amendment.

5 Where Can I Find More Information?

World-Wide-Web Consortium PICS Home Page: http://www.w3.org/PICS

The Pics Incubator Project: http://www.si.umich.edu/~presnick/PICS-incubatorIncubator Project

RSACi: http://www.rsac.org

SafeSurf: http://www.safesurf.com

NetShepherd: http://www.netshepherd.com

CyberPatrol: http://www.cyberpatrol.com

NetNanny: http://www.netnanny.com

Fahrenheit 451.2: Is Cyberspace Burning—The ACLU's Report on Filtering Software: http://www.aclu.org/issues/cyber/burning.html

Peacefire: http://www.peacefire.org

The Censoreware Project: http://www.spectacle.org/cwp/

The Global Internet Liberty Campaign: http://www.gilc.org/speech/ratings

The Internet Free Expression Alliance: http://www.ifea.net

Families Against Internet Censorship: http://home.rmi.net/~fagin/faic

Computer Professionals for Social Responsibility (CPSR): http://www.cpsr.org

6 Credits

6.1)   Who gets the credit?

This document grew out of discussions held by CPSR's Cyber-Rights working group and other concerned individuals during the summer of 1997. Andy Oram, Craig Johnson, Karen Coyle, Marcy Gordon, Bennett Hasleton, Jean-Michel Andre, and Aki Namioka provided invaluable assistance. Please feel free to distribute or copy this document. Comments can be sent to hhochheiser@cpsr.org.

6.2)   Who is CPSR?

CPSR is a public-interest alliance of computer scientists and others concerned about the impact of computer technology on society. We work to influence decisions regarding the development and use of computers because those decisions have far-reaching consequences and reflect our basic values and priorities. As technical experts, CPSR members provide the public and policymakers with realistic assessments of the power, promise, and limitations of computer technology. As concerned citizens, we direct public attention to critical choices concerning the applications of computing and how those choices affect society.

Before You Cite a Site[10]

For uncritical users, the World Wide Web can be a tangle of misinformation. A teacher offers tips to help educators and students to gain insight on the validity of Web sites.

One of my 7th graders was so excited when he got his first computer that he spent much of his time on it. His love of technology led him to the Internet, and he soon built his own Web site. His site is now among the millions of sites on the Internet, and if you search for a site on computer repair and network consultation, you may have to wait for his services— because he needs to be home in time for dinner.

I admire my student's spunk and ingenuity. If I were searching the Internet for a consultant to network my business, however, I would want to know that this entrepreneur is an ambitious 12-year-old. With this, and many other well-developed sites just a mouse click away, how can we determine the correctness of the information we see? More important, how can we teach children to determine the validity of these Internet-based resources?

The Internet, by design, supports freedom of speech. It is a work in progress, and anyone is free to publish information or an opinion on it. There are no editors, and no cyberpolice to steer us away from the unreliable sites (although there is quite a bit of software available now to help us filter out the distasteful sites).

Enter Goals 2000. This push for information technology in our K-12 schools encourages us to weave this information-rich medium into our curriculum. Educators can easily see applications for its use with science and history fairs, literature-based instruction, and information gathering for classroom debates. Most K-12 schools have access to dial-up accounts. Some have more sophisticated access to the Internet. Training is available, but mainly in the form of showing educators the benefits of this information source. Assuming we know how and why to navigate the Internet, have access, and feel the push of Goals 2000, what next?

The Four Ws of Site Validation

Sorting the fluff from the substance is a necessary evil for any teacher or student who decides to use the Internet for

---

10. "Before You Cite a Site," by Carol Caruso for *Educational Leadership* 55, 3:25-5 N '97. Copyright © 1998 Association for Supervision and Curriculum Development. All rights reserved. Reprinted by permission of ASCD.

research. What are some of the things we can teach our teachers and students to look for in a Web site to determine if the information it contains is valid? This brings us to the who, what, when, and where of site validation.

Who wrote the site? Is the author of the site qualified to voice his or her viewpoints about the subject matter? Are the author's credentials mentioned? Is the site sponsored or co-sponsored by an individual or group? If so, have you heard of the group before? Is contact information for the author included in the Web site? An e-mail message to the webmaster can get you the information you need if it is not readily available. Don't be afraid to ask for it. Looking to see who is talking is the first and probably the most important step in site validation. If you can't find an author or webmaster, look for another site. There is plenty of information out there.

What are they saying on the site? What links are on the page and how reliable are they? What is the scope of the topic? Is the information too broad, too shallow, or just the right depth? Do you think the information is factual? Do you suspect any author bias? A gut feeling is probably enough to send you surfing. Is the information you need free, or is it linked to a part that requires access fees? Is what you need to see easy to download, or are the graphics so extensive that the content of the site is lost in download time? Is the text well written? Is what you see worth a bookmark? Is the content age-appropriate? Has the site received any awards? Is the information short enough to be printed out? The content of the site, of course, is only one piece of information. Educators must make certain that learners don't rely solely on Web resources and ignore information available in books, videos, and human resources.

When was the site created? When was it last revised? If the creation date is not posted directly on the site, you can sometimes determine how current it is by clicking on its links. If the links don't work, the site has probably not been updated in a while. The importance of knowing the timeliness of information on a site will vary based on your research needs. Up-to-date information will be important if you are researching an event in progress, but less critical if you are writing a history report on the life and times of Abraham Lincoln. An e-mail message to the author or webmaster can also help you determine how current the information on the site is.

Where is the site from? Where did it originate? Is it buried in someone's Internet account (http://www.mon-

> *Looking to see who is talking is the first and probably the most important step in site validation*

mouth.com/user_pages/malim/) or does it have its own domain name (http://www.rutgers.edu)? Is the domain name reputable? What server houses the site—and why? Is it a paid service provider or part of all organization? What does the URL tell you about the site? Does the URL indicate that this site is an educational institution (.edu) or government (.gov)? If it is a commercial site (.com), is it a source you can trust? If you just did a search and landed on a site with a long URL (http://web.wn.net/%7Eusr/ricter/web/valid.html), what happens when you trace it back to its parent directory (http://web.wn.net)? Many genre categories exist as sources for Internet sites including universities, commercial services, electronic journals and commercial magazines, special interest groups, companies and organizations, advertising pages, personal pages, search engines, software sites, city and state pages, federal government pages, and special interest groups.

We need to teach children about the vastness of the information available to them. They must learn that many reputable sites and many unreliable sites reside side by side

InterNic is also a valuable resource for determining the origins of the information you find. Established in January 1993 as a collaborative project among AT&T, General Atomics, and Network Solutions, Inc., this resource allowed me to search a database and learn the originator's name and the host server of a site. To use this part of the service, visit http://rsl.internic.net/cgi-bin/whois.

Toward Critical Use

Making the Internet available in K-12 schools is not enough. We need to teach children about the vastness of the information available to them. They must learn that many reputable sites and many unreliable sites reside side by side. Equal access is available, and this unbiased medium will voice the opinions of Ivy League professors, as well as your next-door neighbors. I encourage you to visit some of the sites on the Internet that have posted site validation checklists, including *Kathy Schrock's Guide for Educators: Critical Evaluation Surveys* (http://www.capecod.net/schrockguide/eval.htm), *Evaluating Internet Resources: A Checklist* (http://infopeople.berkeley.edu:8000/bkmk/select.html), and *How to Critically Analyze Information Sources* (http://urisref.library.cornell.edu/skill26.htm). Adapt these instruments to your district's research needs, and teach the teachers and students how to use them before they take what they see on the Internet as truth and use it to prove a point.

By the way, my 7th grader's computer repair and network consultation site is pretty nice—and his rates are competitive.

IV. What's Next?

Editor's Introduction

The very nature of the Internet seems more like something from a science fiction novel than something that is a part of everyday life. In fact, some of the terminology of the online world grew from science fiction, most notably from the "cyberpunk" novels of William Gibson. But what lies ahead for this futuristic technology? Looking into the future can never be an exact science, but this chapter includes some glimpses into the future by some people who are not only knowledgeable about the present condition of the Internet, but who may also have a hand in what the future of the Internet will bring. These articles present some mere supposition, some developments that are already well underway, and challenges that must be faced.

The chapter is bookended by articles by people who have played vital roles in the development of the Internet up to this point: Steve Case, the chairman and CEO of the largest online service, America Online, and George Conrades, who until recently was with GTE Internetworking, the branch of GTE that included BBN, which has been a involved in the development of the Internet throughout most of the Internet's short life. With a natural emphasis on America Online, in his "Ten Commandments for Building the Medium," Case discusses where we are now with the Internet, where we have to go, and how we should get there. Drawing on both the successes and failures of America Online, Case is looking at the future mainly from a business point of view, discussing what businesses need to do in order for the Internet to reach its potential.

In "4 Forces that Will Shape the Internet," Andrew Kupfer examines some of the economic realities that will shape the future of the Internet. Noting that "The Net is morphing from ad hoc grassroots semianarchy to mainstream big-money commerce," he explains the effects this change will have on the future direction of the Internet and offers predictions as to what applications will have the most impact. "The Strain for Net Gain" is alone in this chapter in that it deals strictly with plans for the future that are already underway. Gary H. Anthes of *Computerworld* takes a look at the efforts to aid in the development of the technology that will enable the Internet to serve all our needs in the future, whatever those needs may be, by the true parents of the Internet, the government (the Next Generation Internet project) and academic institutions (Internet2). Examining the future needs those groups are striving to meet, Anthes also discusses some of the criticism the government is receiving for these efforts.

The chapter closes with a speech delivered to the Institute of Electrical and Electronics Engineers, by George Conrades, in which he takes a broad view toward the future, touching on the societal effects of the technology, the challenges facing governments and businesses, and technical challenges. He offers some predictions of new uses for the technology and speculates on ways in which it will affect our lives.

All four of these glimpses into the future present fairly consistent opinions concerning the technical and governmental hurdles that must be overcome as the Internet matures, and there is agreement that the potential of the Internet to change our lives cannot be overestimated. However, when it comes to the predicting the exact ways in which our lives will be changed, there is clear no consensus.

Ten Commandments for Building the Medium[1]

Setting Priorities

Gene DeRose, members of our panel here this morning, members of this conference: You know the song: "What a difference a day makes?" Well, in our business, the song we sing is more like "What a difference a nanosecond makes."

It's no secret that this is an industry for the vigorous, not the faint of heart. The technological, social, political and economic forces swirling around the emergence of the Internet, and the challenges those forces present to us are fierce.

What I'd like to do today is give you some of my most recent thinking about where we are as a medium, where we're going, and how we should go about the business of setting priorities in this swirling environment. But first, let me give a little status report from the front lines. The number of people jumping online every day is staggering. At AOL alone, we grew from 10 million to 11 million members in almost three months. That's an extraordinary story about a truly extraordinary trend.

But the trend that we're finding is every bit as significant—more significant in many ways, is what those millions of people are doing once they're connected. In just over a year, on average, we've seen our members more than triple, yes, more than triple, their use of the service. Now, granted, a big piece of that has to do with the transition to unlimited pricing. But frankly, our research tells us that the more significant driver of usage is the integration of interactive features and functionality into people's daily lives. These numbers and trends defy the establishment of any but the crudest predictions. They break every model. They represent a rate of public adoption of a new service that has no precedent. Still, there are those who can't help themselves from making predictions. And I can't help myself from quoting them. Jupiter finds that nearly 50 million people were online by the end of 1997. And it predicts that number will increase to 63.3 by the end of this year. And reach 87.3 million by the year 2000. And these figures refer to the Unites States only!

I don't know about that. What I do know is that those of us in the Internet community have found ourselves on a mission. It's a mission to make this new medium as central to people's lives as the television and the telephone, and even more valuable.

---

1. Address by Steve Case, Chairman and CEO, America Online. Delivered to the Jupiter Communications Annual Conference, New York, New York, March 5, 1998. Reprinted with permission.

And perhaps the most important thing for all of us to remember about this mission, in order for us to succeed, is how far away we still are from realizing it.

The fact is that the Internet has so much mindshare right now, we've created such a big amount of noise, that it's beginning to feel like we've arrived. I compare us to a moon-bound rocketship. Yes, we've had our countdown and we've achieved a spectacularly successful lift-off, but we haven't left the earth's atmosphere yet, much less started walking on the moon.

Or, for those of you who are metaphorically challenged... we're at the top of the 2nd inning.

When I focus on how many people are still not online, on how far we still have to go to reach the mass market, some people say, "Steve, you just can't see this glass as anything but half empty." And, I respond, "no, with 11 million members, we've definitely got a half-full glass. Problem is, we need to fill the whole damn swimming pool."

Recently, I've taken to using what I call the "Fifty, Twenty, One" model to describe where we are. That is, there are those who say AOL has more than 50% of the market. Well, that may be true, of home PC users who are online in the United States. But if you look at us against all us Internet users, we're just at about 20 percent. Or if you look at us against all homeowners of PC's, we're only 20%. And, if you compare us to usage of the cable TV, to the major media and telecommunications companies, our market-share diminishes quickly to less than 1%. Fifty, twenty, one.

I was in Davos, Switzerland, last month on a panel about Internet policy moderated by Eli Noam, and he summed things up very well from my perspective. "Remember," he said "when you add up all of the people around the world who have access to the Internet and interactive services, you are still hovering at around 4 percent of the global audience of *Baywatch*."

The 10 Commandments

The question comes down to how do we get where we want to go from where we are? And the answer I always give is: stay in touch with the consumer. I've said this so much that people have been sending me E-mail advising me to talk about some thing else for a change.

So I've decided to change my tack somewhat today. It occurred to me that, well, the Ten Commandments are something that everybody knows, and yet provide a pretty good basis for discussion when starting a civilized society. And for four thousand years, nobody's criticized them for being tiresome or repetitive.

So let me share my Ten Commandments for building an interactive medium that's central to people's day-to-day lives.

Commandment Number One? What else?

The Mass Market Consumer Is Thy Master.

In reference to this commandment, those who focus only on the fastest, most high-tech, most powerful technologies may find that they are worshiping an idol.

Technology is critical, and at AOL we're using it to allow members to send photos in e-mail, send instant messages, and to personalize their experience, but ultimately technology is an enabler, a means to an end, and not the end in itself. It, too, should serve the mass-market consumer.

The fact is, today, technophobes outnumber technophiles by several orders of magnitude, and it's the technophobes we need to make this new medium truly mass market. The technophiles are already aboard. Which means that "easy-to-use, fun, useful and affordable" will win every time.

Technophobes outnumber technophiles by several orders of magnitude

And we are making significant progress. Ten years ago, when we started, we were 90 percent male and 10 percent female online. Today, I'm very pleased to report that AOL members are 52 percent female, and 48 percent male, roughly identical to the consumer population as a whole.

Of all of the numbers and statistics about our service and our membership and usage, that's the statistic that best illustrates at the true future potential of this medium to reach the true mass market.

The Second Commandment is:

Thou Shalt Not Take Thy Competition for Granted.

There is no more competitive business than that of this emerging interactive medium. And this competition is occurring in an environment that is simultaneously wrenched by both an extraordinary pace of technological innovation and a dramatic convergence of powerful industries, including computing, entertainment and telecommunications. All of this means that the competitive landscape can, and does, change quickly and mercilessly.

Look at the emergence of Yahoo!, Excite and Lycos from unfunded good ideas to heavily capitalized forces in an unheard of period of time. That can happen in this environment and I expect it will happen many more times before the industry settles down.

People today compare AOL with MSN, Prodigy and Earthlink. In that pond. we're pretty big—we have more than 50 percent marketshare. But remember my 50/20/1 rule. Our little pond is merging with some pretty large rivers, lakes and oceans.

We don't look all that big when we're compared with The Walt Disney Company, NewsCorp, Time Warner, IBM, AT&T, Deutsche Telecom, SBC, Sony, and TCI. And, make no mistake, all of those companies and all of their competitors have only just begun to focus on their consumer Internet strategy, and all of them will come after their share of the market.

So anyone—in any piece of this emerging industry—who takes for granted either who their competition is or the ground rules that define that competition is making a fatal error. The competitive winners will be those with the greatest agility, the greatest ability to be flexible and opportunistic, and, of course, the best ability to envision the effect on the underlying experience of consumers.

The Third Commandment is:

Remember the Day Thou Learned Economics 101.

This commandment could just as easily have read: Thou Shalt Consolidate.

Economics 101 tells us that when you have a whole lot of enterprises competing for the same consumers with products that are not significantly differentiated, you will see the total number of companies shrink, and the size of the individual companies increase.

Remember when this happened just ten years ago in the PC industry? We're seeing all of the same signs today.

The fact is the period of consolidation is only beginning. We will see it continue and we'll see it accelerate. The only question is who will be the consolidators and who will be the consolidatees.

The Fourth Commandment is:

Honor Thy Parents, Families, Teachers and Communities.

There are many different ways to judge the ultimate impact and success of a new medium. Clearly one of the most important is the role that the medium plays in expanding opportunities for our children, supporting families and empowering communities.

This is an area that our medium collectively must pay more attention to. And we'd better listen to parents and teachers. They tell us in no uncertain terms that they expect their children to be safe online. The bottom line is that these demands are reasonable. In fact, if Internet online services can't live up to those expectations, we don't deserve to be a mass market medium.

Here, too, we're making good progress. Last December's child safety summit was enormously gratifying for the breadth of participation from the Internet community.

Leaders from entertainment, technology, politics, government, and the private sector all came together to make children's online experiences safer and more rewarding.

As a next step, you'll see this September a major back-to-school public education initiative called America Links Up that will draw national attention to the issues associated with children online.

At AOL, we've also been giving a lot of thought to how we can best use the medium to strengthen civic discourse within our communities and to increase the participation by young people in political discussions.

Frankly, democracy in this country could use a boost. And this medium is tailor made to provide that boost. At AOL we are planning to use the 1998 election cycle to experiment in leveraging the medium to do four things: expand issue education; strengthen one-to-one communications between voters and elected officials and candidates; boost election turnout, particularly among young people; and develop workable models for putting political advertising in context.

Frankly, democracy in this country could use a boost

Then, I believe you'll see that the year 2000 signals an arrival of the Internet in our political culture that is every bit as powerful as the emergence of television was in 1960.

The Fifth Commandment is particularly relevant today:

Thou Shalt Not Spam.

Along with the online consumer, we're fed up with spam and we're not going to take it anymore. Today, in fact, I can share some news with you about how we're stepping up our antispam campaign.

We are adopting a "block and tackle" strategy against spammers. That is, we're going to block as many of their e-mail at the gateway as we can, and we're going to tackle them in court.

And, we're making some headway on the legal front. We have sent more than 500 cease and desist letters to spammers in just the last couple of months and have followed up with lawsuits against many of them.

Today, we're announcing that we've just won two more legal victories against spammers.

Once we bring the legal guns to bear, we have been getting some telling results. One spammer claimed the Fifth Amendment in his deposition. Another literally threw his computer into a swamp to destroy the evidence. Still others are telling us just how little money they have in their bank accounts and saying they want out of the business. Well, the more spammers we can get out of the business the better.

Which is why, today, AOL is releasing a "Ten Most Wanted List" of the worst current spammers. These are the ones we have in our sights. They include such lovely enterprises as:

- The notoriously nasty spammer
- Love-toys-online
- Lose-weight.org

Together, the spammers on our "Ten Most Wanted List" represent a severe impediment to the growth of the medium and are causing a significant depreciation of the experience of the average consumer. We look forward to taking them on one at a time.

The more spam-mers we can get out of the busi-ness the better

Ultimately, however, it may be that a complete solution to the problem of spam may only come about through legislation, and we are actively pursuing that course, too.

The Sixth Commandment is:

Thou Shalt Not Launch Before the Market Is Ready.

There are few more critical questions in the interactive services industry than how and when we will see the emergence of broadband. Broadband technology will enable an even more powerful and magical online experience that can help us reach a wider audience. So, it is a critical personal focus of mine.

Still, let me go on record here and say two things about broadband. First, it won't come as quickly as most people seem to think. And, second, when it does come, it will be available over many more platforms than most people expect.

That doesn't mean we should take our eye off the ball now. In fact, now is when we should be laying the groundwork to ensure that, when broadband gets here, it is easy to use, ubiquitous and inexpensive.

Still, we expect that the availability of broadband will segment the market in the short term. Many customers will prefer to stick with a lower-priced service that is narrowband at a lower cost while heavier or more committed users will pay extra for more speed.

So, we're experimenting with all kinds of new technologies to deliver greater speed, flexibility and ease-of-use for our consumers, from wireless to cable to mindmorphing. And we're watching the equation carefully to understand when speed, platform, and price are in all in alignment for the consumer.

The Seventh Commandment is:

Thou Shalt Not Fail to Take the Business of the Internet Seriously.

Many businesses do not yet understand that their core franchise is dependent on the emerging interactive medium. This underscores a fairly significant cognitive dissonance that persists among many very large companies who see the phenomenal growth of the Internet as something they need to experiment with, rather than as a make or break development for their entire business.

TV viewership is on the decline, for the first time in my lifetime, in proportion to the time being taken up by online activities. And TV audiences are fragmenting among the increasing number of channels. We believe that a significant reassessment of how traditional mass marketers do business is already underway.

Yet, there are still a lot of companies dabbling haphazardly with Internet advertising when they should be preparing for the full-scale transition to interactive marketing and E-commerce. These companies still have a grace period before they significantly disadvantage themselves by missing the trend, but not a long one.

I predict that by the year 2000 we will see several examples of large, complacent companies that no one associated with the Internet suddenly in jeopardy and struggling to catch up in the face of competition that emerged seemingly from nowhere.

The Eighth Commandment is:

Thou Shalt Not Deal with Washington Lightly.

Over the next five years, the future of our emerging medium will be influenced more by the decisions in the area of public policy than by technological development.

In addition to hot-button issues of pornography and privacy, we've got a cacophony of issues to wrestle to the ground, including encryption, spam e-mail, copyright, advertising standards, hate speech, universal service, access fees, tax issues and many more.

There's a simple statistic that vividly illustrates the amount of attention this medium is beginning to get from legislators. In the 103rd congress, 25 bills referenced the Internet. So far, in the 105th congress, that number stands at 151.

We, the entire Internet community, have a critical set of questions to answer about how we want to govern ourselves in the next century. But, as I'll describe when I get to the tenth commandment, we should strive to do more than fend off legislation, taxation, rule making and litigation. Our goal should be to fashion an age worthy of ushering in—not just a new era, or a new century, but a new millennium.

To do that we have to be proactive and aggressive. If we put our head in the sand, we will lose a unique window of opportunity to make this medium something special.

The Ninth Commandment is:

Thou Shalt Not Compromise Thy Neighbor's Online Privacy.

I've already mentioned that privacy is a critical issue for us in Washington, DC. It's also a critical issue for us internationally, especially in light of the European privacy directive which threatens to dramatically affect standard online business practices.

But privacy is one of those issues that transcends the regulatory and legislative challenges and even rises above the public policy discussion.

The ability to build experiences that are highly personalized and valuable for individual members is what gives this medium its power. But that very power of personalization can raise difficult issues of privacy.

The principles that should govern the industry's privacy policies and standards are no big secret. But we must be committed to following them.

They include providing consumers with full notice about how their information is being used and giving them the opportunity to make informed choices.

The privacy of communications like e-mail, instant messages and chat should be uncompromised

The privacy of communications like e-mail, instant messages and chat should be uncompromised, and all of these policies should be reinforced with state of the art internal controls, employee training and enforcement procedures.

Finally, special attention should go to protecting children's privacy, including giving parents the absolute right to choose how information about their children is used.

I know there are those who worry that standards of privacy for the online world are higher than those for the offline world. They probably are. And they probably should be.

And the Tenth and Final Commandment is:

Thou Shalt Build a Medium That Improves the Lives of All People and Benefits Society.

History tells us that when steam technology was first developed, both the French and the British had it around the same time.

The French, focused around their system of absolute monarchy, used the new technology initially to create toys for the children of their royalty and to pump water to the fountains of royal palaces.

The British could have chosen to use this power exclusively for their royalty too. But the British chose instead to use steam technology to power what would become the

Industrial Revolution, the end of one phase of civilization and start of a new one.

I would hate to look back forty years from now and find that we have developed a plaything for the well-to-do.

Likewise, I would hate to look back and find that the Internet [has been] tagged as the television industry has been, perhaps unfairly—as a "vast wasteland." We are at an incredibly unique point in the development of this medium, it's big enough to be relevant, still young enough to shape.

The ways that this medium could benefit society are still emerging. I already mentioned the potential benefits to children and education. The medium also has the ability to elevate and expand civic discourse, including becoming a force for democratization and globalization, and also including healing the communications breakdown between citizens and their elected representatives.

The medium also has the ability to elevate and expand civic discourse

It is not even too much to say that this medium could serve to provide solutions for economic, cultural, geographic disparity. It certainly can bring communities closer together and build greater communications and respect between people.

However, these things will not happen by themselves. It will require vigilance and determination to remain true to the meaning and potential of this medium to build a better, more connected society.

So those are Ten Commandments for realizing our mission of building a mass market medium that is as central and valuable to people's lives as the television and telephone.

Together they represent a sort of compass we can use as we hurtle across unfamiliar terrain at speeds we have never before experienced.

I sometimes feel like I'm behind the wheel of a race car. I need to keep my eyes on the horizon, but I also need to keep my attention on the rear-view mirror to see who's gaining on me. From the passenger seat, consumers are telling me where they want to be dropped off and when, and behind me my shareholders and business partners are engaged in loud back-seat driving. One of the biggest challenges is that there are no road signs to help navigate. And, in fact, every once in a while, a close call reminds me that no one has even yet determined which side of the road we're supposed to be driving on.

And the finish line is a long, long way away.

I look forward to accompanying all of you as we take many, many more exhilarating laps around the track.

4 Forces That Will Shape the Internet[2]

One of the virtues of a virtual place is that it can be what-ever you want it to be. For much of its history, that was the charm of the Internet—a cross between a swimming hole and a cosmological worm hole, a secret place where nerds, geeks, and others in the know could gather, and then, col-lapsing time and distance, travel anywhere in the world, often to the electronic inner sanctums of institutions that would have turned them away if they had shown up in per-son and knocked on the door.

Everyone was equal on the Net. It operated outside the tariffs and rules that governed the rest of telecommunica-tions, even as the Net became the Web and commercial interests began to encroach on it, and Web addresses appeared on magazine covers and movie ads and business cards. The Net took hold of the popular imagination as a way both to connect with others and to hide behind a screen of anonymity. Outsiders became insiders, and they did it almost for free.

It's time to get real.

The Net is morphing from ad hoc grassroots semianarchy to mainstream big-money commerce. With data communi-cations exploding and about to dwarf the volume of ordi-nary phone calls, the Internet's language—Internet Protocol, or IP—is becoming a lingua franca for carrying torrents of digital information: computer files, video, and voice. Huge industries are remaking themselves as this transformation gains momentum—the $700-billion-a-year telecommunications industry, which the Net threatens with irrelevance, and the $1 trillion computer industry, which sees the Net as its best hope for growth.

The furious pace of change means that many things peo-ple have been expecting from the Net are about to hap-pen—not in the distant future but within the next five years. Thanks to the example of companies such as smooth-as-silk Amazon.com, electronic commerce is accel-erating toward widespread acceptance. Businesses are beginning to see the Internet as essential to their opera-tions: Networking giant Cisco Systems, to cite a dramatic example, will no longer do business with suppliers that can't fill orders via the Web. And new technologies are

---

2. Article by Andrew Kupfer. Reprinted from the Jl 6, '98 issue of *Fortune* by special permission; Copyright © 1998, Time Inc.

already helping the Net insinuate itself into everyday life. Grainy and herky-jerky though the video images may be, a Web site operated by the city of Las Vegas posts live feeds from highway surveillance cameras to let drivers plan their morning commute.

The Net will be part of our lives whether we know it or not. The bulk of traffic growth will come from transactions between computers—unmediated by any human. Devices such as boxes atop the television set, palm computers, pagers, cell phones, and perhaps even wearable computers will depend on data automatically transmitted via the Net.

This buzzing undercurrent of data is already baffling institutions accustomed to managing the flow of information, knowledge, and money. Antitrust regulators on two continents are groping to figure out if the far-flung facilities of WorldCom and the potent software of Microsoft give them market-crushing power. In the next five years, governments will have to decide who has jurisdiction over borderless cyberspace, who can tax whom for transactions there, who is responsible when something goes wrong. Corporations will have to decide whether and how to use the Net in manufacturing, distributing, advertising, and recruiting— whether to make it part of the warp and woof of American business, to set off, as Microsoft chief technology officer Nathan Myhrvold predicts, "the era of the recomputerization of America." Like any adolescence, this maturation will proceed in fits and starts, with crazy, hormone-driven flameouts interspersed with flashes of inspiration and surprising growth. Remarkably, what emerges from conversations with dozens of the Net's nervous guardians—network builders, corporate executives, regulators—is consensus on four powerful trends shaping how the Net will grow and what it will do to us.

Walled Gardens

Billion-dollar telecom investments and dazzling technology breakthroughs are coming so fast that, at first blush, networks' capacity for data seems sure to outpace demand. In the first quarter of this year, $20 billion in high-yield debt was issued to finance upstart telecom ventures like Level3 that are building high-speed networks in the U.S. Spurred by the challenge, entrenched telcos like Sprint are announcing multibillion-dollar initiatives designed to pump more data. New laser technology and software enable a single strand of optical fiber to carry light signals on 40 wavelengths simultaneously. Such a strand could, theoretically, carry all the long-distance phone calls in the U.S. Cisco engineers say the time is near when a strand will carry 300 colors, and then 1,000.

Even so, network bandwidth will always be a scarce commodity. A familiar vicious circle applies: New highways built to relieve urban congestion encourage more driving and in turn become choked; so it goes with the Internet. As Lucent optical networking chief Gerry Butters says of the Net, "Every time the size of the pipeline is increased, the growth in traffic blows the forecast, not in a matter of years but in weeks or months." For the past few years, traffic has grown by a factor of ten each year, in part owing to new users. At the end of 1997, about 41 million American adults used the Web, according to Cyber Dialogue, a New York research firm. That figure is up from 14 million only two years before. By 2002, the projection is for at least 92 million users.

Network bandwidth will always be a scarce commodity.

There's no reliable way to predict how many of those 92 million will have high-speed connections from their homes to the Net, similar to the hookups many people now enjoy in their offices. The consensus, though, is that a large percentage will. These empowered home users will devour massive amounts of data, stuff like live video and audio that take forever to download on today's wimpy links into the home. The result will be enormous pressure on what's called the Internet backbone: the fat optical pipes into which Internet service providers feed traffic for transport around the world, and the computers and routers and switches that serve as junctions between the pipes.

Heavy traffic today can cause delays: Web pages take forever to load, and data packets get routed via circuitous pathways. Mostly it doesn't matter; no one cares if an E-mail takes three seconds or three minutes to reach its destination. In the future, though, the backbone will carry phone calls and video and crucial business communications, all of which must reach their destination smoothly, and right away.

So Internet companies are looking for ways to banish nonessential data from the long-haul backbone and move high-priority traffic more efficiently. One way to do that is to price the Internet differently. Today, users pay a flat rate for delivery of any data anywhere in the world. In the future, predicts Microsoft consumer-platforms chief Craig Mundie, "all Internet services will have tiered rates." Providers will create hierarchies of users: Payers of premium prices will fly first class with guaranteed, high-speed service anywhere in the world; the rest will fly coach, with a promise of best effort from their provider.

Owned by a consortium of cable-TV companies including TCI, Comcast, and Cox, @Home Network is addressing this problem by creating the cyber equivalent of a walled garden. Subscribers to @Home will get Internet access via special cable modems, which cost about $40 a month to lease. The payoff: blazingly fast connections to the Net. At least that's the sizzle. But it's not exactly what CEO Thomas Jermoluk provides. "I'm not selling you the Internet," he says. "I'm selling you the service." The service turns out to be high-speed transit to certain Web sites that pay to be warehoused in @Home's computers. Getting data from anywhere else on the Web will be no quicker than it is today. If a high-speed link should someday exist between @Home's servers and far-flung servers caching other Web sites, subscribers might have to pay extra to take that fast road beyond @Home's garden.

Sprint's recent announcement of ION, a completely overhauled network that will carry data, video, and voice over a standard phone line, sounds more democratic. But it may suffer the same limitation that @Home has chosen to impose: high speeds for short runs. If Sprint's plan works, traffic between its customers and its network would travel at lightning speeds; but if the signal must go, say, to another caller not on the Sprint network, or to a Web site linked to a rival backbone, the speed might be much slower.

Even Internet companies with high-speed links around the world will use sleight of hand to divert some traffic. WorldCom, for instance, boasts of the data network it is building around the U.S., beneath the Atlantic, and onward through Europe's major cities. Yet networking chief John Sidgmore says: "Deploy flat-rate broadband service from Denver to Frankfurt? Forget it. It's just too expensive to haul bits long distances." Long-haul travel would be reserved for when WorldCom customers need it—say, for a videoconference between locations that are far apart.

Like others, including @Home's Jermoluk, Sidgmore plans to save space for such high-priority, point-to-point traffic by keeping much more Internet traffic local. Today most Web sites reside on a single server, and any user wishing to visit must travel there electronically, wherever "there" is. The greater the average distance between surfers and Web sites, the more fiber and lasers and switches Internet companies must install and maintain. Sidgmore, like other service providers, plans to push Web sites closer to users by replicating them among many different computers around the world. Without knowing it, surfers will take shorter trips—and faster ones too.

Despite these efforts, Web sites will still be swamped from time to time by floods of traffic. But new software will allow the businesses that operate the sites to discriminate among classes of users, to create walled gardens of their own. Programs that link a firm's Web site with its databases, for example, will use customer information to sort incoming traffic. When the stock market fell in October 1996, traffic was so heavy that Charles Schwab had to turn away 80% of the visitors to its Web site—without knowing whom it was turning back, or whether they had $10,000 on account or $10 million. Charles Giancarlo, vice president of Cisco, says: "Schwab is working with its Internet provider to identify which customer is which while the traffic is coming in. Then it can make sure that the gold customer gets through and the silver and bronze ones are turned away." The latter will get the Net equivalent of a busy signal—an onscreen prompt saying the server is busy—without knowing that others are getting through.

The Net looks to be the first new mass medium since TV

A New Mass Medium

It's a paradox that even as hidden software will keep some Internet customers on the sidewalk behind a velvet rope, the Net looks to be the first new mass medium since TV. Not only are tens of millions of people logging on via PCs, but also tens of millions more will reach the Net in other ways.

In the home, a host of consumer-electronics devices will be wired to the Net, starting with the TV itself. Microsoft's WebTV is a stand-alone box that plugs in to the phone line and delivers Web pages to the set, while WorldGate Communications, in Bensalem, Pa., will do the same using software in cable-TV set-top boxes. Digital cameras will download data to a film processor via the Net, and prints arrive a day or two later in the mail. Baby monitors hooked to the Web will let parents see their children's bedrooms via remote camera.

When they leave their homes and offices, people will take the Net along. Some may stay in constant radio contact with the Web via digital pagers, cell phones, and laptops, perhaps even wearable computers that use new flexible transistors invented by Bell Labs. Users will gather E-mail, directions, maps, and news updates on these devices.

But the application that will really establish the Net as a mass medium is "streaming video," the sending of moving images over the Net in real time. Surfers love PC software that decodes audio and video streams from the Net. Real-Networks, in Seattle, is uploading 100,000 copies of its free "players" each day. Whereas video delivered via the Web is grainy and jerky today, as bandwidths around the Net increase it will become smoother, like TV.

Ordinary Joes may well be the creators of much of this Net video. The Web site www.jennycam.com already offers many links to regularly updated images sent from digital cameras around the country: In Whitefish, Mont., for example, a camera offers live pictures in and around the Great Northern Brewing Co.; from Osage Beach, Mont., you can see who's on the Lake of the Ozarks. As streaming video becomes more widespread, a fan might bring a digital camcorder to a high-school football game and post the video on the Net that night for interested alums.

Such potential has not gone unnoticed by the world's media moguls. Fox, CNN, Sony, Warner Music, and Disney all deploy RealNetworks technology in one form or another. Fox, CNN, and Disney's ABC, for example, let Web users tap in to video clips of network news. The commercial possibilities are vast. Content developed for broadcast will soon be resold on demand via the Net. Shows on WebTV already have Net-borne enhancements—clickable images that let viewers communicate with the studio and with advertisers.

As streaming video proliferates, it will confront advertisers with the same sorts of tough decisions they had to make when TV eclipsed radio. Microsoft's Myhrvold says: "Lots of advertisers never made the transition when consumer products squeezed through the knothole of TV." Companies will have to decide whether to shift billions of dollars in ad budgets to the Internet. Those that do shift will need new kinds of ads that take advantage of the medium: ads that offer viewers options ("Would you like to see a clip about this car's crashworthiness or its speed?") or that are automatically tailored to the spending habits of the viewer.

The Clickable Corporation

When you click "yes" on Dell's Web site, something happens in its plant. The PC maker relays online orders directly to assemblers. That seamless link between user and corporation, hard to imagine five years ago, will gradually become the norm.

The Net also allows companies to anticipate customers' wants with uncanny precision—a hallmark of the Web's slickest bookseller, Amazon.com. CEO Jeff Bezos, a pleasantly rumpled man with a Klaxon laugh, recalls how a year ago, when $2.8-billion-a-year Barnes & Noble launched a rival Web service, an analyst started calling his company Amazon.toast. Since then, Amazon has added nearly a million customers to its rolls (2.25 million have bought books so far) and increased sales from a $65-million-a-year rate to $350 million.

Bezos has stayed a jump ahead of his huge rival by concentrating on customer-friendly technology. One seductive feature of the Web site is a section for book reviews by customers, who sometimes engage in lively debate. Such customer input serves an added purpose. Using so-called collaborative filtering, Amazon's computers track the likes and dislikes of people with similar buying patterns, so when a customer calls up a title onscreen, the Web site helpfully lists other books that have appealed to like-minded readers.

The casbah of cyberspace is changing the social contract with employees and profoundly affecting the notion of what a corporation is

Software embedded in the Web and triggered by the click of a mouse will help turbocharge business-to-business commerce as well. Some programs will help businesses cope with one of the Internet's biggest pitfalls: its anonymity. A company might use the Net to find the lowest price for a year's supply of paper clips, but the buyer would have no way to be sure that the best bid didn't come from a fly-by-night clip joint. Nor could a legitimate office supplier be certain that the buyer would pay the bill. Companies like Concentric Network and IPHighway offer technology for parties in online deals to verify each other's identity.

Web commerce won't be just about buying and selling goods. Companies will use so-called virtual private networks to link employees and even suppliers and customers. A VPN piggybacks on the Internet to create the functional equivalent of a proprietary data network at a fraction of the cost. Employees can log on to a VPN from remote locations. Suppliers and customers who have the right passwords can too.

Aventail of Seattle operates a VPN for a large New York investment bank. Customers in the financial-services industry use the bank to process transactions and get information. Until recently, the bank needed complex and expensive database software to perform routine tasks like clearing checks and trading stocks; clients would put in their requests by fax. Now clients tap into the bank's VPN via the Internet and download software that lets them handle transactions in less time than it used to take merely to put in a bid.

The casbah of cyberspace is changing the social contract with employees and profoundly affecting the notion of what a corporation is. Companies are already using the Net to decentralize; Boeing, for instance, uses video on its intranet for corporate communications, distance learning, and computer training. By untethering work from geography, the Web will let companies farm out functions like human resources and accounting to specialists that can be anywhere in the world.

Indeed, for certain jobs, the competitive edge may lie with people who live as far from the employer as possible, creating a market for what might be called "antipodal commerce." The controller of a California firm with a number-crunching task can send it off to his accountants in Bombay at the end of the day knowing it will be finished when he returns the next morning. Besides getting work done fast, such arrangements can help workers in places that have been isolated from the global economy.

The Net's flexibility may upset some business verities—for instance, that good little companies are always more agile than good big ones, or that large companies win by controlling distribution channels. Instead, expect to see more small companies arise to challenge giants, and to see big companies pursue micromarkets that only local ones could profitably serve before.

Wired Civ

The social consequences of a ubiquitous Internet will take decades to unfold, but in the next five years the Net is sure to cause lots of consternation. With its ability to negate distance, cross borders, and spread information, it means trouble for entrenched hierarchies, and nowhere will that be more apparent than in politics. Cisco CEO John Chambers predicts that streaming video will play the same role in presidential politics that TV has since 1960. He says: "In the elections of 2000 or 2004, voters will go straight to the Net and click on candidates' speeches—and at a fraction of the cost for the politicians."

While changes like that one can help make politics more democratic, the Net can be too much of a good thing. Symptoms of information overload are already endemic.

One recent survey of people who surf found that they read and sleep less than they used to and spend less time with their families. Web-connected jobs can be more stressful too. Robb Eglsaer, director of Internet sales for a Porsche Audi dealership in Cupertino, Calif., finds that customers who contact him via the Net expect a swift reply whenever they happen to write. He says: "I used to have an eight-hour job. Now I work 13 or 14 hours a day."

Not everyone will be plugged in at home, though, and those who can't surf at all may be at a disadvantage, especially if they want certain sorts of products. The Net is fast becoming some companies' preferred way to communicate with customers. MCI's Vinton Cerf recently bought a Macintosh G3 computer, which he likes very much; but it came with a note explaining that some of its software wouldn't work well with the machine's latest operating system, and instructing the buyer to download a compatible version via the Web.

The collision between values and technology stands out most sharply in efforts to control online pornography

"That's chutzpah," says Cerf. "The Web has evolved from an interesting tool into an entity you expect customers to rely on." MCI itself reserves its best long-distance rate—nine cents a minute six days a week and five cents on Sunday—for customers who order, pay, and receive their bills online. Those who can't log on miss out.

The collision between values and technology stands out most sharply in efforts to control online pornography. The landmark Communications Act of 1996 forbade sending certain sorts of X-rated stuff over the Net; the courts quickly struck down that provision on constitutional grounds. Trying to censor online porn with technology won't help much either. Parents can install software filters on their PCs to block access to offending Web sites—those they happen to know about. @Home network chief Milo Medin says: "The amount of material on the Net is growing exponentially. No one group could find all the bad stuff." The only way to be perfectly safe is to let children visit only sites that have been vetted, which means parents would end up restricting their kids' access to good information.

Privacy will be hard to defend as well. The same technology that tells your online broker how good a customer you are can also tell him where you were when you logged on—information that can be sold to interested parties, like marketers. This sort of trade is hardly new; catalogs don't arrive by accident, after all. Nor does everyone think trafficking in tidbits of information gleaned online is evil. Speaking at a recent conference on telecom and the Internet, John McQuillan of McQuillan Consulting in Concord,

Mass., said: "Carrying information, noticing patterns, and selling this knowledge to others isn't bad. It's electronic commerce. That's a good thing, if it's properly managed."

The ease and speed that the Net will give to gathering and conveying information, though, is a change of epoch-making proportions. Indeed, international disagreements on privacy may end up throwing a wrench into some transatlantic Net business plans. After World War II, Europe imposed stringent limits on the distribution of information about consumers and employees. Starting this October the European Union will prohibit transfer of information on any of its citizens—medical information, say, or airline food preferences, and possibly even credit card numbers—to countries that don't meet EU standards of privacy protection. Whether the U.S. will pass the test has not yet been determined; the State Department is negotiating now.

Such uncertainty will typify the coming five years, as people established in hierarchies and rooted behind borders learn to make money and communicate in a realm where ideas and information move freely and can be in all places at once. Their struggle is really the same tension between freedom and control that has run through much of the 20th century. It is reflected in the early picture of the Net—free-form and open—melting into the new one—button-down and tightly managed, probably much better in many ways but with a little less soul.

"The history of the Net has been played out between two poles: central control and everything that tries to evade it," says the English writer Sadie Plant, who has written a book about women and the Internet called *Zeros and Ones*. "Like a lot of contemporary cities, the Net will have some very carefully monitored areas that will be its shiny models. Whether the back streets survive becomes the issue."

The Internet has always seemed a different kind of medium from, say, the phone system. Though state and corporate interests have built it and own its parts, the Net feels like it belongs to the people who use it, even when they do so on the PC in their office. Whether they hold on to that feeling in the 21st century is another matter.

The Strain for Net Gain[3]

Uncle Sam Wants to Lead The Internet Into The 21st Century. But Not Everyone Is Applauding.

To see the Internet's future, look to its past.

A decade ago, the infant Net was for university and government laboratory researchers. There was no World Wide Web, no electronic commerce, no Java applets, no spam. But the phenomenal success of the federally funded Internet propelled the Net into the public's eye, and by the early 1990s, onto the commercial stage.

Now, an adolescent Internet is about to take another big step toward maturity. Technology that supported a few thousand graduate students and rocket scientists in 1988 can't support 25 million Internet hosts, traffic growth of 400% per year or new demands for reliability, security and usability. So Uncle Sam is funding another round of projects in networking technology and applications, which could affect commercial Internet developments in 1998 and beyond.

Chief among them: the Next Generation Internet (NGI) program, a $100 million annual federal initiative that aims to boost the Internet's bandwidth, reliability and flexibility while building sophisticated, distributed applications that can ride over a new and improved infrastructure. A companion university-led effort called Internet 2, has similar goals .

But not everyone believes the government should underwrite and direct Internet developments, even if major technological advances to aid communications and commerce are spun off to industry. Although some government research projects have had "enormous payoffs" in the past, "its track record on anything and everything to do with using computers is so miserable that it's almost an embarrassment to hear them talking about doing applications," say Mike Roberts, founder and the former director of Internet2.

Still, the NGI presses on. Its primary goals are the following:

---

3. Article by Gary H. Anthes from *Computerworld* p38 + D 29 '97. Copyright © Computerworld, Inc. Framingham, MA 01701. Rights reserved. Reprinted with the permission of *Computerworld* Magazine.

Develop advanced networking technologies (with openly published specifications) for security, robustness, ease of use, quality-of-service options and management.

Develop a high-speed, next-generation internetwork that would connect universities and federal laboratories at speeds from 100 to 1,000 times current Internet performance.

Develop advanced distributed applications in areas such as telemedicine, digital libraries, manufacturing and defense that will employ bandwidth-hungry techniques such as full-motion video and virtual reality.

"The routing, quality of service and security demands for multicasting across thousands of networks at speeds 1,000 times faster than today's Internet require network services that are not available with current technology," says White House science adviser John Gibbons.

The Defense Advanced Research Projects Agency (DARPA), which is leading the multiagency NGI, plans by the end of 1998 to have awarded contracts for most of its $122 million three-year effort. David Tennenhouse, director of the Information Technology Office, says DARPA in 1998 will launch the "supernet" project, which will link 10 NGI sites at speeds of more than 1G bit/sec. and pave the way for 2T bit/sec. networking via wavelength division multiplexing.

DARPA also plans in 1998 to define a baseline architecture for quality of service and demonstrate negotiation of quality-of-service "contracts" over wide-area Asynchronous Transfer Mode (ATM) networks. The contracts give applications users confidence bounds on the services they can expect and the trade-offs involved.

Vinton Cerf, one of the founding fathers of the Internet and a senior vice president of MCI Communications Corp. in Washington, says he is looking forward to several technical milestones in 1998 that should make NGI more tangible:

A new and much more powerful version of the Internet Protocol, called IPv6, should begin to appear in commercial products in earnest. Besides expanding the pool of available Internet addresses, it provides for robust security, autoconfiguration, mobility, quality-of-service options and policy-based routing.

Developers will work on protocols for applications with highly distributed databases and software—Java applets, say—that have to be controlled, synchronized, managed and made secure. "Trying to nail down the right protocols for multipoint applications is one of the biggest challenges ahead of us." Cerf says.

Graduating to Internet 2

Internet purists fondly remember when government and academic researchers had ARPAnet all to themselves. In the future, they may have all the bandwidth they need, free from the Net congestion caused by gawkers, gamers and—worst of all—consumers, once a university-sponsored project to develop an Internet fast lane for researchers opens up.

Internet2 is a project of the University Corporation for Advanced Internet Development, a consortium of 115 research universities. It will connect campuses with a high-speed internetwork expected to operate at 2.4G bit/sec. by 2000. It also will develop advanced applications in areas such as media integration and real-time collaboration.

Internet2 schools have pledged $57 million each year over the next three to five years, and vendors have pledged another $8 million over the same period.

Initially, Internet2 universities will use the very high performance backbone network service (VBNS), a 622M bit/sec. network based on ATM switching and SONET transmission. The VBNS is provided by MCI Communications Corp. and funded by the National Science Foundation.

Ways to transparently move traffic from the public switched voice network to the Internet will emerge. "You'll see a lot of corporate use of Internet telephony and Internet fax as a way of gaining efficiency" and lowering cost, he predicts.

Facilitating this will be ATM and IP over Synchronous Optical Network (SONET), which will become the dominant technologies for Internet backbones. For example, Cisco Systems, Inc.'s new "gigabit switch routers" will scale from 622M to 2.4G bit/sec. in 1998 and to 9.6G bit/sec. In 1999, says Richard Palmer, a marketing director at Cisco.

Cisco will also unveil several extensions to The Border Gateway Protocol in 1998 that would increase the stability and robustness of inter-router communications, Palmer says.

And anything that makes the Net more reliable and sturdy will help ease commercial user concerns. Network "quality-of-service," in fact, is a key component of NGI and Internet2 research. The idea is to allow applications to request levels of service based on trade-offs among variables such as bandwidth, timeliness and reliability in order to get predictable performance at specified prices.

For example, Internet telephony might require immediate delivery of data packets but tolerate some data loss, whereas a software transfer might require 100% accuracy but accept some delay.

Service-quality options are a radical departure from today's "best efforts" approach in which users cast data packets into the void and hope they'll get delivered eventually. "If you have an application that's providing real-time interactive video, and it's competing with 7,000 undergraduates looking at the *Playboy* page, you've got to make sure the stuff that's making you money is actually going through," says Scott Bradner, senior technical consultant at Harvard University and a member of the Internet2 technical committee.

Members of the Society for Information Management are "very much in favor" of the service-quality initiatives, even though they may mean higher charges for some services, says Ray Hoving, vice president for issues advocacy. "We knew that the Internet wasn't going to come for free for very long," he says. "But this must be done in a fair, businesslike way in a highly competitive environment."

"We knew that the Internet wasn't going to come for free for very long"

Gartner Group, Inc. in Stamford Conn., predicts that half of all Internet service providers will offer quality-of-service guarantees for traffic within their own networks by the end of 1998.

Performance guarantees across different Internet providers will evolve from metrics developed by industry-specific groups of users, says John Curran, chief technical officer at GTE Internetworking in Cambridge, Mass. For example, he says, the Automotive Industry Action Group—a consortium of automakers and suppliers—is certifying Net providers for adherence to standards in security, reliability and throughput among other things.

Curran says more such industry groups will emerge this year, and "in two or three years, you'll see a set of specs for business-grade Internet service that has commonality among them."

In 1998, the transfer of traffic from the public telephone network to the Net will invite the scrutiny of federal regulators who have until now not touched the Internet, Bradner warns. "It's going to be a wrenching thing when they start putting regulations, taxes, universal access charges, line fees and all that on the data service," he says. "I fully expect it to happen because regulators don't like to see revenue streams go down."

There is broad support in the Internet community for government funding of research in open, "precompetitive" technologies—basic building blocks that can be shared by all users and vendors. But there is less enthusiasm for spending taxpayer dollars on specific applications—about 15% of NGI's budget.

As to the charge that the government shouldn't spend money on things the private sector would do anyway—and do better—NGI supporters insist the program will concentrate on areas industry sees as too risky or too unlikely to produce short-term profits.

For example, it needs to figure out how to ensure manageability, reliability and security in the highly distributed systems likely to be spawned by Java, Cerf says. "That's extremely risky and in many ways unknown territory, so government support is vital because industry is less likely to make investments in it."

Adds Cerf, "The Internet would not have happened in the way it did without government support for an awfully long time—pretty solid support for 20 years."

The Future of the Internet[4]

Predicting the Unpredictable

Thank you Shaygan, [Kheradpir, Program Chair] for that introduction, and good morning everybody. I'm delighted to be with you at the IEEE Network Operations & Management Symposium, and honored to be part of this distinguished event.

Mark Twain once said the only problem with predictions are they involve the future. And he didn't foresee the Internet. In an age when significant change in technology is measured in months, rather than years...and even Moore's Law seems outdated...the future is less predictable than ever. About the only advantage we have over our predecessors is that we can now find out we're wrong faster than ever before.

If technology is science, then the ability to predict the future of technology is surely an art. Like all art, it often raises more questions than it answers. During the past two days you've heard a great deal about the science of networking. So this morning, I'd like to take a different perspective and raise, what I think, are some important questions about the future of the Internet.

The World Wide Web is the fastest growing technology in economic history

I'd like to start by asking you...suppose they held an Internet conference and nobody came?

At first glance, that seems improbable. After all, the number of Internet related seminars, trade shows, road shows, and expos is growing almost as fast as the network itself. It may not be long though, before the Net is such an indispensable part of our organizations, our business processes, and our lifestyles...it essentially disappears.

That's not surprising, because all successful technologies ultimately disappear. They penetrate so deeply into our environment, they become indistinguishable from it. Then we no longer have to think about using them, and can focus instead on related matters.

We've seen it happen to radio, television, and the telephone. (Although the PC has yet to reach that point.) Now it's beginning to happen to the Internet. The World Wide Web is the fastest growing technology in economic history.

---

4. Address by George Conrades, who at the time of this speech was President, GTE Internetworking, and Executive Vice President, GTE Corp. Delivered to the Institute of Electrical and Electronics Engineers, 1998 Network Operations and Management Symposium, New Orleans, Louisiana, February 19, 1998. Reprinted with permission of GTE Internetworking.

Last year, more than 50 million Americans gathered, distributed, and shared information across the Web. They spent an average of 12.8 hours a week on line, compared to 6.5 hours just a year before.

But growth like that is hardly limited to the United States. Canada, for example, is now the most wired country in the world, while Finland has twice as many computers connected to the Internet, per 1,000 residents as we do. Indeed, the number of online users throughout Europe grew last year by nearly double the rate in this country. Moreover, the number of Internet hosts in Japan is currently expanding twice as fast as anywhere else in the world. And one of every four new .com domain-name registrations comes from outside the United States.

By almost every measure, the Internet is exploding, as it continues to attract more financial and intellectual capital than any previous technology.

As events in Asia have dramatically demonstrated, internetworking is also having a serious impact on financial and capital markets. Clearly, the underlying problems plaguing Asian nations have deep historical and cultural roots. But they have reached the crisis stage because of the speed at which investors can learn about...and react to...fluctuations in the global economy. These days, many of the best educated and most affluent investors use the Internet to keep track of events around the world. And thanks to new networking and computer technologies, they can execute trades almost instantaneously.

Just as the nuclear age forever changed the nature of warfare by making it possible to deploy weapons of mass destruction in a matter of minutes, the information age has permanently transformed the world of finance, by enabling vast amounts of data to traverse the globe in a matter of seconds.

For millions of people, the Internet is also becoming a primary source of information on a broad range of other issues. Three decades ago, television emerged as the dominant news medium after two historic events, the death of John F. Kennedy, and the landing of the first man on the moon, History is now repeating itself.

Last summer, when Pathfinder landed on Mars, millions of us here on Earth got our first close-up view of the red planet by visiting a host of Web sites dedicated to the mission. During Pathfinder's excursion, there were 80 million hits a day on the World Wide Web. The Jet Propulsion Laboratory Web site alone, had a record 45 million visitors.

Not long after, millions of people also turned first to the Internet to learn about the tragic death of Princess Diana. Within days of her fatal crash, more than 100 Web sites had been created to memorialize the Princess of Wales.

In both cases, important details were available on the Web before they appeared in other media. The same is true with regard to recent events surrounding the presidency. In trying to explain the reasons for their coverage, many journalists have cited competition from the Internet as a driving force. In fact, according to Forrester Research, *Newsweek*, *The Dallas Morning News*, and *Prime-Time Live* first broke the story on the Net.

Yet the Internet isn't replacing news media. Instead, it is integrating elements of television, radio, and newspapers, along with computers and the telephone, to become the principal means of moving information worldwide. As it does, it will not only change how individuals and institutions use the technology, it will ultimately change the users as well. In time, technical constraints will become secondary concerns, as we confront new economic, political, and social challenges. Then, as scientists and engineers, you will take on new, and important, responsibilities.

Before we reach that point, we will have to make the Internet as easy to use as dialing a telephone or switching channels on a remote control. That means we will have to resolve problems of bandwidth, security, complexity, and quality...that have diverted our attention for so long. All of us here are dealing with these and other technology issues. But to make the Internet disappear, in other words, to enable it to truly succeed, we will have to make sure it meets three other important criteria.

First, it must become ubiquitous.

It wasn't that long ago that most access to the Internet was limited to the desktop. Now, we can reach the Net from just about anywhere. At Chicago's O'Hare International Airport, for instance, travelers can read their e-mail, track their flight schedules, check stock reports, and even look for new jobs, using GTE's new Internet kiosks. Much the same way as motorists in Massachusetts can renew their car registrations; or couples in Arizona and Utah can, believe it or not, file for divorce.

According to a study by MCI Library Link, the number of people who access the Web from alternate locations has almost tripled in the past year. The number will continue to grow as the Web is embedded within an array of business and household appliances. Just as there are more microprocessors in door locks, vending machines, and video-game players, than in PCs, Web server technology may soon permeate everything from copiers and fax machines, to heating, cooling, and electrical systems. As bandwidth expands through new developments such as digital subscriber lines, so will the effectiveness of these appliances. In fact there's already a war going on for access to the home that includes cable, XDSL, wireless, utility lines, and satellites.

For our part, GTE is currently deploying ADSL technology in selected cities across the country, enabling customers to send data over copper wires as much as 50 times faster than today's fastest modems. What's more, ADSL is always connected, which means future Internet appliances will be readily available whenever you need them...no dial-up or busy signals. At that point, the network will disappear in fact, as well as in theory.

New wireless technologies are also making the Internet more accessible, not just to individuals, but to countless organizations and countries. And the advent of low earth orbiting satellite systems will provide small businesses and nations with the kinds of broadband connectivity and global reach that, until now, were limited to their larger counterparts. At the same time, it will enable companies like GTE to extend our services to new markets, with only marginal infrastructure costs, compared to traditional methods.

Still, technology, no matter how ubiquitous, has limited value if it's not easy to use. That's the second factor in the future success of the Internet.

As we all know, the easier a technology is to use, the more complex it is to develop and maintain. Even so, ease of use isn't just a technical matter. It can include how technology is used, and such things as pricing and taxation. Internet technology can also simplify our business processes. It can allow us to reengineer our organizations in entirely new ways. And it reopens the game for everyone, traditional providers and start-ups alike, who want to, *or must*, take part.

That means we must develop a greater understanding of the power of information, and a better appreciation of the value of sharing that power. If you don't get it, ask your children and grandchildren. They get it instinctively especially non-linear, non-hierarchical thinking, and when they start entering the workforce...talk about cultural change! Or ask your parents and grandparents, for that matter. Because people over 50 now represent the fastest-growing segment of PC buyers and online users.

The more children, parents, and grandparents use the Internet, the more they will need easier ways to share a common database of personal interests and communications. One such way might be a "virtual refrigerator door," an idea conceived by Jerry Michalski, the managing editor of Release 1.0. This private, Web-based fridge door would have one section for leaving messages, for example, and another for scheduling, such as a calendar. Family members could post drawings, photographs, video clips, or notes, plus important e-mail addresses and URLs. In this environment, universal messaging becomes the underlying killer application.

Just like the real thing, the virtual refrigerator door would become a focal point for families to share information, ideas, and experiences. And if it could work for families, why not businesses and organizations? We see the beginnings of this already.

In fact, as entire industries converge on the Internet, take buying and selling electrical power, for example, and companies easily operate across borders, they will significantly alter the ways we do business.

Another example of this is the pricing mechanism for communication access and services. As ISPs, telephone companies, cable operators, and other players compete in the same arena, each brings with it a different pricing background. And they are all changing the rules of engagement. We already see how companies like GTE Internetworking and others are moving to usage-based pricing, that is, the amount of bandwidth being used, which we monitor every 15 minutes. In the works are technologies for pricing by Quality of Service, such as being able to charge for prioritization over others on the public Internet.

The virtual refrigerator door would become a focal point for families to share information, ideas, and experiences

In the future, companies may price their services based on the time of day they are used, or the distance information must travel. Of course, if bandwidth becomes so plentiful that costs associated with it are negligible, then flat rates may suffice. And bandwidth is definitely on the way. Again, for our part, GTE is designing, implementing, and has begun to light up a national, high-speed (10 billion bits-per-second), 24-fiber ring network: that will be completed by the end of next year. Here, as elsewhere, the future is still unpredictable. But by planning and preparing for the possible outcomes, we will be ready for whatever structure does emerge.

No doubt, the issue of effectively pricing the Internet is formidable. Yet it may pale next to the challenge of taxing it. Traditionally, taxes are levied according to the location of a commercial activity. For example, there are 30,000 separate taxing jurisdictions in the United States alone. The

Internet, however, is indifferent to geography. So traditional notions of governance, as the basis for taxing digital products and services, are illogical.

Even if we do agree on standards, they will be hard to enforce. Imagine trying to tax goods that are downloaded electronically, such as data, or music, or videos. The marginal cost of these products is close to zero, since it costs little to make or send additional copies. Unlike floppy disks and CD-ROMS, there are also few, if any, ways to cross-check against inventories.

New forms of electronic money may also make tax cheating easier if there's no effective way to trace transactions. That's why the U.S. Controller of Currency requires e-cash providers to report all dealings, so as to reduce anonymity and deter activities such as money laundering.

As you can see, uniform pricing and tax policies will demand a high degree of cooperation and coordination on a global scale. They, in turn, will require an unprecedented level of trust, the third, and most important, criteria for success.

Today, the Internet works because it removes physical barriers so that information can be shared, communities can be established, and transactions can be carried out regardless of geographic boundaries. Our legal systems, on the other hand, are built and practiced within those boundaries, and the differences among them can be daunting.

Let me give you some examples:

Recent efforts to amend America's Uniform Commercial Code would prohibit reverse engineering of software products. Yet that would be in direct violation of public policy throughout Europe, where reverse engineering is permitted so users can achieve interoperability.

Even within the U.S., state laws differ considerably on issues such as requirements for doing business, tobacco sales, charitable donations, and insurance, just to name a few. Further complicating matters is the fact that regulation has traditionally distinguished between public and private communication. You can say things at home you would never broadcast over the air. But the Internet is both private, in the form of e-mail, or the virtual refrigerator door, and public, in the case of Web sites and chat groups.

Once again, the ability to make rules is not the same as the capacity to enforce them. Most countries already have laws protecting copyrights.

Nonetheless, modern day pirates cost publishers and producers billions of dollars every year. The cost of piracy is sure to grow, too, as high-speed networks and new technologies make it easier to download, duplicate, and distribute all kinds of information.

Given the seemingly overwhelming nature of the problem, how do we meet these, and other challenges to making the Internet safer and more trustworthy?

Some legal scholars believe current laws must adapt to the Internet, while others argue for entirely new regulations. I don't believe it's an either/or proposition. As a society, we have developed enormous experience in the ways human beings interact. Here, the challenge is not to change our laws to accommodate technology, but to effectively use technology to enforce the law. Still, new technologies do engender new circumstances, and existing laws are not always appropriate. In these cases, we may have to modify existing regulations or, sometimes, create new ones. But even if organizations and nations could resolve their differences, it would only be a partial response to the question of trust. They would still have to address the needs and concerns of their various constituencies.

A year ago, Internet users were concerned about matters such as access, reliability, and security. But according to the latest survey by the Georgia Institute of Technology, the issues that most trouble them today are privacy and censorship.

It's true, Americans have always provided all kinds of details about themselves. Long before the Internet, credit card companies and frequent flyer programs regularly collected information valuable to marketers. These days though, many consumer and interest groups worry that too much information is too readily available. The same can be said about information available to consumers.

Last year's Communications Decency Act was a direct response to growing concern over Internet content. While the law was overturned, the debate has hardly subsided. Supporters of the original legislation have introduced two new bills to control children's access to the Net.

But the same technologies that present problems can also provide solutions. Projects such as The World Wide Web Consortium's Platform for Privacy Preferences, or P3, will allow users to choose how their personal information is collected and distributed. Likewise, technical standards for filtering electronic information, such as the Platform for Internet Content Selection, or PICS, will enable parents to regulate what content their children see and hear.

Unfortunately, even the solutions are not without controversy. Marketers and civil libertarians alike, argue that the ability to restrict the flow of information *in any direction*, is

The same technologies that present problems can also provide solutions.

a threat to freedom of speech. Meanwhile, observers on all sides of the issue wonder just what role technology should play in influencing public policy.

Indeed, as the questions I've raised indicate, the distinctions between the development of technology, and how technology is used, are also beginning to disappear. Nowhere is this more evident than on the Internet.

How then, can you, the men and women who devise new technologies, participate in designing new systems that effectively address the legal and policy issues surrounding those technologies?

Obviously, one way is by working through organizations like IEEE, to initiate and support engineering advances that will shape our world today, and tomorrow. Another way, is by actively engaging in partnerships with business and government to make certain we have the resources to make that possible. We're beginning to see signs of this in recent initiatives on electronic commerce, and in global efforts to expand and administer the Internet domain name system. We will also have to join together to ensure that we continue to replenish our national treasure of scientists and engineers.

By working with educators, at every level, we can improve the quality of science and math education in our public schools, and attract more first-rate science and engineering majors to our colleges and universities. We can also help university graduates find work in both education and the private sector. Plus, we can educate policy makers, and the public, on the continuing need to develop the vast array of knowledge and skills that will be required to compete in the 21st century.

The Internet today represents the largest and most extensive collaboration in economic history, because no single company, or country, has all the pieces to make it work. It also represents a formidable challenge to the ways we have always worked.

Businesses will have to learn how to operate in an economy where traditional barriers are deteriorating. The integration of intranets, extranets, and the public network, for example, will make it possible, even imperative, for companies to share information among employees, suppliers, partners, and customers.

Governments too, will have to face challenges to their authority to control the flow of information. Some matters, such as copyright and taxation, will have to be dealt with on a global level, while others like privacy and decency will vary from person to person.

Most important, those of us who know the capacity of technology will have to work closely with those who understand the capabilities, concerns, and needs of its users.

As the Internet becomes truly ubiquitous...easier to use... and a source of security and trust...we will have no choice but to turn our efforts to the myriad ways people can learn to use it. In that future, there will be those who focus narrowly on technology...and those who operate within the broader context of how technologies are used. It's not hard to predict who will succeed. Thank you.

Bibliography

Books and Pamphlets

Cate, Fred H. *The Internet and the First Amendment: Schools and Sexually Explicit Expression*. Phi Delta Kappa Educ. Foundation, 1998.

Coyle, Karen. *Coyle's Information Highway Handbook: A Practical File on the New Information Order*. Chicago: American Library Association, 1997.

Ebo, Bosah L. ed. *Cyberghetto or Cybertopia?: Race, Class, and Gender on the Internet*. Westport, CT: Praeger Pubs., 1998.

Gelman, Robert B. and Stanton McCandlish. *Protecting Yourself Online: The Definitive Resource on Safety, Freedom & Privacy in Cyberspace—An Electronic Frontier Foundation Guide*. San Francisco: HarperEdge, 1998.

Grey, Victor. *Web without a Weaver: How the Internet Is Shaping our Future*. Concord, CA: Open Heart Press, 1997.

Hauben, Michael and Ronda Hauben. *Netizens: On the History and Impact of Usenet and the Internet*. Los Alamitos, CA: IEEE Computer Soc. Press, 1997.

Jones, Steve, ed. *Virtual Culture: Identity and Communication in Cybersociety*. London: Sage Publs., 1997.

Kiesler, Sara B., ed. *Culture of the Internet*. Mahwah, NJ: Erlbaum, 1997.

Kizza, Joseph Migga. *Civilizing the Internet: Global Concerns and Efforts Toward Regulation*. Jefferson, NC: McFarland & Co., 1998.

McKnight, Lee W., and Joseph P. Baily, ed. *Internet Economics*. Cambridge, MA: MIT Press, 1997.

Neuman, W. Russell; Lee W. McKnigh and Richard Solomon. *The Gordian Knot: Political Gridlock on the Information Highway*. Cambridge, MA: MIT Press, 1997.

Porter, David, ed. *Internet Culture*. New York: Routledge, 1997.

Rosenoer, Jonathan. *Cyberlaw: The Law of the Internet*. New York: Springer-Verlag, 1997.

Schneider, Karen G. *A Practical Guide to Internet Filters*. New York: Neal-Schuman, 1997.

Simpson, Carol Mann and Sharron L. McElmeel. *Internet for Schools*. Worthington, OH: Linworth Pub., 1997.

Wallace, Jonathan D. and Mark Mangan. *Sex, Laws, and Cyberspace*. New York: M&T Bks., 1996.

Zaleski, Jeffrey P. *The Soul of Cyberspace: How New Technology Is Changing our Spiritual Lives*. San Francisco: HarperEdge, 1997.

Web Sites

For those who wish to find more information online about the Internet, this section contains lists of various Web sites that may be of interest. These sites are only a small fraction of the many sites on the subjects, but we hope these will serve as a good starting point. The sites are grouped according to the type of site they are and/or the subject on which they contain information. Due to the nature of the Internet, the continued existence of a site is never guaranteed, but at the time of publication of this book all of these Internet addresses were in operation.

Search Sites

The various search sites provide the best way to get started when looking for things on the Web. While most of these have similarities, they do have some differences in how they work. You will probably find that each has particular and weaknesses for finding information.

www.altavista
Altavista

www.excite.com
Excite

www.hotbot.com
HotBot

www.infoseek.com
Infoseek

www.looksmart.com
LookSmart

www.lycos.com
Lycos

www.miningco.com
Mining Co.

www.webcrawler.com
Webcrawler

www.vlib.org
WWW Virtual Library

www.yahoo.com
Yahoo

Government

Most federal government agencies (from the U.S. and from countries throughout the world), state governments, and many local governments have their own Web sites. We have listed a few of the major U.S. government sites, a European site, and some sites that point to other government information.

www.whitehouse.gov
White House

www.house.gov
U.S. House of Representatives

www.senate.gov
U.S. Senate

www.uscourts.gov
Federal Judiciary Homepage

www.ecommerce.gov
U.S. Government Electronic Commerce
    Policy

www.usia.gov
United States Information Agency

www.nara.gov
National Archives and Records Administration

europa.eu.int
Europa
    Official Site of the European Union

www.capweb.net
CapWeb
    The Internet Guide to the U.S.
    Congress (not an official U.S. government site)

www.law.vill.edu/Fed-Agency/fedwebloc.html
Federal Web Locator of the Center for
    Information Law and Policy

www.piperinfo.com/state/states.html
State and Local Governments on the
    Net
    Guide to government sponsored
    Internet Sites

www.uncle-sam.com
The Great American Web Site
> Links to government agencies

Libraries

The first items in this list contain links to many other libraries. They are followed by links to a few specific libraries.

sunsite.berkeley.edu/Libweb
Berkeley Digital Library LibWeb
> List of library servers on the Web

**www.nclis.gov/libraries/
stliblst.html**
State Library Agency Websites

**www.capecod.net/epl/public.librar-
ies.html**
U.S. Public Libraries with Websites

www.ala.org
American Library Association

www.ipl.org
The Internet Public Library
> An online library

www.nypl.org
New York Public Library

www.loc.gov
Library of Congress

www.lapl.org
Los Angeles Public Library

www.sil.si.edu
Smithsonian Institution Libraries

www.nlm.nih.gov
U.S. National Library of Medicine

History of the Internet

Among these sites you will find various views of the history of the Internet. Some present an overview or timeline in simple terms, while others delve into more technical details.

**www.davesite.com/webstation/net-
history.shtml**
> A timeline of the history of the Internet

**www.isoc.org/internet/history/
indexes.html**
The Internet Society Internet History
> Links

Contains links to various sites with information on the history of the Internet

www.bbn.com/timeline
BBN Timeline
> A timeline by one of the companies that has been involved with the Internet since its beginning. Lists Internet milestones along with other social, political, and entertainment events.

Social Issues and Technology

While all of these are not specifically devoted to social issues relating to technology, they all contain information on the subject.

www.eff.org
Electronic Frontier Foundation

www.aclu.org
American Civil Liberties Union

www.cdt.org
Center for Democracy and Technology

www.pff.org
Progress and Freedom Foundation

www.mediaacces.org
Media Access Project

www.epic.org
Electronic Privacy Information Center

www.cspr.com
Computer Professionals for Social
> Responsibility

Terminology

www.whatis.com
Whatis.com
> A large dictionary of computer terms and other information

www.hotwired.com/web101
HotWired's Web101
> A glossary and other basic information about the Internet

**www.earthlink.net/internet/glos-
sary**
Earthlink's Computer and Internet
> Glossary

www.matisse.net/files/glossary.html
Internet Literacy Consultants Glossary
of Internet Terms

Infrastructure and Standards

www.w3.org
World Wide Web Consortium
The organization that devises
many of the technical standards
for the World Wide Web
www.isoc.org
Internet Society
An organization whose goal is to
provide "leadership in addressing
issues that confront the future of
the Internet"
www.internic.net
InterNIC
The company that assigns most
domain names
www.nw.com
Network Wizards
They conduct the Internet Domain
Survey, counting Internet hosts

Encryption

www.crypto.com
Encryption Privacy and Security
Resource Page
www.rsa.com/rsalabs/faq/
RSA Laboratories Cryptography FAQ
www.computerprivacy.org
Americans for Computer Privacy

Chat

chatting.miningco.com
The Mining Co. Guide to Chatting
Online
www.chatlist.com
Ultimate Chatlist
chatseek.com
Chat Seek
www.liszt.com/chat/
Liszt's IRC Chat Directory
chat.open24.net
Open 24 Chat

A guide listing chats and events
using ichat software
www.theglobe.com/chat
Chat@The Globe
www.talkcity.com/chat
Talk City
www.thepalace.com
The Palace
chat.yahoo.com
Yahoo! Chat

News

Local, national, and international
news organizations are finding a home
on the Web. Listed here are some sites
that point to a variety of news organizations on the Web, followed by a few
of the major national news presences
on the Web.
www.ajr.newslink.org
American Journalism Review/
Newslink
Links to thousands of media services worldwide
sunsite.unc.edu/slanews/internet/
archives.html
Special Libraries Association News
Division's U.S. News Archives on
the Web
www.ecola.com
Ecola Newsstand
Guide to English-Language Media
Online
www.pointcast.com
Pointcast
Allows you to choose from various
news sources and topics, and automatically updates the news on
your computer
www.abcnews.com
ABC News
www.cnn.com
Cable News Network
www.cbsnews.com
CBS News
www.csmonitor.com
Christian Science Monitor

www.foxnews.com
Fox News
www.latimes.com
Los Angeles Times
www.msnbc.com
MSNBC
www.nando.net
The Nando Times
www.nytimes.com
New York Times
www.usatoday.com
USA Today
www.wsj.com
Wall Street Journal
www.washingtonpost.com
Washington Post

Spam

member.aol.com/emailfaq/email-faq.html
The Email Abuse FAQ
spam.abuse.net
    An anti-spam site
www.jmls.edu/cyber/statutes/email
Federal and State Spam Law Site
    Site is authored the John Marshall
    Law School Center for Informa-
    tion Technology and Privacy Law
www.cauce.org
Coalition Against Unsolicited Commer-
    cial E-mail
maps.vix.com/rbl
Mail Abuse Protection System Real-
    time Blackhole List

Entertainment

www.thesync.com
The Sync
    Offers full-length streaming videos
www.broadcast.com
Broadcast.com
    Live and on-demand Web broad-
    casting
www.onnow.com
On Now
    A guide to live events (chat, music,
    video, etc.) on the Web

www.live-online.com
Live Online
    A guide to music events on the
    Web
www.CDNow.com
CDNow
    Online music store
www.musicboulevard.com
Music Boulevard
    Online music store
www.amazon.com
Amazon
    Online bookstore
www.barnesandnoble.com
Barnes and Noble
    Online bookstore
www.espn.com
ESPN
www.nba.com
National Basketball Association
www.nfl.com
National Football League
www.nhl.com
National Hockey League
www.majorleaguebaseball.com
Major League Baseball

Other

www.cnet.com
CNET The Computer Network
www.feedmag.com
Feed
    An online magazine
www.hotwired.com
HotWired
www.slate.com
Slate
    An online magazine
www.techweb.com
TechWeb
    Technology news site
www.wired.com
Wired
www.zdnet.com
ZDNet
    Computer information, reviews,
    and software downloads

Additional Periodical Articles with Abstracts

For those who wish to read more widely on the subject of the Internet, this section contains abstracts of additional articles on the topic. Readers who require a comprehensive list of materials are advised to consult *Readers' Guide Abstracts* and other Wilson indexes.

These citations are grouped according to the chapter in this book for which they are most closely related, and the citations relating to the "Internet and Society" chapter are further broken down into the following subjects: Age, Race, and Gender Issues; Censorship and Pornography; Chat; Education; Ethics; Human Rights; Privacy; and Society.

What Is the Internet?

Casting the Net. Katie Hafner and Matthew Lyon. *The Sciences* 36:32-6 Se/O '96

The origins of the Internet are discussed. In 1966, Robert Taylor of the federal government's Advanced Research Projects Agency requested funding for a small experimental network that would link four computers. Although Taylor's request truly launched the experiment that gave birth to the Internet, all told, dozens of people helped invent the Internet by improving on the central concept, which is now known as packet switching. In October 1969, a computer at the University of California, Los Angeles, talked for the first time with a computer at the Stanford Research Institute. At the end of 1989, dozens of network pioneers celebrated the ARPANET's 20th anniversary at a gathering in Los Angeles.

The ancient history of the Internet. Edwin Diamond and Stephen Bates. *American Heritage* 46:34-6+ O '95

The Internet is an unintended byproduct of Cold War military research. In the wake of the Sputnik frenzy, the Defense Department established the Advanced Research Projects Agency (ARPA) to dole out high-tech research funds. As part of its research support on command, control, and communication projects, ARPA agreed to fund an experimental computer network, based on new concept called packet switching, that might demonstrate the feasibility of remote computing and test the potential of a post-World War II military communications network. The network would also enable widely dispersed researchers to share supercomputer resources. By the end of 1969, a packet-switched network linking four ARPA research sites was operating. The next milestone came in 1973 with the release of TCP/IP, a set of software protocols to enable different types of computers to exchange packets. By the mid-1980s, TCP/IP was linking ARPAnet with other networks to form what became the Internet.

The birth of the Internet. Barbara Kantrowitz and Adam Rogers. *Newsweek* 124:56-8 Ag. 8 '94

In 1969, a small group of computer scientists laid the foundation for today's international computer network known as the Internet. At the time, there was no standard computer operating system. As a result, machines were generally unable to communicate with one another. The scientists' goal was to build a computer network that would allow researchers around the United States to share ideas. The project was named ARPANET, from the Department of Defense's Advanced Research Project Agency (ARPA) that paid for it. The initial plan was to link four sites—UCLA; the University of California, Santa Barbara; the Stanford Research

Institute; and the University of Utah. By 1971, there were nearly two dozen sites, and other countries were asking to join. Vint Cerf, then a professor at Stanford University, and Robert Kahn, who worked at ARPA, responded by devising a set of technical standards called protocols that multiple networks could use, which paved the way for the Internet.

Greek gods: R. Kahn and V. Cerf. John A. Adam. *Washingtonian* 32:66-71 + N '96

Although Bill Gates is touted as the soothsayer of the Information Age, the ultimate networkers are Vint Cerf and the even more obscure Bob Kahn. Take away Bill Gates, and the computer and networking revolution would be generally unchanged, if not improved. Without Cerf and Kahn, however, and the guiding philosophy of the other 1960s grad students, life in this freewheeling Information Age would be very different indeed. The writer describes how the work of Kahn and Cerf turned a 1960s Pentagon packet-switching network project called Arpanet, named for its high-powered parent agency, Advanced Research Projects Agency, into the Internet and in doing so connected the world.

Guess who was there first: builders of the Internet are bemused by kids who think they own it. Katie Hafner. *New York Times* pG1 + Mr 26 '98

Many of the Internet's inventors and earliest users, now in their middle and late years, are more amused than offended by the proprietary claims of young people who have made themselves at home on the Internet. The early development of the Internet is reviewed.

The Internet and Business

What spammers are really selling. Michael A. Banks. *Home Office Computing* 16:13 Ap '98

The vast majority of online business opportunities advertised via junk e-mail are scams. According to the National Consumer's League, cyberspace business opportunities and franchises are among the ten most common frauds. An overview of the most common e-mail frauds is provided.

Big Web sites to track steps of their users. Saul Hansell. *New York Times* p1 + Sec 1 Ag 16 '98

Some of the largest commercial World Wide Web sites have agreed to put information about their customers' habits into a tracking system in order for advertisements to be aimed at the most likely prospects for goods and services. The system, developed by CMG Information Services, guarantees the anonymity of individual users, but the underlying technology poses concerns among privacy-rights advocates, and the industry collaborative marks the most ambitious effort yet to gather information into a central data base of potentially all Web surfers.

The Net generation is changing the marketplace. Jeffrey H. Epstein. *The Futurist* 32:14 Ap '98

Online merchandising could be transforming shopping trends, especially among younger consumers. Modern teenagers, who are tomorrow's adult consumers, have a greater number of shopping choices than any previous generation, and marketers are finding that they shop differently than a lot of their parents, says Don Tapscott, author of *Growing Up Digital: The Rise of the Net Generation*. This so-called net generation, or N-Gen, tends to be more computer literate than its parents and is, as a result, more likely to shop online, he writes. Five themes the author feels characterize N-Gen consumers are described.

Riding the tech wave: use of the Internet by women and black business owners. Harrold Bevolyn Williams. *Black Enterprise* 28:22 Mr '98

Embracing the Information Age: A Comparison of Women and Men Business Owners, a study carried out by the National Foundation for Women Business Owners, indicates that women are taking the most proactive approach to technology. The study also showed that 30 percent of minority business owners have already invested $5,000-$14,999 in computer software and hardware and that 52 percent of them intended to invest a further $5,000 in equipment before the end of 1997. Other findings include the fact that around one-third of minority entrepreneurs regularly use technology, and another third claim they never surf the Internet.

The Internet and Society

Age, Race, and Gender Issues

Offering curious girls room for exploration. Bronwyn Fryer. *New York Times* pG9 My 21 '98

The Internet has much Las Vegas-style entertainment available that offers little comfort to parents concerned about their daughters finding a safe places on the Web to hang out and have fun. But the Internet does have a few wonderful sites that present utterly absorbing, enjoyable and comparatively safe places for pre-teen-age and teen-age girls. These include Girl Tech, Purple Moon and A Girl's World. These sites gather 1.5 million to 2 million hits per month, making them as attractive as the Disney site. They are successful because they provide a combination of things many young girls love to do in their free time, including the creation and development of fantasy worlds.

A site of one's own. Heather Green. *Business Week* 3587:62 Jl 20 '98

New York-based start-up iVillage is profiting from women's growing presence on the Internet. The iVillage Web site, which provides information on subjects that range from parenting to retirement planning, is the most frequently visited Web site aimed at women. As other sites could challenge iVillage's position, the company plans to broaden its appeal through offering new information areas and Internet commerce.

Gurls' greatest hits. Kim France. *Harper's Bazaar* p98+ Ag '97

The recent spate of female-oriented Web sites may be turning the Internet into one of the most important forums for women's issues. Created mainly by and for women in their 20s, the sites are more raw, spirited, and subversive than professional. There is almost no other type of media that offers more insight into the various concerns and priorities of young women that come straight from the source, unfettered by commercial interests. The majority of the sites receive a few thousand readers daily. A number of the sites are discussed.

The Web: a complete women's guide. Susan Gregory Thomas. *Glamour* 95:248-51 Mr '97

A complete women's guide to using the Internet. The Web is now a low-tech mecca that is attracting millions of nongeeks, 31 percent of whom are female. For those who want to join them, the Web is easy to use, great to look at, and full of goodies. Information is provided on topics that include Web language, the gear required to go online, smart health and fitness sites, glamour on the Web, fantastic sites for women and on art and literature, and things that are easier to do on the Web.

Frank racial dialogue thrives on the Web. Michel Marriott. *New York Times* p1 + Sec 1 Mr 8 '98

As President Clinton urged in his Initiative on Race, Americans are discussing race more openly, honestly, and freely than in the past, but the most common forum is not the town hall meetings that the president recommended, but the Internet. With the rising popularity of Internet bulletin boards and chat rooms, where typed messages can be posted for millions to see and respond to, no one has to know a person's names, age, sex, sexual preference, or race. Wrapped in what many mistakenly assume is a nearly impenetrable anonymity, increasing numbers of people say they feel free on the Internet to truly express themselves about an issue they would otherwise be reluctant to take up face-to-face with someone of another race.

Censorship and Pornography

It's time to tackle cyberporn. John Carr. *New Statesman* 127:24-5 F 20 '98

The writer discusses how to combat pornography on the Internet. There is a tenacious cyber-myth that the Internet is a huge, anarchic forum that is beyond the reach of any government or authority--uncontrolled and uncontrollable. However, the reality is that for all parts of the Internet, there are several potential points of control, and the Internet service providers operating in Britain restrict what they provide as part of their standard service. In addition, the British Internet industry has established the Internet Watch Foundation (IWF), whose remit covers all illegal material on all parts of the Internet, but which has prioritized child pornography. However, the IWF and the police do not have the power to do anything about a huge body of material that, although not illegal, is highly offensive to some, such as hard-core pornography, or else dangerous to others, such as bomb-making information. The writer discusses the debate concerning what should be done with this type of material, the creation of a type of "ratings system" for the Internet, and opposition to such censorship.

Uneasy partners: law enforcers and hackers fight online child pornography. Deborah Radcliff. *Computerworld* 32:58-9 Ag 17 '98

In the fight against child pornography on the Internet, the authorities' best allies may be hackers, the ultimate haters of authority. Although police will not acknowledge them publicly, some hacking groups informally help law enforcement agencies with both technical training and evidence gathering. The efforts of U.S. Customs and the Federal Bureau of Investigation in fighting on-line child pornography are examined.

The cyber vice squad. Randall E. Stross. *U.S. News and World Report* 122:45-6 + Mr 17 '97

Computer software can simultaneously allow parents to restrict children's access to sex-related material on the Internet and permit adults their First Amendment rights. The 1996 law that made posting indecent material on the Internet illegal was declared unconstitutional by a federal district court. Nonetheless, attempting to control material placed on the Internet at either the point of origin or on an intermediate network or on line service is impossible. Some software companies have developed clever Internet filtering systems that work on the receiving PC.

The technology is important both to parents and to corporations that are starting to oversee their employees' Internet access. Various systems available are discussed.

Home Web sites thrust students into censorship disputes. Terry McManus. *New York Times* pG9 Ag 13 '98

According to legal experts, school censorship of student Web sites outside schools is on the rise, giving civil libertarians plenty of reasons to be worried. Sean O'Brien, a 17 year old from Westlake High School in Ohio last spring set up a home-based Web site that insulted his band instructor, Raymond Walczuk. He and his parents sued the school district after the administration suspended O'Brien for ten days, told him to remove the Web site, and threatened to expel him. In an out-of-court settlement, the district reinstated O'Brien, issued an apology, and paid him $30,000 in damages. Other cases of conflict between students with Web sites and school officials are discussed.

Kid-proof your PC. Gail Gabriel. *Home Office Computing* 16:52+ Ap '98

Seven programs that allow computer users to protect their children form the seedier side of the Net are discussed: Cyber Snoop 2.07, WinWhatWhere for Families, Guardian Internet Suite, CYBERsitter 97, CYBERtimer, Cyber Patrol 4.0, Net Nanny, and SurfWatch.

Web censorware. Joshua Quittner. *Time* 152:84 Jl 13 '98

An increasing number of Web sites offer family-friendly surfing. The popular search engine Lycos recently unveiled SafetyNet, an easy-to-use tool. Another approach is Disney's Internet Guide, which offers a preselected list of family-safe Web sites similar to Yahoo's Yahooligans.

Chat

Undercover on the Internet. Leah Rozen. *Good Housekeeping* 225:76+ N '97

Technologically able teenagers are spending long periods chatting online with anonymous strangers via chat rooms. To visit an online chat room, a user only needs a computer, a modem, a telephone line, and a few clicks of a mouse. The problem is that some strangers that teenagers meet in chat rooms are adult perverts looking for sexual trysts with young people. The writer describes conversations in a number of chat rooms and offers advice to parents on protecting their children from potential dangers.

Education

Online learning brings the campus home. Jeffery D. Zbar. *Home Office Computing* 16:24 Jl '98.

Since the emergence of online training in late 1995, interaction via modem has emerged as an electronic alternative to direct schooling. Although it makes up only 2 percent of all information technology training, that number could reach 15 percent of the expected $12.9 billion industry by 2000, according to Christianne Moretti of market research company IDC.

Schools challenge students' Internet talk: A.C.L.U. asserts pupils' expressions on the Web are free speech. Tamar Lewin. *New York Times* p6 Sec 1 Mr 8 '98

Much like the underground newspapers of past generations, student-developed

Web pages are increasingly leading to conflicts between students and schools, with students asserting their right to free speech on their personal sites, while schools seek to control content that concerns them. The American Civil Liberties Union is taking up the students' cause, arguing that students, like anyone else, can't be stopped from saying what they want unless there is a credible threat of imminent harm.

Ethics

Ethics and the Internet. Michael A. Covington. *Electronics Now* 68:42-5 Se '97

The Internet is a loose federation of computer sites that agrees to link its computers together, and therefore it is not regulated by the FCC or any other government agency. Moreover, censoring the content of messages on the Internet is physically impossible because it has no headquarters and has no central site that all messages pass through. The two greatest problems on the Internet today are that the costs are too well concealed, which leads to "spamming"—the massive posting of ads in irrelevant discussion forums—and that there is no proof of the origin of messages. The writer discusses Internet ethics and suggests ways of avoiding various forms of junk mail, hoaxes, fraud, and pornography on the Internet.

Human Rights

Finding liberation in cyberspace. Ella Veres. *New York Times* pG8 Ap 30 '98

The writer, a single mother who grew up in a Transylvanian village under the Ceausescu regime and now struggles to earn a living as a freelance writer in Budapest, describes her discovery and use of the Internet, which has offered her escape and, perhaps, salvation.

Internet fuels human-rights protests. Joseph L. Galloway. *U.S. News and World Report* 125:6 Ag 31 '98

The Internet is being used to fuel worldwide calls for a full accounting of atrocities committed against ethnic Chinese in Indonesia. The atrocities preceded and followed the turmoil that brought down the country's former president, Suharto. Analysts believe the attacks, including numerous deaths and 168 gang rapes, by Muslim mobs on Indonesian Chinese were carefully coordinated and executed. Now, horrific accounts of the atrocities have been disseminated around the globe via Web sites.

Amplifying voices for human rights. Michel Marriott. *New York Times* pG14 F 26 '98

According to Andrew Greenblatt, co-director of Focus on Justice, an online human rights group, Web sites are cost-effective for such groups. Some of the hundreds of human rights organizations that can now be found in cyberspace are discussed.

Home pages for hate: Simon Wiesenthal Center urges limits for hate speech on the Net. Joshua Quittner. *Time* 147:69 Ja 22 '96

Defenders of the First Amendment are concerned about a campaign to limit the voices of white supremacists on the Internet. Racists know that the Internet is a great way to get their message across to a large audience at low cost. In response, Rabbi Abraham Cooper, associate dean of the Simon Wiesenthal Center—the world's largest Jewish human rights organization—has sent letters to Internet access providers, asking them to help draft a code of ethics that would suppress

Websites promoting bigotry and violence. Civil libertarians see Cooper's letter as an assault on free speech in cyberspace, yet Cooper claims it is in keeping with the Constitution and traditional media practice. According to purists, however, the point of the Internet is that it is not traditional media. As a result, Cooper's proposal is provoking opposition from cyberspace denizens on both the Left and the Right, and it has experienced a cold reception from Internet access providers.

Privacy

Gov't must take lead in protecting children: self-regulation in cyberspace has failed badly. Kathryn C. Montgomery. *Advertising Age* 69:40 Jn 22 '98

There is a serious danger that the World Wide Web could become flooded with harmful and misleading marketing practices that endanger not only children's privacy but also the future of E-commerce. Although the on-line industry has argued against any rules and pledged to curtail the invasion of privacy through self-regulation, the shocking findings of a recent Federal Trade Commission study provide strong evidence of just how badly these self-regulatory attempts have failed. The Washington-based Center for Media Education believes that the government must now take the lead in setting limits for on-line marketing and data collection practices.

Is nothing private?: submitting personal data over the Internet. Margaret Mannix. *U.S. News and World Report* 124:59 Jn 15 '98

A recently released Federal Trade Commission (FTC) survey of the Internet is discussed. Of the 674 Internet sites examined, 92 percent collect personal information about visitors and only 14 percent disclose what they do with the information. The majority of the 212 child-oriented sites surveyed gather personally identifiable data directly from children, and only 50 percent say what they do with it. The FTC is recommending federal laws to require such sites to initially notify parents and get consent. For now, Internet users should only disclose necessary information and encrypt sensitive financial data.

Heading off E-voyeurs at the pass. Paul C. Judge. *Business Week* p100 Mr 16 '98

Although few Web sites currently have privacy policies, efforts are under way to improve privacy on the Internet. By May, for example, the World Wide Web Consortium will create a method that enables people to build a personal profile inside a browser and share it selectively with Web site operators they consider trustworthy. In addition, the Direct Marketing Association has assisted 700 companies to draft policies through a service at the association's Web site. The efforts of Web operators to ensure privacy are discussed.

A little privacy, please. Heather Green. *Business Week* p 98-100 Mr 16 '98

Investigators from the Federal Trade Commission (FTC) are to conduct a random check of 1,200 Web sites to see if site operators are are posting privacy notices to explain how personal information is being used and whether it is being protected. If the FTC does not find a sizable number of these protections, the government is threatening to take action. A *Business Week*/Harris poll revealed that the majority of respondents were worried about privacy, and such worries could have a serious impact on the hypergrowth of the Internet. The industry's record has been found lacking to date, and many of the most-frequented sites on the Net still do not post policies. A *Business Week* check of the top 100 Web sites found only 43 percent displayed privacy policies, some of which were hard to find and inconsistent in their explanations.

Society

An ethnologist in cyberspace. *Scientific American* 278:29-30 Ap '98

Sherry Turkle, a professor of sociology at the Massachusetts Institute of Technology, studies the psychology of the relationships and interactions between humans, especially children, and computers. According to Turkle, the Internet allows people subtly—and healthily—to expand the number of ways in which they are able to interact. She is worried, however, about the extent to which people project their emotional needs onto various computer-related phenomena.

Community begins at home: new online communities are grounded in the real world. Anya Sacharow. *Adweek* 39:50+ Se 14 '98

On-line communities that focus on letting users publish their own home pages are being replaced by a new generation that is building interactive communities around off-line interests. For example, Excite's community area on its People/Chat channel uses technology from Redwood, California-based Throw that allows users to interact through accessing a calendar, sharing photo albums or bookmarks, and setting up private chats or bulletin boards. As well as the so-called portal sites from Excite and Yahoo!, there are several local sites sponsored by newspapers.According to Peter Krasilovsky of Bethesda, Maryland-based Arlen Communications, real-world affinity groups that have relationships in the community are better positioned to generate revenue. The services offered by some of the new communities, including the *New York Times* Today site, sponsored by the *The New York Times*, are discussed.

What's Next?

Roadwork ahead: information superhighway gets an express lane. Catherine Greenman. *Home Office Computing* 16:22 Jl '98

A higher-speed, higher-quality Internet service, Internet2, could be available within the next five years. The project was initiated in October 1996 as a cooperative effort among several universities and now involves around 100 universities, government bodies, and U.S. corporations. The objective is to build an advanced network that universities can use for research and education and to develop applications to exploit the network. Internet2 advances will eventually trickle down to the global Internet market, according to Greg Wood of the University Corporation for Advanced Internet Development in Washington, D.C.

Evolution, revolution, or reformation?. Joe Schultz. *Macworld* 13:254 O '96

A number of observers are skeptical or even pessimistic about the potential of the Internet. This is despite the fact that some thinkers welcome the Internet for its democratizing potential. For instance, in *The Gutenberg Elegies: The Fate of Reading in an Electronic Age*, Sven Birkerts expresses his fear that the Internet will bring about the end of literature and not the liberation of information. Moreover, it is possible that electronic communications media of all types could destroy print culture in the same way that print culture destroyed oral culture.

Appendix

The information in the two following charts is from Network Wizards' Internet Domain Surveys (www.nw.com/), which they have been performing since 1987. Their survey is an attempt to count the number of hosts in the domain name system (DNS). For example, hwwilson.com, whitehouse.gov, unc.edu, and antdiv.gov.au are all hosts.

Internet Domain Survey, July 1998

Number of Hosts advertised in the DNS

This chart illustrates the growth in the number of Domain Hosts since 1993. Technological issues forced Network Wizards to alter their method of counting in 1998. The Adjusted Host Count column is an estimate of the count they believe they would have gotten if using the new method, so that the new and old data can be better compared.

Table 1:

Date	Survey Host Count	Adjusted Host Count	Replied To Ping*	
Jul 98	36,739,000		6,529,000	
Jan 98	29,670,000		5,331,640	[first NEW Survey]
Jul 97	19,540,000	26,053,000	4,314,410	[last OLD Survey]
Jan 97	16,146,000	21,819,000	3,392,000	
Jul 96	12,881,000	16,729,000	2,569,000	
Jan 96	9,472,000	14,352,000	1,682,000	
Jul 95	6,642,000	8,200,000	1,149,000	
Jan 95	4,852,000	5,846,000	970,000	
Jul 94	3,212,000		707,000	
Jan 94	2,217,000		576,000	
Jul 93	1,776,000		464,000	
Jan 93	1,313,000			

Produced by Network Wizards. This chart and other data from the Internet Domain Surveys are available online at www.nw.com/.

[* estimated by pinging 1% of all hosts]

[adjusted host count was computed by increasing the old survey host count by the percentage of domains that did not respond to the old survey method]

Distribution by Top-Level Domain Name by NameDomain

This table from Network Wizards presents a list of the top-level domain names listed alphabetically. Most of the names represent countries, but the list also contains the names more familiar in the United States: .com, .net, .gov, .edu, and .org.

Table 2:

Domain	Hosts	All Hosts	Dup Names	Level 2 Domains	Level 3 Domains	
TOTAL	36739151	42606144	5866993	1049865	13062628	
ac	5	5	0	3	4	Ascension Island
ad	477	477	0	30	474	Andorra
ae	13519	13765	246	6	120	United Arab Emirates
af	1	1	0	1	1	Afghanistan
ag	196	197	1	48	161	Antigua And Barbuda
ai	189	224	35	79	41	Anguilla
al	76	76	0	3	76	Albania
am	466	482	16	59	417	Armenia
an	6	6	0	6	4	Netherlands Antilles
ao	2	2	0	1	2	Angola
aq	0	0	0	0	0	Antarctica
ar	57532	59010	1478	22	2990	Argentina
arpa	47910	54677	6767	1	196	Mistakes
as	18	21	3	16	8	American Samoa
at	132202	208146	75944	3084	28113	Austria
au	750327	827191	76864	40	20843	Australia
aw	0	0	0	0	0	Aruba
az	231	231	0	2	3	Azerbaijan
ba	348	348	0	3	6	Bosnia And Herzegowina
bb	45	74	29	8	24	Barbados
be	153760	211691	57931	3160	28574	Belgium
bf	93	93	0	4	93	Burkina Faso
bg	6141	6693	552	200	2590	Bulgaria
bh	337	337	0	2	5	Bahrain

Table 2:

bi	0	0	0	0	0	Burundi
bj	13	13	0	2	13	Benin
bm	1993	1996	3	99	1986	Bermuda
bn	740	740	0	4	726	Brunei Darussalam
bo	506	506	0	8	115	Bolivia
br	163890	174596	10706	344	23941	Brazil
bs	247	247	0	2	247	Bahamas
bt	2	2	0	2	2	Bhutan
bv	0	0	0	0	0	Bouvet Island
bw	578	581	3	27	480	Botswana
by	636	648	12	17	317	Belarus
bz	262	264	2	6	12	Belize
ca	1027571	1229088	201517	4562	230257	Canada
cc	259	269	10	222	131	Cocos (Keeling) Islands
cd	8	9	1	5	6	Congo (Democratic Republic)
cf	0	0	0	0	0	Central African Republic
cg	1	1	0	1	1	Congo (Republic)
ch	205593	211836	6243	12715	183067	Switzerland
ci	265	265	0	6	17	Cote D'Ivoire
ck	33	33	0	2	10	Cook Islands
cl	22889	23820	931	806	8194	Chile
cm	5	5	0	5	5	Cameroon
cn	19313	19550	237	41	494	China
co	11864	12069	205	30	548	Colombia
com	10301570	13506865	3205295	742472	5266752	Commercial
cr	2844	2879	35	13	305	Costa Rica
cu	85	87	2	14	77	Cuba
cv	1	1	0	1	0	Cape Verde
cx	11	11	0	3	11	Christmas Island
cy	3286	3517	231	9	268	Cyprus
cz	65672	72120	6448	4960	39993	Czech Republic
de	1154340	1265163	110823	61105	344826	Germany
dj	0	0	0	0	0	Djibouti
dk	190293	203308	13015	8516	117594	Denmark
dm	79	79	0	6	76	Dominica

Table 2:

do	4917	4927	10	23	190	Dominican Republic
dz	19	19	0	2	18	Algeria
ec	1227	1237	10	13	387	Ecuador
edu	4464216	4699401	235185	3489	1504988	Educational
ee	18948	19856	908	977	14038	Estonia
eg	2043	18554	16511	7	196	Egypt
er	0	0	0	0	0	Eritrea
es	243436	247982	4546	3514	127151	Spain
et	76	76	0	1	1	Ethiopia
fi	513527	524185	10658	5624	330742	Finland
fj	127	127	0	5	33	Fiji
fk	1	1	0	1	1	Falkland Islands (Malvinas)
fm	95	95	0	92	5	Micronesia, Federated States Of
fo	560	567	7	74	530	Faroe Islands
fr	431045	512516	81471	7816	238518	France
ga	1	1	0	1	1	Gabon
gb	81	81	0	1	1	United Kingdom
gd	0	0	0	0	0	Grenada
ge	632	655	23	12	392	Georgia
gf	121	121	0	1	121	French Guiana
gg	13	13	0	7	11	Guernsey
gh	241	243	2	1	6	Ghana
gi	191	192	1	34	191	Gibraltar
gl	515	515	0	16	303	Greenland
gm	0	0	0	0	0	Gambia
gn	0	0	0	0	0	Guinea
gov	612725	744269	131544	419	249717	Government
gp	115	115	0	73	114	Guadeloupe
gq	0	0	0	0	0	Equatorial Guinea
gr	40061	41618	1557	1693	16660	Greece
gs	1	1	0	1	0	South Georgia And The South Sandwich Islands
gt	1046	1052	6	7	74	Guatemala
gu	89	90	1	6	49	Guam
gw	13	13	0	4	10	Guinea-Bissau
gy	58	58	0	3	4	Guyana

Table 2:

hk	72232	72820	588	12	11107	Hong Kong
hm	1	1	0	1	1	Heard And Mc Donald Islands
hn	106	110	4	23	92	Honduras
hr	6117	6173	56	392	5183	Croatia (local name: Hrvatska)
ht	0	0	0	0	0	Haiti
hu	73987	76143	2156	1416	31272	Hungary
id	10691	11765	1074	10	611	Indonesia
ie	44840	45195	355	1494	26789	Ireland
il	87642	92387	4745	11	2580	Israel
im	21	21	0	6	21	Isle of Man
in	10436	11041	605	12	153	India
int	853	64522	63669	25	100	International Organizations
io	56	56	0	5	54	British Indian Ocean Territory
iq	0	0	0	0	0	Iraq
ir	262	264	2	5	20	Iran (Islamic Republic Of)
is	20678	20977	299	989	17501	Iceland
it	320725	382703	61978	13948	171213	Italy
je	14	14	0	4	6	Jersey
jm	253	256	3	6	30	Jamaica
jo	360	364	4	4	17	Jordan
jp	1352200	1368313	16113	97	30316	Japan
ke	692	697	5	4	60	Kenya
kg	182	182	0	10	63	Kyrgyzstan
kh	58	58	0	2	12	Cambodia
ki	0	0	0	0	0	Kiribati
km	9	11	2	3	8	Comoros
kn	1	1	0	1	1	Saint Kitts And Nevis
kr	174800	180286	5486	32	3362	Korea, Republic Of
kw	5597	6653	1056	7	4354	Kuwait
ky	359	376	17	8	54	Cayman Islands
kz	1397	1438	41	80	1169	Kazakhstan
la	0	0	0	0	0	Lao People's Democratic Republic
lb	1400	1552	152	7	53	Lebanon
lc	24	24	0	5	23	Saint Lucia

Table 2:

li	402	408	6	95	186	Liechtenstein
lk	580	590	10	10	199	Sri Lanka
lr	1	1	0	1	0	Liberia
ls	17	17	0	2	17	Lesotho
lt	8746	8893	147	341	6991	Lithuania
lu	6145	10313	4168	345	5667	Luxembourg
lv	8115	8439	324	473	5316	Latvia
ly	1	2	1	1	1	Libyan Arab Jamahiriya
ma	478	511	33	5	360	Morocco
mc	154	154	0	33	153	Monaco
md	370	645	275	21	347	Moldova, Republic Of
mg	18	18	0	2	18	Madagascar
mh	2	2	0	1	2	Marshall Islands
mil	1359153	1504600	145447	72	121216	US Military
mk	407	407	0	5	70	Macedonia, The Former Yugoslav Republic Of
ml	1	1	0	1	1	Mali
mm	0	0	0	0	0	Myanmar
mn	17	17	0	12	8	Mongolia
mo	143	144	1	4	25	Macau
mp	8	8	0	2	6	Northern Mariana Islands
mq	17	17	0	13	16	Martinique
mr	22	22	0	6	22	Mauritania
ms	7	7	0	6	3	Montserrat
mt	785	790	5	9	51	Malta
mu	370	370	0	1	370	Mauritius
mv	70	70	0	1	2	Maldives
mw	0	0	0	0	0	Malawi
mx	83949	92467	8518	125	8525	Mexico
my	40758	40891	133	19	2270	Malaysia
mz	83	83	0	12	79	Mozambique
na	665	668	3	6	71	Namibia
nc	141	141	0	53	122	New Caledonia
ne	5	5	0	3	5	Niger
net	7054863	7567384	512521	48584	2448432	Networks
nf	55	55	0	14	33	Norfolk Island
ng	91	91	0	4	11	Nigeria

Table 2:

ni	692	698	6	7	81	Nicaragua
nl	514660	523148	8488	15566	276608	Netherlands
no	312441	318773	6332	5534	188976	Norway
np	123	123	0	3	5	Nepal
nr	0	0	0	0	0	Nauru
nu	1608	1656	48	1234	941	Niue
nz	177753	182407	4654	15	4143	New Zealand
om	666	667	1	13	18	Oman
org	644971	726335	81364	64276	535298	Organizations
pa	766	780	14	11	35	Panama
pe	3763	3830	67	9	543	Peru
pf	273	274	1	25	264	French Polynesia
pg	62	62	0	4	8	Papua New Guinea
ph	7602	7793	191	6	239	Philippines
pk	1923	2193	270	7	295	Pakistan
pl	98798	106663	7865	777	11486	Poland
pm	0	0	0	0	0	St. Pierre And Miquelon
pn	0	0	0	0	0	Pitcairn
pr	123	123	0	3	44	Puerto Rico
pt	45113	46177	1064	922	24385	Portugal
pw	1	2	1	1	1	Palau
py	855	930	75	7	128	Paraguay
qa	23	24	1	5	10	Qatar
re	1	1	0	1	1	Reunion
ro	13697	22359	8662	640	10151	Romania
ru	130422	137178	6756	3889	69305	Russian Federation
rw	0	0	0	0	0	Rwanda
sa	42	42	0	6	9	Saudi Arabia
sb	24	24	0	1	5	Solomon Islands
sc	7	7	0	3	4	Seychelles
sd	0	0	0	0	0	Sudan
se	380634	391346	10712	8058	150315	Sweden
sg	59469	115776	56307	13	1795	Singapore
sh	1	1	0	1	0	St. Helena
si	18084	18537	453	780	9275	Slovenia
sj	0	0	0	0	0	Svalbard And Jan Mayen Islands

Table 2:

sk	14154	14805	651	893	9985	Slovakia (Slovak Republic)
sl	0	0	0	0	0	Sierra Leone
sm	154	155	1	30	154	San Marino
sn	189	192	3	14	187	Senegal
so	0	0	0	0	0	Somalia
sr	0	0	0	0	0	Suriname
st	64	65	1	45	45	Sao Tome And Principe
su	20024	20745	721	66	2524	Soviet Union
sv	647	653	6	5	41	El Salvador
sy	0	0	0	0	0	Syrian Arab Republic
sz	397	398	1	8	73	Swaziland
tc	129	129	0	60	121	Turks And Caicos Islands
td	0	0	0	0	0	Chad
tf	7	7	0	1	5	French Southern Territories
tg	83	84	1	3	50	Togo
th	25459	25679	220	11	867	Thailand
tj	57	57	0	36	22	Tajikistan
tk	0	0	0	0	0	Tokelau
tm	296	305	9	181	200	Turkmenistan
tn	57	57	0	6	57	Tunisia
to	1446	1497	51	797	1103	Tonga
tp	1	1	0	1	0	East Timor
tr	27861	28618	757	10	1812	Turkey
tt	1531	1536	5	6	74	Trinidad And Tobago
tv	0	0	0	0	0	Tuvalu
tw	103661	107882	4221	13	3418	Taiwan, Province Of China
tz	137	143	6	4	9	Tanzania, United Republic Of
ua	13271	16278	3007	46	1200	Ukraine
ug	41	41	0	7	18	Uganda
uk	1190663	1453507	262844	39	33215	United Kingdom
um	0	0	0	0	0	United States Minor Outlying Islands

Table 2:

unknown	23610	193043	169433	9884	9240	Unknown
us	1302204	1372109	69905	76	3001	United States
uy	16345	16444	99	6	210	Uruguay
uz	198	198	0	31	92	Uzbekistan
va	9	9	0	3	9	Vatican City State (Holy See)
vc	0	0	0	0	0	Saint Vincent And The Grenadines
ve	6825	7093	268	27	920	Venezuela
vg	13	13	0	10	5	Virgin Islands (British)
vi	514	538	24	49	437	Virgin Islands (U.S.)
vn	25	25	0	6	17	Viet Nam
vu	47	47	0	3	14	Vanuatu
wf	0	0	0	0	0	Wallis And Futuna Islands
ws	0	0	0	0	0	Samoa
ye	14	14	0	7	10	Yemen
yt	0	0	0	0	0	Mayotte
yu	5270	5416	146	21	1395	Yugoslavia
za	140577	213818	73241	25	10899	South Africa
zm	236	241	5	13	208	Zambia
zr	0	0	0	0	0	Zaire
zw	836	844	8	4	135	Zimbabwe

Produced by Network Wizards. This chart and other data from the Internet Domain Surveys are available online at www.nw.com/

Index